Microprocessor 4

Series Editor
Jean-Charles Pomerol

Microprocessor 4

Core Concepts – Software Aspects

Philippe Darche

WILEY

First published 2020 in Great Britain and the United States by ISTE Ltd and John Wiley & Sons, Inc.

ISTE Ltd
27-37 St George's Road
London SW19 4EU
UK

www.iste.co.uk

John Wiley & Sons, Inc.
111 River Street
Hoboken, NJ 07030
USA

www.wiley.com

Library of Congress Control Number: 2020943937

British Library Cataloguing-in-Publication Data
A CIP record for this book is available from the British Library
ISBN 978-1-78630-566-4

Contents

Quotation

Every advantage has its disadvantages and vice versa.

Shadokian philosophy[1]

---

1 The Shadoks are the main characters from an experimental cartoon produced by the Research Office of the Office de Radiodiffusion-Télévision Française (ORTF). The two-minute-long episodes of this daily cult series were broadcast on ORTF's first channel (the only one at the time!) beginning in 1968. The birds were drawn simply and quickly using an experimental device called an *animograph.*

The Shadoks are ridiculous, stupid and mean. Their intellectual capacities are completely unusual. For example, they are known for bouncing up and down, but it is not clear why! Their vocabulary consists of four words: GA, BU, ZO and MEU, which are also the four digits in their number system (base 4) and the musical notes in their four-tone scale. Their philosophy is comprised of famous mottos such as the one cited in this book.

Preface

Computer systems (hardware and software) are becoming increasingly complex, embedded and transparent. It therefore is becoming difficult to delve into basic concepts in order to fully understand how they work. In order to accomplish this, one approach is to take an interest in the history of the domain. A second way is to soak up technology by reading datasheets for electronic components and patents. Last but not least is reading research articles. I have tried to follow all three paths throughout the writing of this series of books, with the aim of explaining the hardware and software operations of the microprocessor, the modern and integrated form of the central unit.

About the book

This five-volume series deals with the general operating principles of the microprocessor. It focuses in particular on the first two generations of this programmable component, that is, those that handle integers in 4- and 8-bit formats. In adopting a historical angle of study, this deliberate decision allows us to return to its basic operation without the conceptual overload of current models. The more advanced concepts, such as the mechanisms of virtual memories and cache memory or the different forms of parallelism, will be detailed in a future book with the presentation of subsequent generations, that is, 16-, 32- and 64-bit systems.

The first volume addresses the field's introductory concepts. As in music theory, we cannot understand the advent of the microprocessor without talking about the history of computers and technologies, which is presented in the first chapter. The second chapter deals with storage, the second function of the computer present in the microprocessor. The concepts of computational models and computer architecture will be the subject of the final chapter.

The second volume is devoted to aspects of communication in digital systems from the point of view of buses. Their main characteristics are presented, as well as their communication, access arbitration, and transaction protocols, their interfaces and their electrical characteristics. A classification is proposed and the main buses are described.

The third volume deals with the hardware aspects of the microprocessor. It first details the component's external interface and then its internal organization. It then presents the various commercial generations and certain specific families such as the Digital Signal Processor (DSP) and the microcontroller. The volume ends with a presentation of the datasheet.

The fourth volume deals with the software aspects of this component. The main characteristics of the Instruction Set Architecture (ISA) of a generic component are detailed. We then study the two ways to alter the execution flow with both classic and interrupt function call mechanisms.

The final volume presents the hardware and software aspects of the development chain for a digital system as well as the architectures of the first microcomputers in the historical perspective.

Multi-level organization

This book gradually transitions from conceptual to physical implementation. Pedagogy was my main concern, without neglecting formal aspects. Reading can take place on several levels. Each reader will be presented with introductory information before being asked to understand more difficult topics. Knowledge, with a few exceptions, has been presented linearly and as comprehensively as possible. Concrete examples drawn from former and current technologies illustrate the theoretical concepts.

When necessary, exercises complete the learning process by examining certain mechanisms in more depth. Each volume ends with bibliographic references including research articles, works and patents at the origin of the concepts and more recent ones reflecting the state of the art. These references allow the reader to find additional and more theoretical information. There is also a list of acronyms used and an index covering the entire work.

This series of books on computer architecture is the fruit of over 30 years of travels in the electronic, microelectronic and computer worlds. I hope that it will provide you with sufficient knowledge, both practical and theoretical, to then specialize in one of these fields. I wish you a pleasant stroll through these different worlds.

IMPORTANT NOTES.– As this book presents an introduction to the field of microprocessors, references to components from all periods are cited, as well as references to computers from generations before this component appeared.

Original company names have been used, although some have merged. This will allow readers to find specification sheets and original documentation for the mentioned integrated circuits on the Internet and to study them in relation to this work.

The concepts presented are based on the concepts studied in selected earlier works (Darche 2000, 2002, 2003, 2004, 2012), which I recommend reading beforehand.

Philippe DARCHE
August 2020

Introduction

This volume details how to program a microprocessor in five chapters. The first two chapters demonstrate the three characteristics of ISA (Instruction Set Architecture, *cf.* § V1-3.5), which are: instruction encoding, addressing modes and the instruction set of a generic component. Then, additional notions linked to the instruction set and execution are discussed in the third chapter. This primarily involves the notion of illegal, invalid, reserved and trusted instructions, the notion of memory alignment, orthogonality and the symmetry of the instruction set, as well as the notion of pure, re-entrant and relocatable code. Then, the subjects of execution time, memory requirements, execution modes, portability and virtualization will be discussed. Finally, it ends with aspects that are very important in industry, their hardware and software compatibilities, how to measure execution performances and the criteria for choosing a microprocessor or MPU (MicroProcessor Unit). The last two chapters study two ways of altering execution flow. These are the concepts of the sub-program and interruption.

NOTE.– The choice has been made to write the names of registers in upper case in the text and figures but in lower case in assembly language, since the norm (IEEE 1985) does not specify which case to use. The name of the instructions is in lower case in the text and programs (MIPS (Microprocessor without Interlocked Pipeline Stages) style), sometimes also in upper case (Motorola or Arm® style). Moreover, the examples given refer to current and older microprocessors and computer processors for the purposes of instruction. This chapter is not intended to be exhaustive. It mainly presents the functions of the first MPUs. It will be completed by the following two books. The instructions cited will be complemented by MPU documentation or in a specialist work.

Coding and Addressing Modes

This chapter focuses on two important characteristics of Instruction Set Architecture (ISA) (*cf.* § V1-3.5), which are instruction encoding and addressing modes.

1.1. Encoding and formatting an instruction

The instruction[1] is represented in a computer using a binary word in the format i bits, a multiple of the format n of the data and, in general, a multiple of the byte. We use the expression *machine code* to mean all those binary words representing the instruction to be executed. Instruction encoding depends on the architecture of the target processor. It is formed at least of an instruction code and, potentially, of one or more operands as Figure 1.1 illustrates.

An instruction

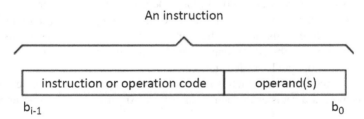

instruction or operation code	operand(s)

b_{i-1} b_0

Figure 1.1. *Breakdown of an instruction*

---

1 In the context of a microprogrammed architecture (this will be covered in a future book by the author on microprocessors), it is sometimes called a macro-instruction to differentiate it from the micro-instruction, which is internal to the processor.

This instruction can be broken down into fields[2]. The instruction code, also called operation code (abridged to opcode), in format c, has one or more fields. The essential one is the function code. It defines the operation to be executed. Its format of f bits defines the maximum number of instructions F ($= 2^f$) in the instruction set[3]. Other fields can be added to this such as, for example, one that specifies the addressing mode (the addressing mode field) of the operands to the format as Figure 1.2 illustrates (VAX[4] approach from the Digital Equipment Corporation (DEC)). The processor therefore has 2^a addressing modes. Besides simplifying the encoding, one benefit is to separate the encoding of the function from that of the address, which makes it possible to make the instruction set symmetrical (*cf.* § 3.1.3). This instruction code generally takes the format of the data n of the processor to optimize access to primary memory. Since in our example n is fixed, the architect of the microprocessor or MPU (MicroProcessor Unit) must therefore compromise between the number of instructions and the number of addressing modes if the field exists. One field may be favored to the detriment of the other.

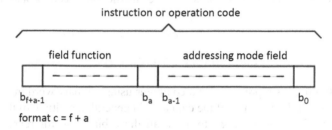

Figure 1.2. *An example of the structure of an operation code*

If the instruction requires, the operation code is followed by one or more operand fields (Figure 1.3), and their number is dependent on the operation (unary or binary) and the architecture. This operand field in the format o bits makes it possible to specify, depending on the addressing mode chosen, the value of the reference of the location of the operand needed for calculation or, potentially, the result. An operand's storage location, which is imposed by the programmer, compiler or linker or architecture, is a register or memory location. An instruction to one operand is

2 Although these fields exist, they cannot be documented or can only be documented partially, as for MC6800 from Motorola.

3 We can choose not to code the instruction (an uncoded instruction). This means that one bit is assigned to each of the possible operations. The gain lies in eliminating the logic of classic decoding and the corresponding stage in a pipelined architecture (this will be covered in a future book by the author on microprocessors). The immediate counterpart is an increase in its format.

4 VAX for Virtual Addressed eXtended.

called a "monadic", and one with two operands, "dyadic". When there are two operands, we speak of source and destination operands or sink operands or sometimes simply left and right operands. We cite the VAX mini-computer with a variable format as an example of encoding. The operation code included one to two bytes. It was eventually followed by no more than six operand specifiers, mainly address specifiers, making it possible to design the operand. The MPU MC6800 instruction format included one to three bytes, the first being an operation code indicating the addressing mode.

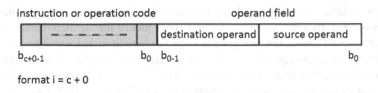

format i = c + 0

Figure 1.3. *Format of an instruction with two operands*

Table 1.1 shows the different address combinations for IA-32 instruction set (IA for Intel Architecture, also called i386). Combinations not indicated are not possible either due to the architecture or to their incoherence. We cite impossible memory (to) memory combinations in most architectures, as it is necessary to pass through a register and an immediate-register or immediate-memory, which cannot be done because of the impossibility of allocating a value to a constant.

Operands	
Destination	**Source**
Register	Immediate
Memory	Immediate
Register	Register
Memory	Register
Register	Memory

Table 1.1. *Possible address combinations in family IA-32*

The identification field (ID) of the operand(s) specifies the format and addressing mode (register or memory reference) as well as the direction of transfer (Figure 1.4). In a RISC microprocessor (Reduced Instruction Set Computer, this will be covered in a future book by the author on microprocessors), this field is included in the instruction's code through simplification and in view of the reduced number of instructions and addressing modes.

Figure 1.4. *An instruction with several operands*

By construction, the format of the instruction is fixed (fixed length), short or long, or variable (variable length). The value of a fixed format is a multiple of the byte in general. Its value will have a direct consequence for the incrementation value of the Program Counter (PC, *cf.* § V3-3.1.3). The benefit is that it will be possible to align the instructions (*cf.* § 3.1.2), thus accelerating memory reading or writing by reducing the number of memory accesses. The division of the instruction into sub-fields, for example, one for the instruction class (*cf.* Chapter 2), the second for the function, the third for the type of operands and the last for the operands and a unique format allowing simplification of the hardware, the counterpart being a larger format. A variable format, a multiple of the MPU data format, complicates the Control Unit (CU), and it has an impact on the number of machine cycles (*cf.* § V3-2.4.1) needed for decoding. During this phase, the decoder should determine the size of the instruction as quickly as possible. This information is needed, for example, for debugging, to determine the instruction boundaries or limits in the machine code (*interruptible "at instruction boundaries"*). On the other hand, it has the advantage of obtaining programs that take up less memory. In fact, a simple instruction such as nop (no operation, *cf.* § 2.8.5) will classically take up one byte compared to a word with several bytes with a fixed format. The format's variability makes it difficult to use a pipeline or a superscalar execution (this will be covered in a future book by the author on microprocessors). As an example of a fixed format, we cite the format n = 32 bits for MIPS Technologies microprocessors. Even if the format is fixed, the number of fields may vary as well as the format. Encoding uses three types, which are *Register (R-type), Immediate (I-type)* and *Jump (J-type) format* (Figure 1.5). The operation code, completed possibly by the function field, specifies the instruction. For the first type, the second field is a specifier of the source register (rs). The following specifies the target or destination register (rt or rd), which receives the result or branching condition. The last field is an immediate value, a jump or address displacement. For the J type, the operand is the jump address in a 26-bit format. For the last type, the third field is a destination register specifier (rd). The penultimate field indicates the value of a possible shift (0 = no shift). Note the conventions rt = rs + immediate and rd = rs + rt. This simple encoding should be compared with that of the Arm® family, which can show as many as 21 types (Arm 2000).

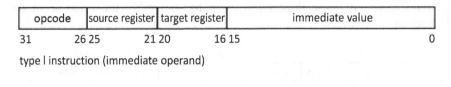

opcode	source register	target register	immediate value
31 26	25 21	20 16	15 0

type I instruction (immediate operand)

opcode	jump address
31 26	25 0

type J instruction (jump)

opcode	source register	target register	dest. register	shift	function
31 26	25 21	20 16	15 11	10 6	5 0

type R instruction (register operand)

Figure 1.5. *Three fixed formats for MIPS instructions*

None of these different fields have been standardized and are dependent on the manufacturer and the MPU family. For example, for Bayliss *et al.* (1981), an instruction is formed of four fields, which are the function fields (opcode), reference fields, and format and class fields. The class specifies the number of operands and their types. The necessary format field if there is at least one operand indicates their location (memory, register or pile, for example). The reference field gives their location explicitly. Their operation code field specifies the operation to be executed.

Figure 1.6 shows the typical variable instruction of an existing microprocessor. The instruction code has a format of 6 bits. The direction bit D indicates the direction of transfer (0 = source specified by the field reg, 1 = destination specified by the field). The bit W specifies the transfer format (0 = byte, 1 = word of 16 bits). The 2rd byte is called a "post-byte". The mode field indicates whether the transfer involves only the registers or if the memory is involved, the two displacement fields therefore indicate the length of the latter. We recognize the Little Endian byte order (LE (Cohen 1981), *cf.* § 2.6.2 from Darche (2012)) typical of Intel architecture since the *Least Significant Byte* (LSB) is first stored in the memory, in the order of the increasing addresses. To finish, the R/M (Register/Memory) field, poorly named, specifies the addressing mode, that is, the method of calculating the effective address (*cf.* § 1.2). Another format exists where the instruction is coded on a single byte. Thus, the format of these instructions can vary from 1 to 6 bytes. It is possible to add to these three types of prefix to modify the behavior of the instruction.

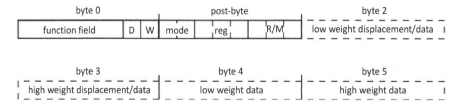

Figure 1.6. *Typical instruction format from 8086/88*

The architecture can also add a field, before or after the operation code to code the instruction class (called an extension of the operation code) or to specify a variable format. One example is the central IBM System/370 computer with its first 2 bits. The encoding of one instruction of the i486 by Intel is a typical example of the CISC approach (Complex Instruction Set Computer, this will be covered in a future book by the author on microprocessors). This type of instruction has a size ranging from 1 to 13 bytes. The word-code is therefore formed of one or two bytes for the operational code, a modify Register or Memory (mod R/M) byte, a Scale-Index-Base (SIB) byte, the bytes for displacement and the bytes for the immediate values. The reg/operation code field specifies a register or makes it possible to add information for the operation code. The R/M field specifies a register (2^3 at most) or, if it is combined with the mode field, makes it possible to specify a mode of address (24 maximum). The SIB byte makes it possible to specify the scale factor (0, 2, 4 or 8), an index register number and the base register number. In addition, one or more prefix bytes (in any order except for REX, see below) can change how the following instruction is interpreted. Figure 1.7 shows the instruction format for Intel IA-32 and Intel 64 architectures, which has changed with the evolution of MPUs. For example, the operation code for Pentium had a maximum size of two bytes. Today, the maximum length of an instruction is 15 bytes. The format for the instructions has not ceased growing.

Another example is Arm® architecture, which, to the left of the operation code, adds a condition field (Figure 2.23). Today, there are sets of instructions in multiple formats, a sort of compromise between fixed and variable formats with only two formats, for example, 32 bits and another value such as 16 bits with 19 different forms of encoding for Thumb® (Arm®) technology linked to the compression of these instruction codes (*cf.* § 1.1.1).

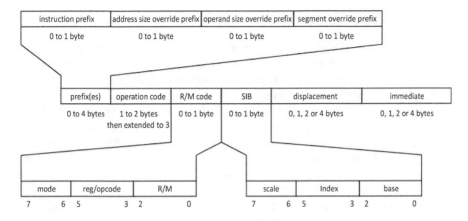

Figure 1.7. *Variable instruction format Intel IA-32 and Intel 64 (Intel 2016) architectures*

Several technical solutions exist for retaining ascending binary compatibility (*cf.* § 3.3.3). Intel has chosen the instruction prefix. It affects how the instruction is interpreted. For example, a REX (Register Extension) prefix in 64-bit mode that indicates that the instruction uses extended registers is a valid instruction (inc or dec) in IA-32 mode. This solution had already been used by Z80 with four non-assigned machine codes (hexadecimal values CB, DD, ED and FD as prefix) to expand its compatible instruction set with 8080. Another solution was to add a post-byte to distinguish between the sets of instructions. One recent example is the VEX prefix for Vector Extensions, which makes it possible to encode the AVX (Advanced Vector eXtensions, *cf.* § 2.7.1) extension from Intel.

The number of instructions, type of architecture (stack-based, register-based, etc.), the number of addressable registers, the number of internal busses and the type, format and location of the operands will have an influence on the format i of an instruction. For access to primary memory, the memory organization, in particular the exchange format (byte or word), byte order (remember the Endian story! *cf.* § V1-2.2.1) and the alignment (*cf.* § 2.6.1 from Darche (2012)), will have some influence. The ISA can be evaluated by the number of instructions F, their complexity, their format i and the memory space they occupy. The designer's choice will depend on the function of the desired performances (execution time, memory requirement, etc.), of the usage domains and the manufacturing cost. Complexity, if it is not material, could affect the software, in particular the compiler as in the RISC approach and in the programmer. The appendix shows the instruction encoding table for MPU 6809E from Motorola. For information, the aspect of decoding an instruction has been discussed in the previous volume.

1.1.1. *Code compression*

In order to limit the programs' memory footprint for reasons of cost, memory size, performance or, in particular, power saving, one solution is to compress the machine code at compilation and its decompression at execution, for example, when it is loaded in the MPU cache memory (Wolfe and Chanin 1992). One benefit lies in the fact that the compiler has not been modified. For implementation, the Huffman (1952) (de)compression algorithm can be used, for example. Because of its objectives, it is intended especially for embedded systems with an MPU/MCU[5] RISC. Two industrial examples are Thumb® and Thumb-2 for which the 16-bit instruction word is a compression of the classic version of Arm® processors, which have a 32-bit format. RISC-V (Waterman 2016) has a compressed version of its code suggested by (Waterman 2011). A comparison between MPUs can be made using a measurement of the code density.

The principle can quite clearly be applied to data and to buses (*cf.* V2) for the same aims.

1.2. Addressing modes

We recall that the address is a whole number that makes it possible to identify (we also say locate or spot) a place in the memory (*cf.* § V1-2.1). This, generated by an MPU, is termed "physical" (PA for Physical Address) since it is this that will be carried by the address bus. This physical address can be positive (i.e. natural integer) or also negative (i.e. relative integer) in the case of an address in Assembly Language (AL) or machine language, for example, for a displacement relative to the current value of the PC (Program Counter). Addressing is the mechanism for accessing information (data and instructions) stored in MPU registers or in other levels of the memory hierarchy (*cf.* § V1-2.3). The addressing or referencing mode specifies how to reach the instruction (code addressing mode) and its operands (operand addressing mode) during its execution. This distinction between the addressing code and its operands, which may moreover be an instruction classification (*cf.* § 2.1), may not exist (which is the most common scenario). One of the difficulties of using the concept is that its designation and its semantics vary depending on the architecture and on the designer of the CU (Control Unit). Thus, it involves sometimes only the memory address (memory address calculation mode) or it also covers the registers (operand addressing mode). The definition is taken in its widest sense. It does not therefore only involve access to the primary memory. The different addressing modes add to the wealth of a processor, and their number still varies depending on the architectures and designers. Addressing modes are one of

---

5 For MicroController Unit, i.e. a microcontroller (*cf.* § V3-5.3).

the ISA specification points (*cf.* § V1-3.5). For example, the IBM System/360 mainframe computer only has three (immediate, register and memory), but the Pentium microprocessor has nine. The more possibilities there are, the less the assembly language programmer will have to write the lines of code to carry out the desired operation. The argument refers today to the compiler designer, as assembly language is used less and less, except for teaching purposes or to meet a specific need in the use domain (*cf.* § V2-1.3). The other side of the coin is a more complex control unit and a longer execution for the instruction using it. We will see what the consequences of this will be covered in a future book by the author on microprocessors, which studies, among others, the RISC approach. If necessary, it specifies the means used to calculate the effective address (EA), also called the target address. This address is the result of the evaluation of an address according to its addressing mode. It will be applied on the address bus to reference the memory location if there is no virtual address mechanism at work (a mechanism that will be covered in a future book by the author on microprocessors). A synonym for EA (Effective Address) is "physical address". In the contrary scenario, the effective address is a logical address that should then be translated into a physical address in the case of the Virtual Memory (VM) mechanism. Depending on the manufacturers, the name may also be different or there may be other nuances. To finish, some microprocessors distinguish access to instructions and to their operands from access to Input–Output (I/O) registers with specialized instructions (I/O addressing mode), thus making it possible to address different Address Space (AS) (*cf.* § V3-2.1.1.1). One example is shown in § 2.8.2.

We define four modes of basic (i.e. simple) addressing, which are immediate addressing, implicit and explicit addressing and memory addressing. Memory addressing is broken down into direct, relative, indirect, indexed and based addressing. These modes indicate the way to fetch or store the operand. The storage of one value can only be done in a register or memory location. There can then exist combinations of these basic addressings, called complex addressings that can be replaced using a sequence of instructions with simple addressing. The other modes involve primary memory, the stack, the bit, the registers and those specific to a particular MPU family. To illustrate these, we have chosen some instructions that are representative of various MPUs. In these examples, all digital data will be expressed on base 10 (implicit base) with the exception of indications in the form of a character prefixing or post-fixing the value or of a number in subscript. To define the operand, the rules of syntax inspired by those of the MC6809 microprocessor will be the following:

#: immediate value

$: hexadecimal base

%: binary base

The registers will be the following:

PC: Program Counter

A: accumulator

The conventions for the pseudo-code will be the following:

← or =: assignment of the right-hand value (similar to an *rvalue*) in the left identifier (similar to an *lvalue*). The symbol used means "receives" or "takes the value". This left–right positional information avoids using parentheses, but it makes use of them for the right-hand value; they mean "contained in".

(): address access, of which the value is framed.

@: (calculation of) the two-point symbol address: concatenation

1.2.1. *Immediate addressing*

Immediate addressing mode, also called immediate data addressing mode, makes it possible to initialize a register or a memory location with a constant value d, which is specified after the instruction mnemonic (*cf.* § 2.1) (Figure 1.8), hence its other name "literal addressing mode". There is no effective address here since the memory is not addressed, but (DEC 1983) called it "PC immediate mode with auto-increment" as the PC (Program Counter) is used to address the value memorized immediately after the instruction code. One example is LDA #%10101010 from MC6802 from Motorola, which means that the accumulator A receives the immediate binary value 10101010b (b for binary) in byte format.

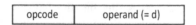

Figure 1.8. *Instruction with an operand field*

It is one of the fastest addressing modes since the value is included in the instruction and there is therefore no additional access to the main memory to fetch the operand accessed by another addressing. But this value is a constant. In addition, from the perspective of programming, the change of value means a modification in the program since the value field cannot be a destination. The extent of the values (in the sense of Chapter 2 of Darche (2000)) is limited by the number of bits remaining after subtraction of those bits reserved for coding the operation itself (a similar limitation for the address for direct and relative addressing). In its extended or long version, the format is double that of a short format. The possibility of choosing makes it possible to decrease the number of clock cycles to fetch the operand. An alternative to this mode is register addressing, which contains a constant value, which is materially fixed. This is the current practice with RISC microprocessors (this will be covered in a future book by the author on microprocessors) such as Arm®, whose register r0 contains the null value (*cf.* § V3-3.1), which can serve for initialization and avoids time-consuming external access to the main memory.

1.2.2. *Register addressing*

The use of registers makes it possible not to slow the microprocessor down since the registers are integrated. An instruction that uses them in addressing mode will only require external access to fetch the instruction code. It is possible to address a register in two ways, explicitly and implicitly.

1.2.2.1. *Explicit addressing*

The operand field operand(s) R specifies the registers used for execution. It is sometimes called register (direct) addressing, the term "direct" indicating that the referencing in the register is found in the instruction coding, as for the direct memory address (Figure 1.9). These registers are accessible to the programmer. There is no effective address since the memory is not addressed, hence a fast execution of the instruction using it and a small instruction format. It is for this reason that RISC microprocessors prefer to use this mode. For other architectures, the number of registers accessible to the programmer is limited (order of size: about 20).

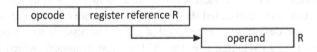

Figure 1.9. *Execution of an instruction using register addressing from one register*

The example below shows an addition in an Arm® microprocessor, which uses three registers: r0, r1 and r2:

ADD r0,r1,r2; r0 ← r1 + r2

Note, a distinction can be made between Data Register Direct Addressing and Address Register Direct Addressing as for MC68000 (*cf.* § V3-3.1.1).

1.2.2.2. *Implicit register addressing*

To simplify the programming, some instructions use one or more registers in an extended or implicit manner. In this addressing mode, also called implicit or implied addressing mode, no operand is specified after the instruction mnemonic (*cf.* § 2.1). Execution of the instruction involves the reference to operand that is not joined to the operating code. One synonym is implication (Brooks 1962). The instruction format is reduced by it. One example is the dex instruction from MCS6502, which decrements its index register X. The name of this appears in the mnemonic to facilitate programming. Sometimes when the accumulators are used, this mode is called "accumulator addressing". The example below applied to MC6809. The accumulator B specified by the last letter of the mnemonic receives a value expressed in hexadecimal base.

LDB #$FA; B ← FA$_{16}$

If the name of the registers does not appear in the mnemonic, then only a detailed reading of the technical documentation can specify the name of these registers. In the example below (MC6809), the instruction for multiplication mul (without operands) implicitly uses both implicit accumulator registers A and B and stores the concatenated result in these same registers, and the MSB (Most Significant Byte) is found in accumulator A, which in pseudo-code gives: A:B ← A × B.

Another example is the instruction from 8086 mul bl, which uses the implicit register A as source and destination operands in the case of multiplication in 8-bit format (ax ← bl × al for this example).

To generalize, an instruction lacking one or more operands found in a register (an accumulator for example) or in memory uses implicit addressing. We find this mode in machines with a single address called an accumulator or in the extreme case of zero-operand computers also called stack or pushdown-store machine (*cf.* § V1-2.7.1). By broadening the definition to registers that are not accessible to the programmer, any instruction for its execution uses the PC (Program Counter), which is therefore implicit.

1.2.3. *Memory addressing modes*

It is possible to address the memory in a direct, relative, indirect, indexed or based manner. Combinations of these modes are possible. Other specific modes are then presented.

1.2.3.1. *Direct addressing*

Direct or absolute addressing is without doubt the most natural. It can access a memory address location A defined (i.e. arranged immediately) after the instruction code in the operand field (Figure 1.10). It can therefore be considered a constant. The effective address EA is given by the following formula:

$$EA = A \hspace{10cm} [1.1]$$

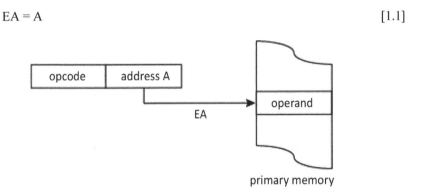

primary memory

Figure 1.10. *Instruction with direct addressing*

It can be used by jump instruction to branch to a set location in the program. This mode is in fact an indirect mode with auto-incrementation using the PC (Program Counter) as an indirection register (*cf.* § 1.2.3.3 for indirection).

This mode allows for variations depending on the format of the address provided, the benefit lies in reducing the instruction's memory size. Some manufacturers thus distinguish the short mode from the extended mode, known as long mode, depending on the format of the address A, provided. In the short mode (absolute short, page zero, also known direct at Motorola, a base page (IEEE 1985)) illustrated in Figure 1.11, the address is expressed in a smaller format than that of a microprocessor. The address field may also be smaller than 3 bits, one example being the 8021 microcontroller from Intel or, classically, 8 bits in 8-bit MPUs. Page zero can be seen as a bank of registers (RF for Register File, *cf.* § V3-3.1.11.1). The MIPS firm speaks of pseudo-direct addressing. Aside from a smaller format, the second benefit lies in decreasing the number of memory accesses to fetch the instruction code and the operand address. It is equivalent to a basic addressing + displacement, as in the IBM System/370 architecture, with a null base address. One example is the MC6802 microprocessor where the address is in byte format, while the format of the MPU address bus is double. This then limits the address space to the interval $[00, FF]_{16}$, hence the term "absolute short addressing" or "page zero"[6] (if the size of the memory page is 256 bytes). In the example below, the A register receives the content of memory location 00.

04F0 96 04 LDA $00; A ← (00)

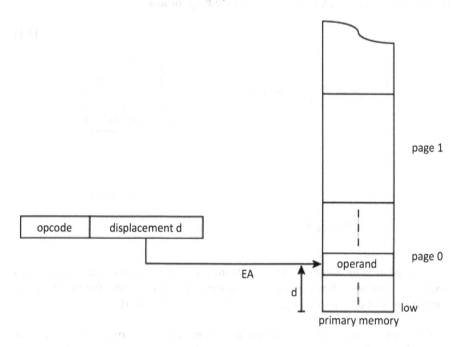

opcode | displacement d

EA

d

operand   page 1

page 0

low

primary memory

Figure 1.11. *Instruction with an address at page 0*

The concept of page zero addressing has been improved with direct page addressing. The direct page is now movable in a larger memory page. The start of the page is addressed by a specialized register (*cf.* § V3-3.1.1). We cite MC6809 (a page of 256 bytes in a space of 64 KiB, addressing capacity of the MPU itself, direct page (DP) register), the 65CE02 from Commodore Semiconductor Group or CSG (the same as before except that its addressing capacity is higher, base page register B) and the 65816 from the firm Western Digital Corporation (WDC) with an address over 16 bits in the direct page register D.

A direct addressing is limited in its extent for a given instruction format; there are bits reserved for coding the instruction, which should be subtracted from the bits

6 The mini-computer PDP-8 for Programmable Data Processor from DEC introduced in 1965 used this term.

reserved for the addressing. This limitation can be lifted if the instruction format is not limited (i.e. variable format). With extended addressing, the address belongs to the microprocessor's address space without restriction. The format is that of the address bus. It should be noted that the absolute address can be implemented with a basic address + displacement with a basic register with zero content base.

1.2.3.2. *Relative addressing*

Relative addressing, implied in PC (Program Counter-relative addressing), makes it possible to access a memory location relating to the current position of the program counter that, we recall, contains the address of the next instruction to be executed (Figure 1.12) after the decoding stage. This mode is in fact an indexed mode using the PC (*cf.* § 1.2.3.4 on indexing). With the following formula, we see that the effective address of the data or instruction relates to the PC by a value of d:

$$EA = PC_{\text{following instruction}} + d \qquad\qquad [1.2]$$

This is the favored mode for jump instructions, whether conditional or not (PC-relative branch). The relative displacement d is expressed in a signed integer representation, which is always the complement to 2^n (two's complement, *cf.* § II.2.5 from Darche (2000)). Depending on the size of the displacement, the extent of the jump will be limited to $(-2^{n-1}, 2^{n-1} -1)$, with n being the format of the address field. Depending on the value of n of the relative address, we will call it a short or long jump. When the processor uses segmentation (this will be covered in a future book by the author on memories), jumps can be made within a single segment (intra-segment jump) or between two segments (extra-segment jump).

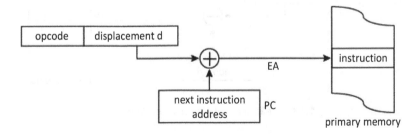

Figure 1.12. *Execution of an instruction in relative addressing*

The example below (x86) is a negative jump. The hexadecimal value F9 represents -7 in base 10. This means that the processor will connect 5 bytes higher than the instruction address, the difference of two bytes arising from the fact that the

PC has changed while the instruction was executed (incrementation of the size of this instruction, here, two bytes):

73 F9 jnc loop; PC ← PC + F916

Two particular cases should be cited: jmp 00, which jumps to the following instruction since the program counter has been incremented during the decoding phase of the execution cycle (*cf.* § V1-3.2 and V1-3.3.2) to direct the following instruction and jump −n, where n is the instruction format (in words) underway, which implements an infinite loop. This mode is linked to PC (PC with displacement or Program Counter with Displacement for MC68000). It can be seen as an indexed mode, the indexation register being the PC (*cf.* § 1.2.3.4).

This mode is useful for generating the independent code of implantation in memory (position-independent code). We also speak of a translatable code (relocatable code), a topic discussed in § 3.1.4. It is also at the root of implantation of classic control structures of high-level languages (if_<condition>_then_else, iterative   structures   (i.e.   loops)   such   as   while_<condition>_do, repeat_until_<condition>, for_<condition>_do, etc.) in assembly language.

This mode can even be used to address an operand (Figure 1.13). We cite x86 64-bit architectures with addressing called RIP (Instruction Pointer Register)-relative, ARMv8 with literal mode and MPU MC6809 with the program counter-relative mode.

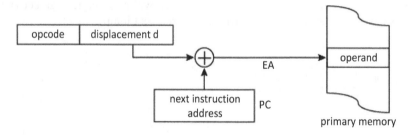

Figure 1.13. *Seeking an operand in relative addressing*

This mode can be seen as an indirect mode auto-incrementation using the PC (Program Counter) as an indirection register (*cf.* § 1.2.3.3).

1.2.3.3. *Indirect addressing*

It is useful to dissociate addressing of the operand from that of the instruction code. The address may thus vary without changing the reference indicated in the instruction. This mode is used to implement the mechanism of the High-Level (programming) Language (HLL) pointer. In assembly language, the square brackets "[" and "]" are generally used to employ this mode. Some constructors use parentheses or the character @. A memory location or register contains the address of the operand. In indirect mode or register deferred mode (register indirect or register deferred addressing[7]) illustrated in Figure 1.14, the effective address EA is given by the following formula:

$$EA = R \hspace{4cm} [1.3]$$

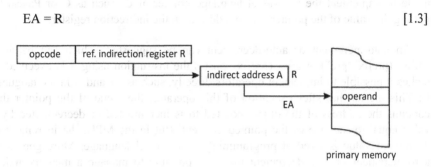

Figure 1.14. *Instruction with indirect register addressing*

In memory indirect addressing illustrated in Figure 1.15, the final effective address EA is given by formula [1.5]. Here, it is a double indirection:

$$EA' = A \hspace{4cm} [1.4]$$

$$EA = (A) = A' \hspace{3cm} [1.5]$$

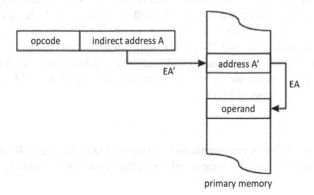

Figure 1.15. *Instruction with indirect memory addressing*

---

7 Vocabulary from DEC (1983).

This mode of addressing generally has a greater extent than direct addressing since the addressing format m is the same as that of the data format n. It was therefore useful for the first computers, which had a restricted addressing capacity (in the case of mini-PDP-8 computers from the DEC firm of the NOVA series from Data General, for example). Another advantage is the decrease in the instruction format, thus increasing the instruction throughput. For MC6809, the constructor speaks of "extended indirect addressing". The compiler will doubtlessly use this mode to implement the high-level language pointer mode such as C or Pascal by putting the value of the pointer (i.e. an address) in the indirection register.

An auto-increment or auto-decrement can be suggested, which can be done before (prefix "pre") or after (prefix "post") the instruction using it is executed. It makes it possible to implement operators directly, such as ++ and -- in the language C. This means that after execution of this operator, the value of the pointer that contains the address of the object pointed to is incremented or decremented by a value equal to the size of the pointed element. But in the MPU, the increment or decrement value is fixed at programming in low-level language. More generally, auto-increment or auto-decrement makes it possible to manage a memory index, which is useful, for example, in displacement in a data structure such as an array. Register indirect addressing with post- or pre-increment/decrement is adapted for digital signal processing to address samples.

This mode is in fact the one that makes it possible to implement absolute addressing mode using the PC (Program Counter) as an indirection register. It is for this reason that DEC (1983) with PDP series, which used the PC as a General-Purpose Register (GPR, *cf.* § V3-3.1), called it "PC absolute mode", equivalent to an immediate indirect addressing (immediate[8] deferred mode or auto-increment deferred mode). The term "immediate" means that the value immediately following the instruction code addressed by the PC will be used to fetch the address of the operand (EA = PC + 2 bytes in the case of the PDP-11 mini-computer) with, afterwards, an update to the PC. This same manufacturer proposed a relative deferred mode PC addressing, that is, indirect relative addressing, which uses the PC added to a displacement to fetch the operand's address (EA = $(PC_{instruction + 1} +$ displacement) in the case of PDP-11).

1.2.3.4. *Indexed and based addressing modes*

Indexed addressing is characterized by using an Index Register (IR) that contains a reference address, called a base or offset address, making it possible to access a

---

8 Here this means an immediate value following the instruction code that will serve as the address.

memory location. The content of this register, here R, is added to a displacement A specified with the instruction (Figure 1.16). The effective address EA is equal to:

$$EA = R + A \qquad\qquad\qquad [1.6]$$

Indexed addressing with null displacement is identical to register indirect addressing. This mode is equivalent to relative addressing if the index register is replaced by the PC (Program Counter). The index register may be implicit or designed explicitly as an operand. It can be dedicated specifically to this usage or it can be a GPR. In the former case, it is generally named X or Y (in the case of MCS6502). From the perspective of execution complexity, it adds an operation (addition) compared to the indirection. The @ symbol is generally used in assembly language to indicate this mode.

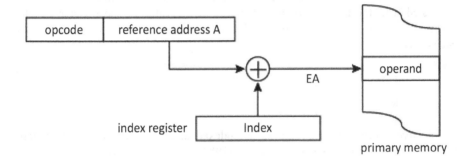

Figure 1.16. *Execution of an instruction in indexed addressing with displacement (indexation "true")*

Cushman (1975) speaks of "true" and "false" indexing. Indexing is called "true" when the index address is the operand, the case in Figure 1.16 and MPUs MCS6502 and 2650 (Signetics). In the second case, the index address is in the dedicated register and the operand is the index, one example being the MC6802/MC6809 (Figure 1.17). The second field of the instruction word, called a "modifier" in Simpson and Terrell (1987) has an 8-bit format, while the index register format has 16 bits. Some manufacturers such as Motorola consider the relative address as an indexed mode, the indirection register being the PC (Program Counter, *cf.* § 1.2.3.3).

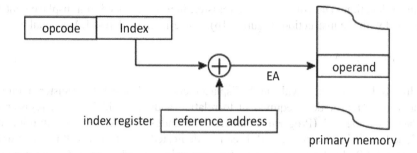

Figure 1.17. *Execution of an instruction in indexed addressing with displacement (false indexing)*

As for indirection with auto-increment or auto-decrement, auto-indexing can be suggested with the addition of an integer A to the value of the register R. The designer of M68HC12 speaks of pre-decrement and post-decrement indexed. At each execution, we will have:

$$EA = R + A \qquad\qquad [1.7]$$

$$R = R + 1$$

Relative addressing is similar to an indexed addressing by the PC (Program Counter). It is for this reason that DEC (1983) called it "PC-relative addressing mode".

Scaled indexed addressing mode makes it possible to multiply the content of the index register by a constant 1, 2, 4 or 8, for example, for 80386. This facilitates management of data structures in high-level languages as an array, a structure or record.

Base (plus) offset addressing arises from the principle above except that the index register is replaced by a base register (Figure 1.18), hence its other name: base register addressing. Intel uses the BX and BP (Base Pointer) for x86, the first addresses the data segment and the second addresses the stack. The IBM z System mainframe computer uses 16 General-Purpose Registers (GPR) in 64-bit format as a base register and the displacement is specific to the 12-bit format. At its origin, this mode made it possible to extend the address space. Today, this is no longer necessary.

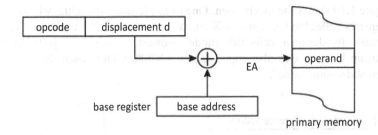

Figure 1.18. *Execution of an instruction in base addressing with displacement*

The difference between these two modes is more semantic than applicable to calculating the effective address. The index varies starting from a given index address with the instruction, while the base address is constant (hence its name) and an offset is provided with the instruction. Moreover, Intel uses the terms "base" and "indexed" for base addressing. Moreover, if no offset is specified with the instruction, Intel (1989) names the 8086 base and indexed addressing without offset "indirect register addressing". Often, in RISC microprocessors such as Arm®, the r0 register contains the constant 0, thus avoiding an immediate addressing using a main memory access that takes a great deal of time. If it is used as a base register, the addressing becomes absolute. The base mode is similar to segmented addressing (this will be covered in a future book by the author on memories). Another means of differentiating these two addressings is that there is no auto-increment with base addressing.

Calculation of the effective addressing depends on the storage order or endianness (*cf.* § V1-2.2.1) of the address' bytes. Thus, MCS6502 with a little-endian order is favored because the addition is carried out starting from the LSBs.

1.2.3.5. *Combinations of addressing modes*

It is possible to combine the addressing modes above. Some processors offer indirect addressing with indexing. The associated terms "pre-indexing" and "post-indexing" will qualify at what step of the address calculation the indexing will apply. Pre-indexing means that indexing is carried out on the indirection address (*pre-indexed indirect addressing mode*), hence the second name, "indexed indirect addressing mode".

We will have:

$$EA' = A + R \qquad\qquad [1.8]$$

$$EA = (EA')$$

Figure 1.19 shows the mechanism. One example was MCS6502, which included two registers called "index registers X and Y" even though X has already served for indirection. Its designer calls this mode (indirect,X), which is justified by the relationship [1.8]. It was also suggested by MC6809. DEC used the term "index deferred addressing mode".

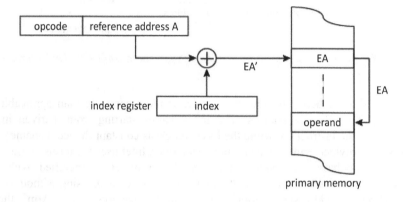

Figure 1.19. *Indirect indexed addressing or pre-indexing*

Post-indexed indirect addressing mode or indirect indexed addressing mode applies indexing after indirection, as illustrated in Figure 1.20. We will have:

$$EA' = A \tag{1.9}$$

$$EA = (A) + R \tag{1.10}$$

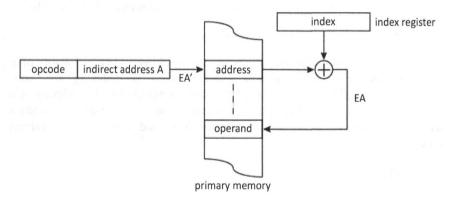

Figure 1.20. *Indirect indexed addressing or post-indexing*

The peculiarity of MCS6502 is that it used zero-page addressing as the address field was limited to 8 bits and the indexing occurred only on the lower part of the address (Figure 1.21). Its designer calls this mode (indirect),Y, which is justified by the relationship [1.10].

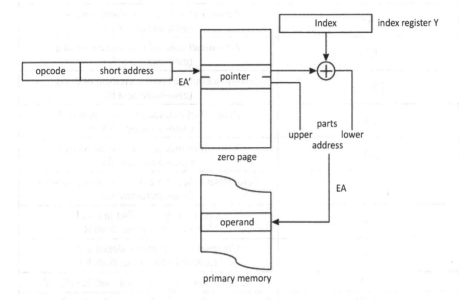

Figure 1.21. *Indirect indexed zero-page addressing of MCS6502*

A representative, penultimate example is MC6809, which offers 18 variations in mode, combining indexed and indirect addressings with the possibility of automatic post-increment or pre-decrement. This post-increment or pre-decrement is useful for managing a stack's pointer. Table 1.2 summarizes the possible combinations. R represents one of the four registers that can be used for indexing, the classics X and Y and the stack pointers user U and material S. Note the addressings using the program counter at the end. The offset is expressed in complement to 2^n representation.

Indexed and based addressings with or without offset (based indexed plus displacement addressing mode) can be combined, thus offering, for example, 17 possible variations in the case of microprocessor x86. One example of this use is addressing an array of records, of a vector or of a structure, the base pointing the start of the array and index, an element of the array and the displacement, a field of the element.

MC6809 assembly language notation	Description
,R	Zero-offset indexed
[,R]	Zero-offset indexed indirect
,R+	Zero-offset indexed post-increment of 1 (auto-increment R)
,R++	Zero-offset indexed post-increment of 2 (auto-increment R)
[,R++]	Zero-offset indexed post-increment of 2 indirect (auto-increment R)
,-R	Zero-offset indexed pre-decrement of 1 (auto-decrement R)
,--R	Zero-offset indexed pre-decrement of 2 (auto-decrement R)
[,--R]	Zero-offset indexed pre-decrement of 2 indirect (auto-decrement R)
n,R	Constant signed offset indexed (5, 8 or 16 bits offset from R)
[n,R]	Constant signed offset indexed indirect (5, 8 or 16 bits offset from R)
A,R	Accumulator A signed offset from R indexed
[A,R]	Accumulator A signed offset from R indexed indirect
B,R	Accumulator B signed offset from R indexed
[B,R]	Accumulator B signed offset from R indexed indirect
D,R	Accumulator D signed offset from R indexed
[D,R]	Accumulator D signed offset from R indexed indirect
n,PCR	Constant signed offset from PC indexed (8 or 16 bits)
[n,PCR]	Constant signed offset from PC indexed indirect (8 or 16 bits offset)
[n]	Extended indirect

Table 1.2. *Combined MC6809 addressing modes*

1.2.4. *Other addressing modes*

Other modes have been introduced to provide a high-level functionality or to adapt to a specific domain such as digital signal processing (*cf.* § V3-5.2), to a specific mechanism of a processor or to a component such as an I/O controller (*cf.* Chapter 3 of Darche (2003)) or a microcontroller (*cf.* § V3-5.3). Moreover, other modes belong to high-level languages. To finish, some obsolete modes are presented.

1.2.4.1. *Memory-to-memory addressing*

The memory-to-memory transfer functionality is possible in a von Neumann-inspired MPU, but it should be seen as exceptional. This is the continuity of the tendency of CISC processors to implement high-level functionalities in the material. Intel calls this mode "string addressing" for its 8086. It involves addressing the characters of a string, that is, of an array of characters by indirection using both its pointer registers SI (Source Index) and DI (Destination Index). It makes it possible, among other things, to read or write a character and, whether the repeat prefix is conditional or not, to make a copy of it in the main memory. The search function in a string is also available.

1.2.4.2. *(Implicit) stack addressing*

Operands are found implicitly (i.e. they are not named) on the stack which is, we recall (*cf.* § 4.1), access to LIFO (Last-In/First-Out, push-in/pop-out or push-down/pop-up memory) and implemented in primary memory in modern MPU. The two primitives (i.e. functions) to access it are stacking() and unstacking(), translated into instructions respectively by `push()` and `pop()`, for example, in x86 architecture. These instructions implement, internally, an indirect addressing mechanism with the Stack Pointer register (SP), which memorizes the address at the top of the stack. The stack is implemented in main memory, but it can be implemented in the processor. The stacked element is specified with the operand. There are also specific instructions to a register, such as `pha/pla` (push/pull accumulator onto/from stack) from MC6800, which makes it possible to stack/destack this MPU's accumulator. MCS6502 uses `php/plp` (push/pull processor status on/from stack) this time for the MPU's context. By extension, stack computers do not explicitly name the operands (zero-operand, one-operand or two-operand addressing). For reading on this subject, see Koopman (1989).

The NS3200 (Hunter 1987) from National Semiconductor (NS) has broadened access to the stack by offering a mode called top-of-stack, literally "stack top", which makes it possible to access the data of the so-called summit, since modification of the pointer is not systematic (i.e. dependent on the operation). To finish with this topic, MPUs such as the families Arm®, PowerPC or MC68000 make it possible to use General-Purpose Registers (GPR) as stack pointers. The addressing mode is of indirect type with auto-increment/decrement.

1.2.4.3. *Bit addressing*

The first GPPs (for General-Purpose Processor, *cf.* § V3-1.1) did not have specialized instructions to manipulate (set at one/zero or extraction) or to test individually the bits of an operand by conditional branching (*cf.* § 2.4.1). It is generally microcontrollers that possess them as they have to read or modify binary information in memory or at the input–output ports (*cf.* § 3.1 from Darche (2003)). Thus, the microcontroller 68HC12 from the MC6800 family from Motorola has the instructions bclr (bit clear) and bset (bit set) that initialize respectively at 0 or at 1 one position bit specified with the help of a binary mask (see exercise E2.4) in an address word A. These instructions use this mode associated with pre-studied conventional addressing modes. It should be noted that the addressing space is limited compared to other modes. The example in Figure 1.22 shows a reset at 0 for the MSb (Most Significant bit) of an I/O port in byte format implanted at the address $0F_{16}$.

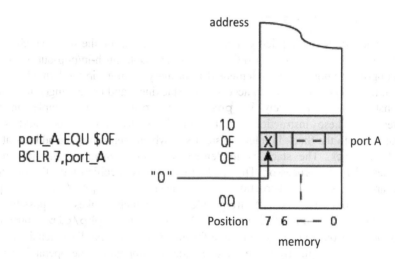

Figure 1.22. *Execution of an instruction in bit addressing*

1.2.4.4. *MMR addressing*

One possibility is to manipulate I/O registers as conventional addresses (MMR for Memory-Mapped Register, literally, registers projected into memory, *cf.* § V3-3.1.1 and V3-2.1.1.1) in reduced format (page zero addressing) with fast specialized access instructions. One example is the Digital Signal Processor (DSP), reference C5000 from Texas Instruments (TI).

1.2.4.5. *Addressing modes specific to the digital signal processor*

Other than indirect register addressing with post- or pre-increment/decrement, two other modes are particularly adapted to digital signal processing, which justifies their implementation in DSPs. This is circular addressing and (address) bit-reversed addressing.

1.2.4.5.1. Circular addressing

Digital signal processing consists of digitizing samples x_i ($i \in [0, \infty]$) of the signal that are stored in memory, then carrying out a mathematical processing such as filtering on them to then reconstruct the analog signal. To simplify the discourse, memorization of coefficients needed for the calculation is not attempted. The sample flow is of infinite length, and the calculation is only made on a limited number of consecutive samples on the sampled sequence. This set is called a "window". Linear addressing of the buffer FIFO (First In, First Out) illustrated in Figure 1.23a is not well adapted as it is necessary to test whether the pointers have reached the end. Moreover, the size of the buffer is necessarily high. The circular buffer (ring or cyclic buffer, circular queue), that Figure 1.23b shows, is a much better solution as it makes it possible to decrease its size to that of the window of samples needed for the calculation.

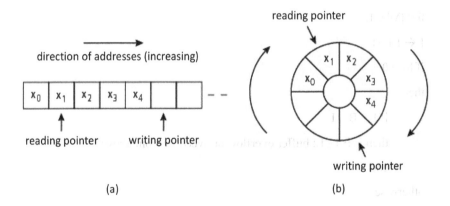

Figure 1.23. *Window of five samples*

Circular or modulo addressing makes it possible to implement a circular buffer in a Random Access Memory (RAM). As shown in Figure 1.24, it is necessary to have four pieces of information that are the size of the circular buffer L, the address of the base of buffer B, the index pointer of the buffer I and increment (relative integer) M. This addressing uses modular arithmetic where the extent of the values is finite to calculate the pointer addresses. The benefit of using it lies in the fact that a block of L contiguous memory words is addressed by a pointer that uses a modulo addressing L. This means that once a pointer arrives at the end of a buffer, it is reinitialized to point the other end (more precisely, modulo addressing is the capacity to memorize the buffer).

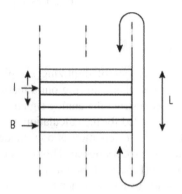

Figure 1.24. *Circular buffer*

This is conveyed in algorithmic form by:

$0 < |M| \leq L$

$I \leftarrow I + M$

if M > 0

then

> if $I \geq B + L$
>
> then I ← I - L; buffer overflow or overflow from above
>
> end_if

otherwise

> if I < B
>
> then I ← I + L; buffer overflow or overflow from below
>
> end_if
>
> end_if

Management logic detects a buffer overflow when there is a wraparound. It then generates an interrupt request (see Chapter 5) to warn the handler. This automatic management avoids a costly rearrangement of data by shifting them (Figure 1.25(a)) and a permanent monitoring of the pointer value to know whether it has reached an end of the buffer in order to reinitialize it. It frees useful calculating power for processing. For example, as soon as the top of the buffer is reached, the following sample is stored at its start (Figure 1.25(b)).

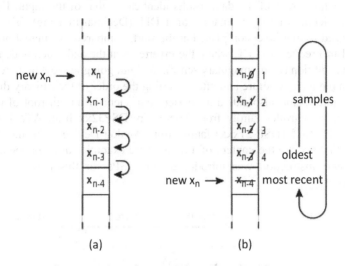

(a)   (b)

Figure 1.25. *Comparison between linear and circular addressings (from Rao (2001))*

The use domain is digital signal filtering carried out by a DSP where digital values, the results of a quantification of an analog signal, are stored in a delay line that can be implemented with a circular buffer in place of carrying out costly temporal shifts. The DSP ADSP-210xx family from Analog Devices uses this mode. One example of use is implementation of a Finite Impulse Response (FIR) described in § V3-5.2.

1.2.4.5.2. Reverse bit order addressing

Bit-reversed addressing makes it possible to manipulate materially the address without changing the source address. When the processor is set in this specific mode by the positioning of a flag (*cf.* § V3-3.1.5) in a control register, the address generator (AGU for Address Generation Unit, also called DAG for Data Address Generator or ACU for Address Computation Unit) generates bit-reversed addressing. This means that the LSbs (Least Significant bits) and MSb are exchanged, position 1 and m-2 bits are exchanged and so on (change from little-endian order to big-endian order or vice versa). This mode is used in implementation of the Fast Fourier Transform (FFT) algorithm (Cooley and Tukey 1965), an effective method for calculating a Discrete Fourier Transform (DFT), used for filtering or spectral analysis. Remember that the FFT makes it possible to change the time domain to the frequency domain and vice versa. The problem is that the result output order differs from that of the input or vice versa. This mode makes it possible to preserve the initial order of the data by choosing out-of-order input samples to keep the output order of the data results identical to that of the input. Figure 1.26 shows the details of the calculation of a DIT (Decimal-In-Time) FFT, which is characterized by the inversion placed at the start, compared to calculation of a DIF (Decimal-In-Frequency) FFT, where the inverter is at the end. Each node represents a complex addition (in an imaginary sense). Without going into detail, note the value of the sample indices before and after inverting the order of their binary digits. W_K^{nk} is the twiddle factor, also called a Fourier coefficient or an nth root of unity. The dsPIC® microcontroller family from Microchip, DSP32xx from AT&T and DSPs from the SHARC® (DSP-21xxx) family from Analog Devices with the instruction bitrev that reverse the content of a register are examples of components offering it. The mac instruction was introduced into DSPs for this type of calculation (cf. § 2.8.4.2).

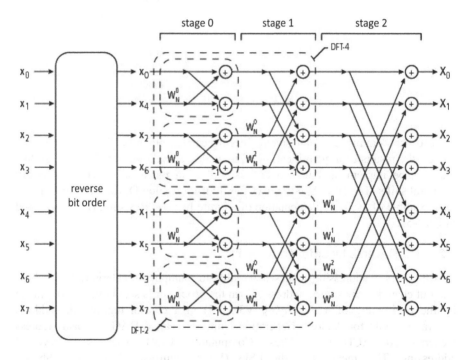

Figure 1.26. *Flow diagram of the algorithm of an 8-point FFT DIT in base 2*

To carry out this inversion of the address bit order, Reverse-Carry Arithmetic (RCA) is used. The sub-set managing the address or AGU (*cf.* § V3-3.4.4) reverses the direction of the bits retained when an increment is added to the value of an address register. Two processors that implement it are DSP32xx from AT&T and DSP56000 (Motorola 1992). The AGU also implements linear and modulo arithmetic.

1.2.4.5.3. Linear addressing

The DSP56000 uses a – perhaps poorly named – address modifier. It makes it possible to jump address at each access with a stored constant memorization in a register. The benefit is easy access to the elements of a complex data structure.

1.2.4.6. *Modes specific to the assembler*

The assembler can offer addressing modes that do not exist in the MPU. Each instruction using them will be replaced by an equivalent logical sequence. One example is symbolic addressing, which facilitates programming of a jump to a specific location in the code marked by a symbolic name called a label (*cf.* § V5-1.3.3). This mode belongs to assembly language (*cf.* § V5-1.3), unlike those seen previously in this chapter which belong to machine language. It is used to make a jump to a precise place in the code marked by this symbolic name. One example is MPU MIPS R2000/R3000 (Kane 1988).

1.2.4.7. *Obsolete modes*

The modes studied so far are those that are currently available. Some modes have been abandoned because they are complex or not useful. For example, page-zero and direct paged modes (microprocessor IM6100 from Intersil) with current memory sizes are no longer required. We also mention truncation, which consists of deleting the most significant address bits to adapt to addressing capacity in the storage hierarchy considered (Brooks 1962).

1.2.4.8. *Note*

Sequential execution of instructions in von Neumann architecture (*cf.* § V1-3.2.2) can be seen as a sequential addressing mode (source: Wikipedia).

1.2.5. *Summary on addressing*

Addressing modes have evolved to meet needs in the software industry to improve efficiency of programs and facilitate implementing functionalities of high-level languages as their control structures. It is useful to class addressing modes depending on their content, code or data. Simple code addressing modes are

Program Counter (PC)-relative absolute addressings and indirect register addressings. Sequential execution by nop instruction can be seen as an addressing mode. Sample data addressing modes are immediate, (direct) register, implicit and base plus offset modes. Mixed (code/data) modes are direct absolute and indexed, base plus index modes with or without offset (base plus index plus offset), scaled indexed modes, register indirect modes, indirect register modes with auto-increment, indirect memory and PC-relative modes.

Making the programmer accessible to registers that are not conventional, such as PC and SP, makes it possible to enrich addressing modes. Thus, some modes can be implemented using others, such as, for example, absolute and relative modes with respectively indirect and indexed modes.

The trend has been towards multiplying addressing modes, making it possible to adapt to complex data structures such as those of high-level languages or application domains such as digital signal processing with its operations such as convolution or correlation. This wealth of modes facilitates the life of the assembly language programmer and makes it possible for the code to be compact during compilation. The counterpart is the complexity of the CU (Control Unit), one of the defects of the CISC approach (this will be covered in a future book by the author on microprocessors). The number of possibilities of machine codes depends on the number of instructions and associated addressing modes. Therefore, MC6809 had 59 instructions and 1,464 machine codes (Motorola 1981, 1983). A reverse tendency was that of reduced instruction set architectures (RISC, this will be covered in a future book by the author on microprocessors).

1.3. Conclusion

The following chapter focuses on the instruction set for a generic microprocessor by presenting the different instruction families and extensions in this set.

Instruction Set and Class

This chapter focuses on perhaps the most important characteristic of an ISA (Instruction Set Architecture, *cf.* § V1-3.5), which is a processor's instruction set. We define and propose how to classify instructions, and then present the different instruction families for a generic microprocessor as well as the possible extensions for this set.

2.1. Definitions

Instructions differ depending on their designers in their number, name, mnemonic, the number of operands and addressing modes and in their syntax. From their designation (i.e. name and mnemonic), these characteristics depend on the type of architecture and ISA (*cf.* § V1-3.5). We must distinguish the instruction name, which always begins with an action verb indicating the operation to be executed (e.g. move) from its symbolic or mnemonic name, which is either its abridged instruction name (e.g. mov) or an acronym that always begins with the first letter of the action verb according to IEEE standard (Std) 694-1985 (IEEE 1985) (*cf.* § V5-1.3.2). One benefit of this choice is that the alphabetical order corresponds to the function, with some exceptions. This facilitates a modern microprocessor's (MPU for MicroProcessor Unit) reading of several thousand pages of documents. Still following the recommendations of this standard, it should not include any integrated addressing mode specification, or integrated operand name. The execution conditions are integrated. The type of operand specified in the suffix begins from a point in the mnemonic or, in some cases, in the operand. There may be synonyms of mnemonics for a single operation, one example being arithmetic and logical left shifts (sal[1] and shl from the x86 family). A processor's instruction set is grouped within the instructions or IS (Instruction Set), and a microprocessor that executes

---

1 Instruction shla (SHift Left Arithmetical) in the standard.

instructions from a fixed IS is called an ISP (Instruction Set Processor). The instruction set can be extended and complex, or, on the contrary, it may be reduced and simple, hence the names for the respective microprocessor families CISC and RISC (respectively Complex and Reduced Instruction Set Computer, this will be covered in a future book by the author on microprocessors). Instructions that are complex in their function, variable format, transfer type, etc., complicate the compiler's task because of the various cases to be taken into account. A compromise, depending on the applications targeted and the complexity of the control unit, should therefore be found when choosing instructions. To be comprehensive, the Application-Specific Processor (ASP, *cf.* § V3-1.1) has a specific instruction set, hence the acronym ASIP for Application-Specific Instruction set Processor.

The process of classifying instructions generally relies on the locality of execution or processing. We can thus classify instructions into three main families or classes, one for data transfers, one for arithmetic processing instructions for integers and logical instructions and one for control transfers (Figures 2.1a and b).

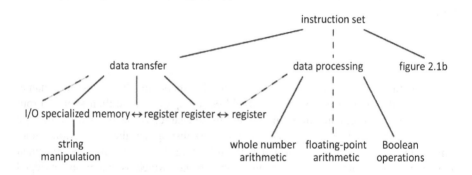

Figure 2.1a. *Instruction classification in modern MPUs*

A fourth class is that of system control, which Kaeli and Yew (2005) call "the environmental instructions class", that is, those executed in most cases in privileged mode (if this exists) by the Operating System or SE (InTerruption (IT), management of hardware resources, etc.) to control the MPU. Execution parallelism instructions such as atomic instructions (*cf.* § 2.6.1) were introduced subsequently in microprocessors. A final class is that of extensions to the instruction set for a particular application such as multimedia application. Figure 2.1(b) completes this classification.

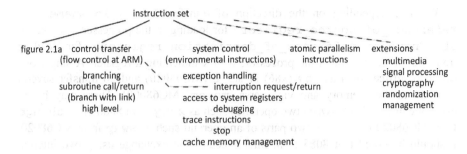

Figure 2.1b. *Classifying instructions in modern MPUs (continuation and end)*

An instruction set can also be subdivided into several sub-sets depending on the execution rights or modes, of which there are generally two, administrator and simple user (*cf.* § 3.2.2). Another criteria for classification is the number of operands (0, 1, 2, etc.). A component such as the microcontroller or Digital Signal Processor (DSP) will add the bit manipulation instruction family.

We will now see the instructions for these classes in detail. To present them in a readable and generic form, the Assembly Language (AL) mnemonics (*cf.* § V5-1.3) used are those from IEEE Std 694-1985 (IEEE 1985) or those of industrial components.

2.2. Transfer instructions

One of the three MPU functions, aside from their processing (i.e. calculation) and storage, is data transfer. An additional function is manipulation of the address itself.

2.2.1. *Data transfer*

Data transfer, also called "information-moving instructions", can be made from memory to register and vice versa (memory access instructions), as well as from register to register, per word or per block of memory words. For the first two forms, the reason linked to architecture comes from the basic operating cycle that permits only a single access to the memory per cycle (the golden rule of access, *cf.* § V1-3.3.3), for example, for accumulator architectures (single-bus structure, *cf.* § V1-3.4). A register such as an accumulator should then be used as an intermediary for transfer and exchange. It is also possible to load a literal in a register or memory. Depending on the architectures and designers, there may be an instruction for each type of transfer.

We list, depending on the direction of transfer, `ldx` or `ld` <name_or_reference_of_source_register> for loading in the processor and `stx` or `st` <name_or_reference_of_destination_register> for loading from the memory towards the processor, with x indicating a register. A single one can also suffice, such as `mov` (x86) or `move` (MC68020) and, to transfer several registers to the memory and vice versa, `movem` (MC68000). There may be an exchange instruction between two operands such as `xchg` from 8086 or `exchange` from MC68020 or between two parts of an operand such as `swap` from MC68020. It should be noted that 8085 from Intel executes the exchange using two internal registers, W and Z allowing temporary storage of operands.

Traditionally, the transfer instruction does not update the status register (*cf.* § V3-3.1.5), but there are counter-examples such as with the VAX (Virtual Addressed eXtended) mini-computer from the Digital Equipment Corporation (DEC) whose transfer instructions position the flags. Another example is the instruction `move` from MC68020 that positions indicators N and Z depending on the value of the operand, fixes C and V at zero and does not modify the flag X (eXtend flag).

Stack manipulation instructions are a special case. The stack, with LIFO (Last-In/First-Out) memory access, is generated by two primitives that are, we recall (*cf.* § 4.1), stack() and unstack(). On the contrary, Arm® uses two traditional transfer instructions instead of the specialist instructions `push` and `pop`. We will explain in detail how these operate in a future book by the author on microprocessors.

Advanced modes have been implemented, such as transfer between two memory areas or regions, either of a whole word or a part of this word with the aid of a logical mask or the transfer of several words (block transfer). These are character manipulation instructions (Zilog family or Intel, for example) enabling transfer of a block of bytes as well as a search for a binary pattern within it. The associated instructions are described in § 2.8.1. Another example with P6 architecture, with Pentium Pro as the first representative in 1995, introduced conditional transfer depending on the state of one or more flags (instructions `cmovcc`, cc indicating the condition).

Depending on the address spaces (*cf.* § V3-2.1.1.1), specialist instructions are sometimes available for input–output (input/output) transfers (*cf.* § 2.8.2).

Moreover, to carry out transfers in a multiprocessor environment with shared memory, some MPUs, such as the DSP TMS320C3x family, offer (inter-)locked (un)loading instructions for integer and floating-point numbers respectively `ldfi` (load floating-point value into a register, interlocked), `ldii` (load integer into a register, interlocked), `sigi` (signal, interlocked), `stfi` (store floating-point value to memory, interlocked) and `stii` (store integer to memory, interlocked), which are linked to two signal synchronization hardwares XF[1:0].

2.2.2. Address manipulation instructions

Some processors have an instruction that can recover the effective address, as in architectures x86 and IBM System/390 (mainframe, *cf.* § V1-1.2). With Intel, it is called `lea` for Load Effective Address. One application is to decide the address from the start of a data structure, for example, an array, to be able to pass it to a function (passing by reference). Being able to manipulate the Effective Address (EA, *cf.* § 1.2) makes it possible to implement a complex addressing mode such as based indexed addressing with offset (*cf.* § 1.2.3.4), which makes it possible to add two register values with one constant, which is useful for signal processing.

2.3. Data processing instructions

The main function of an MPU is to process information. (Data) processing instructions are also called transformational instructions. For this sub-set, we need to distinguish arithmetic instructions for integers and for bit manipulation.

2.3.1. Arithmetic instructions for integers

Arithmetic instructions, which were the first to be implemented in microprocessors, involved integers with addition (`add`) and subtraction (`sub`). Multiplication (`mul`) and division (`div`) appeared much later with MC6809 from Motorola. Particular forms of addition and subtraction are respectively incrementation operators (`inc`) and decrementation operators (`dec`) where the implicit implement value is the unit. Exercises V3-E3.2 and V3-E3.3 suggest studying their respective logic function. Addition and subtraction can take account of a previous carry (in the x86 architecture, respectively `addc` – addition with carry and `sbb` – subtract with borrow), useful in chained operations (RCA for Ripple-Carry Addition). Moreover, the comparison (`cmp`) executes a subtraction without giving a result that positions the indicators. It traditionally precedes a conditional jump instruction (*cf.* § 2.4.1). It should be noted that instruction `cmp2` from the 68,000 family makes it possible to test whether a value belongs to a range.

The operations are carried out in the format n. This type of arithmetic is called "modular" (modular arithmetic) or more rarely called wraparound arithmetic, literally enveloping arithmetic (i.e. that loops). This means that if there is a format overflow (in the case of a natural integer) or capacity overflow (in the case of a relative integer), the result will be false but not blocking (i.e. execution continues).

All these operations can be signed or unsigned. The two representations of whole numbers in a binary code that have been kept are respectively Natural Binary Code (NBC) and two's complement representation. The distinction for addition and subtraction is made by coding the operands and reading the carry flags C and overflow flags V for the validity of the result. The instruction `neg` (Negate) subtracts a zero-operand to calculate its opposite in two's complement representation. For multiplication and division, distinct mnemonics are proposed for the unsigned version, for example, respectively `imul` (Integer Multiply) and `idiv` (Integer Divide).

Some MPUs do not position the indicators by default. We cite the Arm® family that requires suffixing the mnemonic by one S, which forces it to position the indicators on the result. This avoids side effects (*cf.* § V3-3.1.12.1.).

Adjustment instructions make it possible to use these arithmetic instructions for whole numbers coded in other representations such as BCD code (Binary-Coded Decimal, *cf.* § II.1.2 from Darche (2000)). We take the example of the x86 architecture. For compact BCD (format n = 2 digits, so one byte), there is `daa` (Decimal Adjust for Addition) and `das` (Decimal Adjust for Subtraction). In the non-compacted version (n = 1), there are the badly named[2] `aaa` (ASCII Adjust for Addition) and `aas` (ASCII Adjust for Subtraction). Correction consists of adding 6 to each invalid digit result (*cf.* exercises E2.1 and E2.2). To conclude, we cite for non-compacted BCD (n = 1) only `aam` (ASCII Adjust for Multiply) and `aad` (ASCII Adjust for Division).

Format extension instructions make it possible to extend the sign to higher formats while nonetheless not modifying the indicators. We cite version x86 `cbw` (Convert Byte to Word) and `cwd` (Convert Word to Doubleword).

2.3.2. *Bit manipulation instructions*

Figures 2.2(a) and (b) show the different operations for the bits in one word. We recognize the classic base operators, those from basic combinatorial logic (i.e. Boolean) as well as non-parallel operations, which are shifts and rotation. We call the latter scale operators or, better, bitwise operators.

---

2 The acronym ASCII (American Standard Code for Information Interchange, *cf.* § III.3.4 from Darche (2000)) is deceptive here, since the underlying representation is BCD.

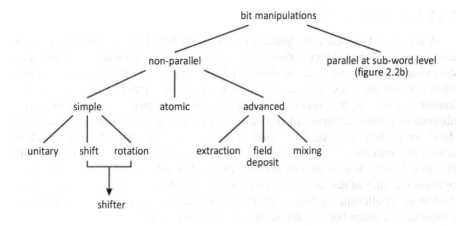

Figure 2.2a. *Classification of the main bit manipulation operations*

Today, with the integration of a vector unit in microprocessors, in particular for multimedia[3] applications, we must consider changed and advanced bit manipulation instructions. These two adjectives are used to distinguish the complexity of manipulations and the dates they appeared. Atomic instructions are studied in § 2.6.1.

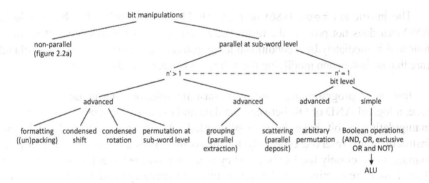

Figure 2.2b. *Classification of the main bit manipulation operations (continuation and end)*

Prior to presenting operations, it is necessary to define three terms relating to binary data.

---

3 Multimedia covers several data representation modes, visual 2D and 3D (text, video, still or moving graphic images) and audio (music, voice and sound) by linking them with interaction.

2.3.2.1. *Preliminary definitions*

A superword is used to designate a vector. A bit field in a word in format n is a contiguous sequence of bits in the format $1 \le n' \le n$. We can consider this field as a data structure formed of any number n' of consecutive bits (chain of consecutive bits). A sub-word of a word in the format n is a word of length $n' = 2^k$ with k natural integer and $n' < n$. It is this word's unit of subdivision that has consequences on alignments within it. Sub-word type data will be called "condensed or compacted data[4]" or packed. The word to which it belongs will be called "a word (broken down) into packets". This organization is adapted to multimedia data such as RGB (for Red–Green–Blue) data with pixel attributes. The sub-word becomes the atomic operand (i.e. unit of decomposition) for parallel calculation. This approach is called "sub-word parallelism" or "MicroSIMD type parallelism" by Lee (1999) and will be explained in a future book by the author on microprocessors.

2.3.2.2. *Basic Boolean operators*

The combinatorial logic base operators (*cf.* Chapter 2 of Darche (2002)), which are `and`, `or`, `exclusive or` (`xor`[5] or `eor`) and `not`, apply to each bitwise operation. Equivalent operators in C language are respectively &, |, ^ and ~. Aside from the last, these are Boolean operators with type 2-arity, that is, with two operands. They are used in particular for masking and logical bit forcing to the state "1" or "0" (*cf.* exercises E2.4 and E2.5 and § 2.2 from Darche (2002)).

The instruction `test` (x86) or `bit` (HC11 microcontroller family) is a logical AND that does not provide the result but which positions the indicators. It should be followed immediately by a conditional jump instruction, or, in any case, we should take care that no instruction modifying the indicators is intercalated (*cf.* § 2.4.1).

Instead of programming a software masking solution, that is, depending on the case, a logical AND or OR between the data and the mask, specialist instructions for manipulating a bit have been implemented. As explained in § 1.2.4.3, these instructions are reserved especially for microcontrollers as they make it possible to manage more closely the I/O lines. They make it possible to set the bits of a word at 0 or 1 logic respectively `bclr` (clear bit(s) in memory) and `bset` (set bit(s) in memory) for 68HC11 family do so in the memory, with an operand playing the role of mask. They also offer the possibility of branching on a bit state. In the same family, we cite `brclr` (branch if bit(s) clear) and `brset` (branch if bit(s) set). But classic MPUs generally have instructions for setting binary indicators from the status register (*cf.* § V3-3.1.5) at 1 or at 0. More particularly, the instructions `set`

---

4 To return to the vocabulary of BCD representation (Binary-Coded Decimal, *cf.* § II.1.2 from Darche (2000)).

5 Note that the mnemonic violates the rule of naming a mnemonic from standard (*cf.* § 2.1).

and `clr` respectively force the specified operand to "1" and "0". IEEE Std 694-1985 (IEEE 1985) proposes respectively suffixes -C and -V used with these two last instructions (*cf.* § V5-1.3.2) and the instruction `not` to modify the value of the binary indicators carry flag (CF) and (capacity) overflow flag (OF). Some MPUs have specialized flag instructions. For example, we cite `cli` (Clear Interrupt Flag) and `sti` (Set Interrupt Flag) which position the interrupt mask in x86 family to respectively inhibit or authorize external interruption requests (*cf.* § 5.2). It should be noted that some MPUs such as x86 family make it possible to test the value of a particular bit of an operand and extract or initialize it (`bt/btc/btr/bts`, *cf.* § 2.6.1). In the same architecture, the instruction `bzhi` (for zero high bits starting with specified bit position) makes it possible to copy the bits of the source operands while still setting the most significant bits of the destination operand at zero avoiding software masking.

For the record, mainframe computers of the 1960s offered a set of logical combined instructions less refined than those of System-10 from DEC (Table 2.1).

No.	Mnemonics	Operations
0	setz	0
1	and	$A \cdot B$
2	andca	$\bar{A} \cdot B$
3	setm	B
4	andcm	$A \cdot \bar{B}$
5	seta	A
6	xor	$A \oplus B$
7	ior	$A + B$
8	andcb	$\bar{A} \cdot \bar{B}$
9	eqv	$\overline{A \oplus B}$
10	setca	$\bar{A}$
11	orca	$\bar{A} + B$
12	setcm	$\bar{B}$
13	orcm	$A + \bar{B}$
14	orcb	$\bar{A} + \bar{B}$
15	seto	1

Table 2.1. *Logical instructions from DEC System-10*

2.3.2.3. *Basic non-parallel manipulations*

Simple, non-parallel base operators are unitary operators, (open) shifts and rotations. These last two operations can be made on the left and on the right. A number of operations can be specified with the operand involved (so the right operand).

Unitary operations are Boolean, but they consider a non-null word as a logical "1" and the null value as a logical "0". Their implementation gives, for example, the operators && and || in C language.

In the shifts, we should distinguish logical and arithmetic variants. The logical shift does not consider the leftmost bit as a sign bit but instead as an ordinary bit. A zero (kill value, *cf.* § V3-3.3) is injected in the register. It takes the place of the vacated bit. The outgoing bit goes in the status register carry flag. Equivalent operators in C language for left shifts (lsl for Logical Shift Left or asl) and (lsr for Logical Shift Right or shr) are respectively << and >>, the symbol chosen suggesting the direction. Figure 2.3 illustrates our idea. In the x86 architecture (386 and above), left and right shift instructions, respectively shld and shrd (Bitwise Double-Precision Shift), make it possible to carry out a shift between two operands specified in the instruction without changing the source.

Figure 2.3. *Logical left and right shifts*

The arithmetic shift, when it is made to the right (sar for Shift Arithmetic Right; Figure 2.4), duplicates the sign (i.e. the vacated bit takes the value of the sign). This propagation of the sign makes it possible to preserve the operand's polarity. The outgoing bit is stored in the carry indicator (not proposed by the standard). Shift Arithmetic Left (sal or shla) is equivalent to a logical shift in the same direction (*cf.* Figure 2.3).

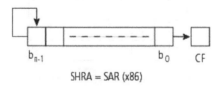

Figure 2.4. *Shift arithmetic right*

The shift function is generally used to multiply or divide a number (by 2), to make a mantissa alignment[6] or normalization (*cf.* § II.4.2.7.1 in Darche (2000)) in floating-point representation or to insert or extract a field from a binary word. The particular instance for this function is to isolate a bit in order to test it (*cf.* exercise E2.5).

Rotation is a shift looped on itself, as Figure 2.5 illustrates, hence the rarely used name "cyclic shift" compared to the open shift. The outgoing bit is re-injected at the other end.

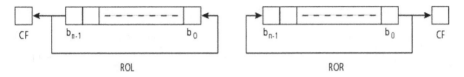

Figure 2.5. *Left and right rotations*

If required, a link bit can be inserted in the rotation loop. In most cases, this is the carry flag, as Figure 2.6 illustrates. This makes it possible, for example, to make a conditional jump onto the value.

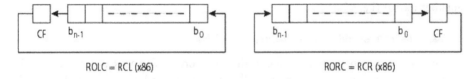

Figure 2.6. *Left and right rotations through carry*

Figure 2.7 shows an example of shift and an example of rotation for s bits.

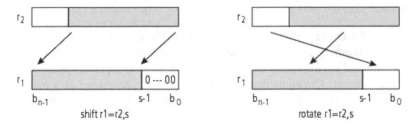

Figure 2.7. *Generic examples of multiple shifts and rotation*

6 This should not be confused with the alignment of information seen in § 3.1.2.

Some processors can have particular shifts. 386 from Intel and the following generations offer a double shift by linking one register with another or a memory location with the instructions `shrd` (Shift Right Double) and `shld` (Shift Left Double), thus doubling the format (Figure 2.8). Along the same lines, PDP-10 offered a double rotation by linking two consecutive registers.

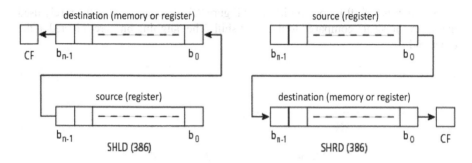

Figure 2.8. *Double shift with a 386*

Another particular example is Z80, which offers a left or right rotation (instructions `rld` and `rrd` – rotate left/right digit) in packed BCD representation in number format (i.e. 4 bits).

2.3.2.4. *Advanced bit manipulation instructions*

Shifts and rotations can be made in the sub-words. We speak of a packed shift and packed rotation. There is also the instruction `rldimi` from PowerPC (Performance Optimization With Enhanced RISC Performance Computing), which makes possible a rotation with insertion masking in a 64-bit format. The masking can be carried out by inserting a bit field at a set position. Aside from shift and rotation, other more advanced bit manipulation operations have been imagined. These are extraction, field deposit and shuffle.

Figure 2.9 shows an example for the first two. Field extract consists of selecting a bit field of arbitrary length from a source word and position, starting at position p (p^{th} + 1 bit) and storing it, right-justified, in a destination operand initially at zero (sub-word extract). The equivalent operation with base operations is a masking to select the field and a logical right shift of p bits applied to the source operand. The equivalent expression in C language is the following:

$$\text{dest} = (\text{src} >> \text{start}) \mathbin{\&} (1 << (\text{len-1})) \qquad [2.1]$$

The instruction `bextr` (Bit Field Extract) from the BMI 1 (Bit Manipulation Instructions) extension from Intel is one example. In version 2 of this set (i.e. BMI 2), Intel offers a "word" version with the instruction `pextrw` (Packed Extract Word) from the SSE (Streaming SIMD Extensions) set. Another example is the instruction `u/sbfx` ((un)signed bit field extract) from the ARMv7 architecture or the instructions found in the Arm® Cortex-M3 microcontroller that may or may not include the sign.

Field deposit is the symmetrical operation. It consists of selecting the l first bits of a source operand and depositing them at position p in a destination operand initially at zero (sub-word deposit). The equivalent operation with base operations is masking to select the field and a logical left shift of p bits applied to the source operand. One example is the instruction `bfi` (bit field insert) from the ARMv7 set. Intel with the instruction `pinsrw` (Packed Insert Word) from the SSE set offers a "word" version. We can also list the instructions `bfins bfextu` from MC68020.

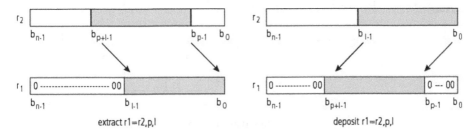

Figure 2.9. *Field extract and field deposit operations*

Shuffle allows partial interleaving of sub-words from two source words in a destination word. There are two kinds, left and right, as Figures 2.10 and 2.11 illustrate. Traditional sub-word formats are typically 8, 16 and 32 bits for a 64-bit word but, generally, the format n' of a sub-word from a word in n format is given by the inequation $0 < n' < n$. It appeared with PA-RISC[7] (Lee 1996) to accelerate calculation of multimedia applications, it is also found in Itanium from Intel (Lee *et al.* 2001). One example of shuffle is `mix` from the PA-RISC 2.0 architecture (Lee and Huck 1996), which is found in the IA-64 architecture (Intel Architecture). Another example is `pshufw/pshufb` from the SSE extension versions 1 and 3 (*cf.* § 2.6.1), versions for condensed floating numbers also exist in SSE2.

Reverse instructions also exist. Figure 2.12 shows instructions `rev, rev16` and `rev32` from the Arm® and Thumb® family applied on a 64-bit word as an example. A square represents a byte. They can apply only to one word, at least in double format. There is also a bit-level version (complete reversal of the order of the word) with `rbit`.

---

7 PA for Precision Architecture.

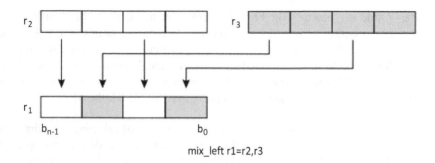

mix_left r1=r2,r3

Figure 2.10. *Left shuffle operation (interleaving)*

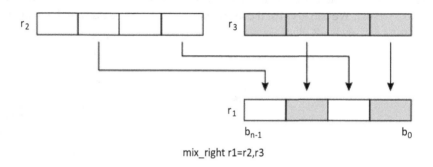

mix_right r1=r2,r3

Figure 2.11. *Right shuffle operation (interleaving)*

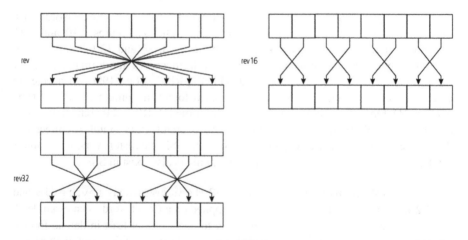

Figure 2.12. *Reverse instructions from the Arm® and Thumb® family (n = 64)*

To conclude, and for information, counting instructions makes it possible to count the number of bits at 1 or 0 (`lzcnt`, `tzcnt` and `popcnt` with Intel).

2.3.2.5. *Advanced bit manipulation instructions*

There are three Advanced Bit Manipulation (ABM[8]) instructions. There are bit gather, bit scatter and bit permutation operations (Figure 2.13).

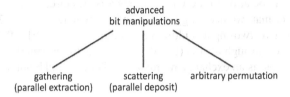

Figure 2.13. *Classifying advanced bit manipulations*

The two previous advanced operations, which are field extract and field deposit, may exist in multiple forms. The gathering of bits, also called parallel extract, consists of making several extractions of groups (or fields) of bits and regrouping them. The scattering of bits or parallel deposit consists of carrying out the reverse operation, that is, extracting groups of bits and dispersing them. For these operations, a stuffing of 0 is made if necessary (bit stuffing). Figure 2.14 illustrates both these operations. Signaling using "1"s indicates respectively the bits to be gathered or the locations that will receive the bits to be scattered. We also cite as industrial examples respectively the instructions `pext` (*Parallel Bits Extract*) and `pdep` (*Parallel Bits Deposit*) from the BMI 2 set from Intel.

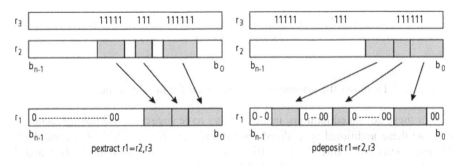

Figure 2.14. *Field extract and field deposit operations of parallel bits*

---

8 This should not be confused with technology from AMD (see below).

An example of the permutation instruction is `permute` from the PA-RISC 2.0 architecture (Lee and Huck 1996). One permutation at the bits (of one word) is an arbitrary rearrangement of these in this word (cardinality = n!). This operation is beneficial, for example, in the domain of cryptography. Any permutation in the format n bits can be carried out, as Hilewitz and Lee (2006, 2008) have shown, by passing only once through two units that carries out a butterfly permutation, a normal (instruction butterfly or `bfly`) then an inverse butterfly or `ibfly` instruction. The association of these units forms a Benes circuit (Benes 1964). To do this in an n-bit format, we need $\log_2(n)$ steps of n/2 switches (Figure 2.15a), each of them formed of two two-input multiplexers (Figure 2.15b) (2:1 MUX), where the information passes through as it is (E = 0, variables a and b underlined in the figure on the right) or there is an exchange of inputs (variables a and b not underlined).

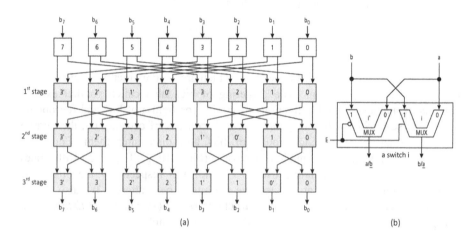

(a)   (b)

Figure 2.15. *Normal butterfly circuit in n = 8 bits format (a) and associated switch (b)*

Figure 2.16 shows the symmetrical circuit from the previous one.

For these advanced families, manufacturers have suggested technology names to indicate these additional specialized instruction sets. We cite ABM (Advanced Bit Manipulation) and TBM (Trailing Bit Manipulation) for AMD and BMI 1 and 2 from Intel. These sets are specialized ISA extensions such as SSE at Intel.

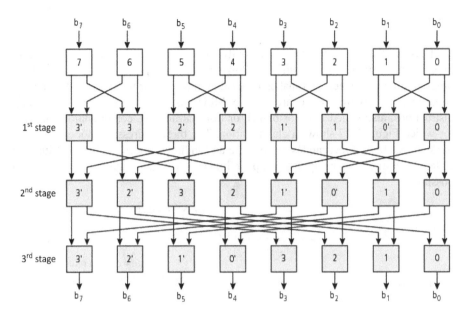

Figure 2.16. *Reverse butterfly circuit in n = 8 bits format*

2.4. Control transfer instructions

In the Von Neumann architecture, the execution of instructions is sequential in origin (*cf.* § V1-3.2). To be able to implement, among others, high-level language control structures such as, for example, if_then_else, control-flow instructions are needed, also called program control instructions or program transfer instructions. They will alter the execution's sequentiality, hence a final name, sequence breaking. The rupture of flow control or of the execution sequence is simply obtained by changing the value of the Program Counter (PC), which makes it possible to "break" this sequentially of the execution model. It is necessary to distinguish conditional and unconditional (de)branching instructions[9] (of the execution sequence); the latter includes subroutine call and return instructions and, to conclude, those for handling (or processing) hardware and software interruptions with, among others, exceptions (*cf.* § 5.4).

---

9 Some authors, as Etiemble (2016) and Clements (2014) explain, distinguish the jump (the Program Counter (PC) receives an absolute address) from the branch (addition of a relative address to the PC). This distinction will not be made in this book as the two names have an identical meaning. The context will be enough to show whether it is a conditional operation or not.

2.4.1. *Branchings*

These instructions alter the sequentially of execution by making it possible to jump to an instruction other than the following one. They play a fundamental role in programming languages as it makes it possible in particular to achieve a branch-on-condition. To do this, there are, in the MPU instruction set, specialized jump instructions, also called jump or branch or test instructions, conditional or not, and for which Figure 2.17 shows a classification. The three addressing modes currently used are relative, direct modes or absolute and indirect modes. An indirect jump is called an indirect or computed jump or branch. A register-indirect jump is also possible.

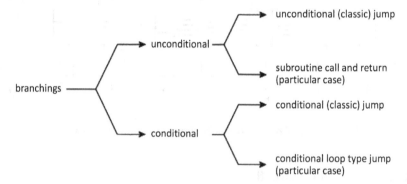

Figure 2.17. *Branching instructions*

Any jump – backward or forward – can be made in the code (Figure 2.18). The first sub-class of jump is the unconditional jump (instruction jmp from Intel). It makes it possible to understand the branching mechanism in all the forms cited previously. Executing it unconditionally initializes the program counter at the calculated address, depending on the addressing mode. Thus, the next instruction to be executed will be that of the specified address. The unconditional jump represents 30% of jumps made in programs (Cragon 1992).

One conditional branching instruction is similar to the high-level control structure if <Boolean_condition> then <go_to target_address>. It makes it possible, depending on the conditions, to perform an execution sequence branching. The condition is called a predicate[10]. A predicate is the expression of a condition. Figure 2.19 shows the different steps of executing if the condition is true.

---

10 This should not be confused with an assertion or proposition, which is a phrase to which it is possible to attribute a truth value, that is, one that is either true or false.

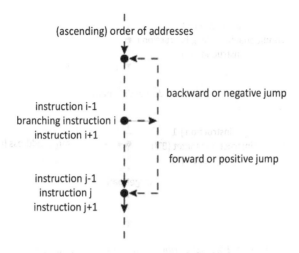

Figure 2.18. *Execution paths for a jump*

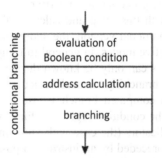

Figure 2.19. *Execution steps for a conditional jump*

As Figure 2.20 illustrates, the execution path is divided by the branching instruction (or node) into two paths, the fall-through path and the target path. If the condition is true, then the control transfer is made at the instruction on the branch target address (BTA for Branch Target Address). The microprocessor will execute this targeted instruction known by the acronym BTI (Branch Target Instruction). We say the branching is called "taken". If the condition is a constant, then it is an unconditional jump. If it is a Boolean variable, then it is a conditional jump. Where there are several successive jumps, the branch path is the code between two executed branchings. The number of instructions involved is, on average, three to nine (Uht *et al.* 1997).

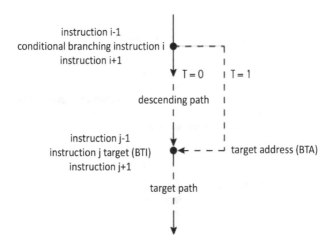

Figure 2.20. *Execution paths for a conditional jump*

During its execution, the processor must carry out two tasks: they must evaluate the condition associated with this jump and calculate the jump address (i.e. target address). As for the unconditional version, the addressing modes traditionally used are absolute mode and relative modes, in general to Program Counter (PC) relative. Moreover, the jump address can only be known during execution. This is true, for example, for a multiple branching control structure such as switch() from C language. We speak of a computed branch whose address should be calculated dynamically. The role of the condition register is fundamental as the jump is made on the condition of its indicators (the case with x86). In this case, any conditional jump should therefore be preceded by an instruction positioning the indicators. The comparison instructions and conditional branching use the traditional four condition code bits N, Z, O (or V) and C (NZVC flags). When the condition is not verified, execution of the instruction is equivalent to a nop (*cf.* § 2.8.5). The first use is to verify the validity of a result (i.e. its exactitude). A second is to compare two values, digitally. Any comparison operator comp_op ($<$, $>$, $=$, LGE for Less, Greater and Equal and combinations and complementation, which gives GT, GE, EQ, LT, LE, NE, etc.) is reduced to a subtraction followed by the test compared to zero (formula 2.2). It justifies the presence of a status register and, in particular, of the ZF (Zero Flag).

$$\text{op1 comp\_op op2} \Leftrightarrow \text{op1 - op2 comp\_op 0} \qquad [2.2]$$

The mnemonic of a conditional jump instruction takes the form jcc (jump on condition code) or bcc (branch on condition code). This respects the naming standards rule since the first character of the mnemonic should be that of the action verb and it should contain the condition (role of cc). The test can be carried out simply on an indicator. We list the five tested indicators from the x86 family, jc (jump on carry) – jnc (jump on not carry), jo (jump on overflow) – jno (jump on not overflow), jp (jump on parity) – jnp (jump on not parity), js (jump on sign) – jns (jump on not sign) and jz (jump on zero) – jnz (jump on not zero). The test can be complex, involving several indicators. This makes it possible to make digital comparisons, but the digital representation should be considered. Table 2.2 summarizes them. Note the mnemonic synonyms for a single test. This means that the corresponding machine codes will be identical. The two other jump possibilities occur on the condition of testing a register's value (the case with MIPS) and on condition of exception.

Mnemonics	Names	Tests and digital groups involved	Conditions
ja jnbe	Jump on above jump on not below or equal	$>$, $\mathbb{N}$	$\overline{C \cdot Z}$
jae jnb	Jump on above or equal jump on not below	$\geq$, $\mathbb{N}$	$\bar{C}$
jb jnae	Jump on below jump on not above or equal	$<$, $\mathbb{N}$	C
jbe jna	Jump on below or equal jump on not above	$\leq$, $\mathbb{N}$	$C + Z$
je jz	Jump on equal jump on zero	$=$, $\mathbb{N}$ and $\mathbb{Z}$	Z
jne jnz	Jump on not equal jump on not zero	$\neq$, $\mathbb{N}$ and $\mathbb{Z}$	$\bar{Z}$
jg jnle	Jump on greater jump on not less or equal	$>$, $\mathbb{Z}$	$\overline{(S \oplus O) + Z}$ $\overline{((\bar{S} \cdot \bar{O}) + (S \cdot O)) + \bar{Z}}$
jge jnl	Jump on greater or equal jump on not less	$\geq$, $\mathbb{Z}$	$\overline{S \oplus O}$ $(\bar{S} \cdot \bar{O}) + (S \cdot O)$
Jl jnge	Jump on less jump on not greater or equal	$<$, $\mathbb{Z}$	$S \oplus O$
Jle jng	Jump on less or equal jump on not greater	$\leq$, $\mathbb{Z}$	$(S \oplus O) + Z$

Table 2.2. *Conditional jump instructions for 8086 for whole numbers*

A coprocessor can provide support to a jump mechanism. Therefore, the x87 coprocessor can carry out a comparison between two numbers represented in floating point (instructions fcom, fcomp, fcompp, ftst, fucompp, ficom and ficomp, the difference influencing how the flags are handled). It makes the comparison by positioning its indicators, which are then recopied in the master processor's status register (an old mechanism before the P6 microarchitecture from Intel). The new form of execution (with the P6) directly positions the indicators of the master processor's status register (instructions fcomi, fcomip, fucomi and fucomip). In both cases, it is always the latter that actually carries out the jump.

The control schema for the execution for an instruction, which is shown, is based on updated binary indicators (i.e. NZVC flags, mainly) on a specialized register, the status register. These indicators are then tested by a conditional branching instruction. This well-established schema is called result state checking. The advantage of a status register is that it factorizes the code for calculating the flags, but it is adapted to a purely sequential execution model. It is a real and harmful side effect of parallel execution, and it makes the instruction set non-orthogonal (*cf.* § 3.1.3). This schema is for mainframe computers (IBM System/360 and /370 for example), PDP-11 and VAX mini-computers, the first CISC microprocessor families (families x86 and MC68000, for example) and some RISC (families RISC-II and RISC-II, SPARC[11], PowerPC and Arm®, for example). For Arm®, the mnemonics should be suffixed by the letter S to update the flags after execution. Moreover, the instructions support conditional execution.

To accelerate execution, execution parallelism has been suggested with, for example, ILP (Instruction-Level Parallelism, this will be covered in a future book by the author on microprocessors) whose pipelined execution is a mechanism. With a pipelined architecture, a conditional branching instruction will have to wait until the instructions preceding it in the pipeline have been executed so that it can be executed itself, which takes a great deal of time. In this implementation, it is therefore necessary to avoid intercalating instructions between the test and the conditional jump instruction, which is a constraint for the compiler. If there are a small number of instructions involved, then a specialized software can determine how to anticipate the state of the flags of the instructions that precede it. Hence, positioning of indicators may be optional for arithmetic and logical instructions. In this context, an alternative to state control implementation is the direct check concept (Sima *et al.* 1997). No state is therefore saved in a status register during a comparison. Blaauw and Brooks (1997) propose the concept of explicit and implicit evaluations (Figure 2.21).

In case (a) of Figure 2.22, the arithmetic operation positions status flags after calculation. The instruction that follows will be a jump on condition(s) of these flags. In case (b) of the figure, the state result check follows the calculation instruction. The test and branching are made either in a single instruction or in two.

---

11 SPARC for Scalable Processor ARChitecture.

A single instruction (test of the result then branching) in place of two separate instructions makes it possible to optimize execution, in particular in current parallel architectures.

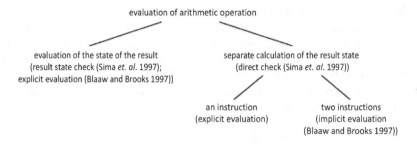

Figure 2.21. *Left: result state check; right: direct check*

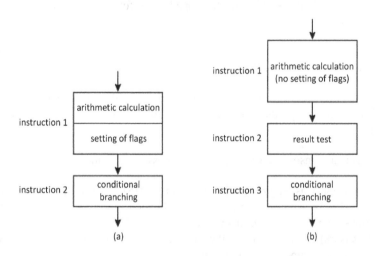

Figure 2.22. *Schema for evaluating a calculation*

The first form is that of the RISC AMD 29000 microprocessor. This test schema always uses two instructions, one for comparison positioning a Boolean result (and not the classic NZVC flags) in a GPR, which is then tested by a jump instruction (an approach using two instructions). It should be noted that it offers a comparison instruction `assert`, which traps[12] if its result is false. The second type tests and makes the jump in a single instruction (notion of atomic operation, *cf.* § 2.6.1). Cragon (1992) calls this type TB for Test and Branch. It is the one used by

_____

12 For the concept, *cf.* § 5.4.

supercalculators CYBER/70 and Cray, mini-computers PDP-8 and PDP-10 (instructions `skip`) and microprocessor families RISC MIPS, HP PA (Precision Architecture) and DEC Alpha. One drawback is that is uses many registers.

It should be noted that processors such as family SPARC from version 9 use both control schemas. In addition, it should be noted that the microprocessor cannot execute the code that follows the branch instruction as it is linked to its result. It is called a branch effect, which has a prejudicial effect on a processor's performance in the context of parallelism (*cf.* § 2.6.1). For example, the pipeline should stall and, eventually, purge itself if branching, limiting the execution parallelism. There will, on the other hand, be techniques for reducing these effects or BERT for Branch Effect Reduction Techniques. One example is IBM S/360 model 91, which, at the moment of decoding, positions a 2-bit tag in the instruction's code called cc for condition code, which indicates at execution that the instructions already decoded should not be executed before the conditional branching instruction (Anderson *et al.* 1967). These techniques will be developed in a future book by the author on microprocessors.

2.4.2. *Conditional execution*

Conditional execution, also called guarded or predicated execution, makes it possible to attribute a predicate to a traditional instruction according to the following schema:

$$\text{Predicated instruction <conditional expression > ? <instruction>} \qquad [2.3]$$

The concept was suggested by Dijkstra (1975). Hsu (1986) and Hsu and Davidson (1986) suggested the first application for ILP scalar processors (Instruction-Level Parallelism, this will be covered in a future book by the author on microprocessors) to get around the problems of branching, which slows the operation of their superscalar and superpipelined architectures. It generalizes the conditional control transfer mechanism (branch prediction). The condition affects the value of the flags. Execution of a predicated instruction is effective when the qualifying predicate is true. We say that the execution is gated by a qualifying predicate. This happens after the flags have been updated by a specialized instruction such as a comparison, instructions that have not updated these flags will be able to intercalate with one another. If the condition is not verified, then the instruction does not execute, no result is given (i.e. no writing), no flag is modified and no interruption is lifted. The instruction is then equivalent to a nop. It should be noted that predicting any instruction set complicates the Control Unit (CU). Discussion of this mechanism will be covered in a future book by the author on microprocessors.

In the Arm® architecture, each mnemonic can be suffixed by the condition. This will correspond to a value of a quadruplet of flags (N, Z, C, V) called predicate flags. This quadruplet is on the left of the predicated instruction code (most significant digits of the 32-bit word). For the condition to be verified, the values must be equal to those of the corresponding flags in the state PSR (Program Status Register) updated following execution of the instruction involved. In assembly language, the mnemonic is suffixed by an abbreviation that recalls the condition. Table 2.3 summarizes these uses in this architecture.

Codes	Suffixes	Logical conditions	Description	Symbols
0000	EQ	$Z == 1$ (Z)	EQual	$=$
0001	NE	$Z == 0$ $(\bar{Z})$	Not equal	$\neq$
0010	CS/HS	$C == 1$ (C)	Carry set/unsigned higher or same	Unsigned $\geq$
0011	CC/LO	$C == 0$ $(\bar{C})$	Carry clear/unsigned LOwer	Unsigned $<$
0100	MI	$N == 1$ (N)	MInus/negative	< 0
0101	PL	$N == 0$ $(\bar{N})$	PLus/positive or zero	≥ 0
0110	VS	$V == 1$ (V)	Overflow	$-$
0111	VC	$V == 0$ $(\bar{V})$	No overflow	$-$
1000	HI	$(C == 1) \bullet (Z == 0)$ $C \bullet \bar{Z}$	Unsigned higher	Unsigned $>$
1001	LS	$(C == 0) \bullet (Z == 1)$ $\bar{C} + Z$	Unsigned lower or same	Unsigned $\leq$
1010	GE	$N == V$ $\overline{N \oplus V}$	Signed greater than or equal	Signed $\geq$
1011	LT	$N \neq V$ $N \oplus V$	Signed less than	Signed $<$
1100	GT	$\bar{Z} \bullet (\overline{N \oplus V})$	Signed greater than	Signed $>$
1101	LE	$Z + (N \oplus V)$	Signed less than or equal	Signed $\leq$
1110	AL	1	ALways (flags ignored)	$-$
1111	NV/-	$0 / -$	NeVer[a]/unpredictable	$-$

a. NV before version 3 of the architecture, otherwise unpredictable.

Table 2.3. *Condition codes from the Arm® architecture*

One industrial use is that of the Arm® family that results in the instruction code by a binary quadruplet (Figure 2.23). The value of the condition field is one of those in the table above.

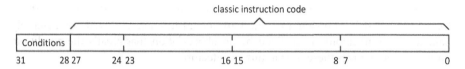

Figure 2.23. *Condition field from MPU Arm® VL86C010*

The aim of predicting instructions is to delete conditional branchings. The guarded execution has the advantage of allowing for fewer dependencies. This facilitates the work of the compiler. There is less prediction to be done, and there are fewer poor predictions. In terms of limitations, guarded execution and extension to the ISA and specific handling by the compiler, support for the execution by the ISA may be full or partial. In fact, some instruction sets do not support conditional execution for all instructions for reasons of complexity or performance. It was first applied to conditional move. This was the case with SPARC V9 (conditional transfer instructions for whole numbers MOVcc and floating point FMOVcc only), from the Alpha processor or the ISA x86. The A64 set from ISA ARMv8 also offers a reduced number of conditional branching instructions. In the case of a conditional structure if_then_else with blocks of more than 10 instructions, the compiler can operate the parallelism better but the classic conditional jump (i.e. not predicated) is better in terms of execution time (addition of the time corresponding to the execution of the two blocks). The number of instructions executed increases, as it makes compatible the instructions of the path crossed as well as those that would not have had to be executed in the classic approach. Additionally, not all MPUs offer this. The IA-64 architecture (that of the MPU Itanium) from Intel is another example of guarded execution similar to the Arm® architecture, except that is based on the idea of a PR (Predicate Register), of which there are 64 (p[63:0]) which each stores a condition test result. The instruction is written in the form:

$$(p_i) \text{ instruction} \hspace{4cm} [2.4]$$

For information, predicated execution is also used in software for speculative execution (this will be covered in a future book by the author on microprocessors). Moreover, vector processors such as Cray-1 (Russel 1978) used a similar principle with the notion of a vector mask that controlled execution of the instruction on the elements of the vector. VLIW (Very Long Instruction Word) architectures such as the Cydra-5 computer (Rau *et al.* 1989; Beck *et al.* 1993) have their entire set predicated.

2.4.3. *Iteration control*

One particular case with the conditional jump is the loop-closing conditional branch, which is a backward jump that is always made, except on the last iteration. This conditional loop closure jump was initially a classic conditional branching instruction with explicit handling of the loop counter. A specialized conditional jump instruction may be available, such as jcxz in the x86 architecture.

So as not to lose time in handling, a simple technique called loop unrolling is traditionally used in digital calculation. It consists of replacing a loop by repeating its code as many times as necessary. Loop unrolling is useful for reducing control but is prohibitive in terms of the number of lines of code.

To facilitate programming in assembly language and to decrease execution time, the classic instruction set of a microprocessor has been completed with instructions whose operation is similar to those of high-level languages (CISC approach). Those placed at the end of the loop use either a specialist or general register as a counter, which is decremented and tested to carry out a conditional jump at the start of the loop. We cite as an example the instruction loop from the x86 family that makes it possible to implement easily control structures such as the loop for var = i to j do. An implicit register, CX or its format variants, is decremented and tested compared to zero. Other existing versions also test the value of the ZF indicator, called loope/loopz and loopne/loopnz. MC68000 offered an equivalent instruction DBcc (Test Condition, Decrement and Branch), cc being the output condition. As another industrial example, RISC PowerPC uses handling with three specialized registers that serve to handle branchings. This is the CR (Condition Register), CTR (CounT Register) and the LR (Link Register). CR serves as a loop counter as CX previously, but it can also contain the target branching address for the loop handling instruction Bcctrx (Branch Conditional to Count Register) just like LR for the instruction Bclrx (Branch Conditional to Link Register). The HLL (High-Level (programming) Language) compiler or the assembly language programmer explicitly generates loop control instructions. Loop control instructions can be seen as a jump instruction sub-family. Software management (i.e. incrementation or decrementation of the counter, test of its value an eventual jump) is carried out with a time penalty (i.e. with the addition of machine cycles) as the corresponding instructions are executed. Moreover, it has a cost in terms of latency in the case of a jump, since the processor must empty the pipeline by terminating the remaining instructions. There is therefore an overhead with, in addition, requisition of a register, dedicated or not. These additions of high-level instructions, which are not without consequence on the complexity of the CU (Control Unit), are typical of the CISC approach. Loop handling has a time penalty as well as an energy penalty that must be taken into account.

Moreover, digital signal processing, omnipresent in modern-day digital devices, makes massive use of loops. Designers of specialized processors in this domain or DSP (*cf.* § V3-5.2) have gone further by adding specialized functional blocks to loop handling. The material approach makes it possible to remove the software management overhead, hence the name zero-overhead hardware looping. This can be done with no time penalty and transparently. In the case of nested loops, the first approach is first-level hardware management (i.e. the most external), the internal loops being handled by software. The second is complete management by the hardware. An internal stack stores the loop handling parameters. Tsao *et al.* (2003) shows an example. To do this, a buffer instruction internal to the processor, called a hardware loop buffer, makes it possible to store instructions from the body of the loop (i.e. to repeat), the loop's execution time to avoid access to the external memory costs time. It acts almost as a cache memory if the addressing mode is not taken into account. Initialization of this local memory occurs at the first execution of the loop body or before during the prefetch step. It is intercalated between the instruction fetch unit and the decoding unit (Figure 2.24).

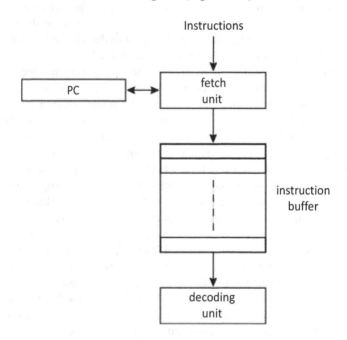

Figure 2.24. *Instruction buffer*

Three registers are needed: BRC, RSA and REA (Figure 2.25). BRC for Block Repeat Counter contains the required number of repetitions of the loop body. (Repeat Start Address registers and REA (Repeat End Address) store respectively the address for the start and the end of the loop body. The associated instructions are do m,n, where m is the number of instructions that follow to be executed in a loop n times and break, which makes it possible to leave the loop abruptly. One example of a component using this approach is TMS320c54x from Texas Instruments.

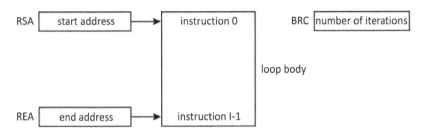

Figure 2.25. *Hardware management of a loop*

Figure 2.26 shows a block diagram of a loop manager. The comparator at the bottom of the figure compares the value of the program counter with the loop end address. When the two values are equal, the BRC loop counter is decremented. If this is not null (the role of the upper comparator), then the PC (Program Counter) is initialized at the loop start address. A flag called BRAF for Block-Repeat-Active Flag associated with loop handling authorizes this looping. If the BRC passes to zero, the flag is deactivated.

As an industrial example, TMS320C80 from TI (Texas Instruments) has three special registers. These are registers LC (Loop Counter) and LS (Loop Start), which point the first instruction of the loop, and LE (Loop End), which points the last. These registers take another name in TMS320C31 with respectively RC (Repeat Counter), RS (Repeat Start Address register) and RE (Repeat End Address register).

Another handling method is that used by the DSP56000 family. Associated with the two instructions do (Start Hardware Loop) and enddo (End Current DO Loop) are two LA (end-of-Loop Address) registers and LC handle loops (test to 1 to leave). This makes it possible to implement a control structure "for". It should be noted that a bit called LF (Loop Flag) in the SR (Status Register) indicates that a loop is being executed. To implement a "while", two other instructions have been introduced in this same family. These are brkcc (Conditionally Break the current Hardware Loop) equivalent to break in C language, and do_forever (Start Infinite Hardware Loop). These instructions manipulate (i.e. backup and restore depending on the case) the context which is formed here of registers LA, LC, SR and PC (Program Counter).

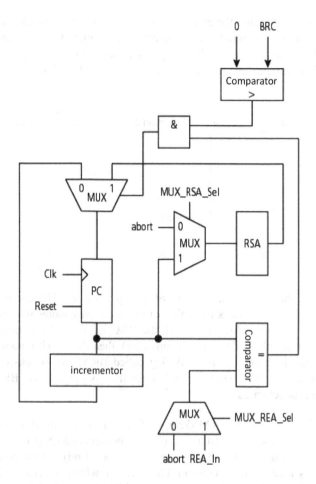

Figure 2.26. *Functional block diagram showing a hardware loop manager (from Tsao et al. (2003))*

2.4.4. *Subroutine call and return instructions*

There is a possibility of factorizing the code in the form of a subroutine (*cf.* Chapter 4). This subroutine makes it possible to implement a function or procedure, code structuration primitives from high-level languages respectively C and Pascal. Subroutine call and return instructions can be unconditional or conditional.

For execution of this subroutine to be transparent, it is necessary to save information gathered during execution (*cf.* § 4.2.2). A call instruction to a subroutine can be seen as a macro-instruction (Blaauw and Brooks 1997) as it behaves like a normal instruction by making transparent the execution of the block of instructions representing the subroutine. The minimal context needed, which is saved, is the return address stacked on the stack (instruction `call` from the x86 family) or stored in a register (the case of the instruction `jal` (jump-and-link instruction) from MIPS). The execution context is important in the contexts of (quasi-) parallel execution, memory handling and I/O handling. Thus, it is saved during a switching of Heavy-Weight (i.e. classic) or Light-Weight (i.e. thread) Processes (HWP/LWP), when the memory fails (page or segment, this will be covered in a future book by the author on memories) or during an external or internal interrupt request (i.e. exception and system call, *cf.* § 5.4).

Note that both these instructions can be seen as a particular instance of a jump as in PowerPC or PA-RISC architectures where these instructions are distinguished by the value of a bit (LK (LinK) bit). When its value is 1, then the processor has saved the return address in a dedicated register called an LK register, which will be resumed on return. This circumvents the need to use a stack (*cf.* § 4.1) in main memory for which access is slower.

2.5. Environmental instructions

This section gathers the instructions that makes it possible to control a system in a broad sense. These are instructions that handle interruptions, those that make it possible to stop the MPU and those that are used for debugging.

2.5.1. *Interrupt request and interrupt return instructions*[13]

To manage I/O events, a particular form of subroutine called interrupt handler, or ISR for Interrupt Service Routine, is known as a form of interrupt request. This concept will be addressed in detail in Chapter 5.

2.5.2. *Stopping instructions*

The instruction `break` makes it possible to initialize an interruption sequence. The instruction `wai` from MPU MC6802 suspends execution of the program in expectation of an interrupt request. The processor state is stored on the stack, and the PC (Program Counter) points the following instruction. On an external interruption, the MPU restarts. It is used, for example, in operating systems. It is named `hlt` in the x86 family or `halt` for Z80, and they have almost identical functions. For Z80,

---

13 This paragraph could be included in § 5.2.

the component does not stop, but it executes nops to ensure that the memory is correctly refreshed. This is because of its core, implemented in dynamic logic, the consequence is therefore an absence of energy saving. The instruction stop from MC68020 saves the associated operand in the status register and stops, awaiting a classic interruption of trace or a RESET type. One logical condition can be added to put it on hold with the instruction cwai from MC6809, which carries out a logical AND with the status register.

These stopping instructions make it possible ensure synchronization with an external component such as coprocessor or an I/O controller. We cite the instruction wait, which puts the 8086 processor into an idle state waiting for the signal #TEST to become active or until there is an external interrupt request. With architecture development and the demand for lower energy consumption in autonomous applications, for example, mobiles, the number of stopping possibilities has increased. Microcontrollers (MCU for MicroController Unit) use these specialized instructions in particular to handle dynamic consumption as well as possibly by stopping the whole processor or some of its sub-components (*cf.* § V3-6.1.4).

2.5.3. *Processor management*

Some instructions make it possible to control the processor's execution environment by carrying out an operation on the control flags. The instructions lmsw (Load Machine Status Word) and smsw (Store Machine Status Word) that make it possible to access the content of the computer's status register MSW (Machine Status Word), called CR0 in the IA-32 architecture, from Intel, are one example. By changing, for example, the stat of the PE (Protected Mode Enable) flag, it is possible to move from real mode to protected mode.

2.5.4. *Memory management*

By memory, we should understand all memory integrate in the MPU. This means the cache memory and the Translation Lookaside Buffer (TLB) of the virtual addressing mechanism. Specialized handling instructions make it possible to take the best of the operation of this type of memory, with which mid- and high-range MPUs are equipped. These are clearly preferable instructions. Since the ways they operate these memories are complex, they will be detailed in a future book by the author on memories.

2.5.4.1. *Cache management*

These instructions make it possible to manage block allocation by initializing it to zero, to load or flush a block, to write a block in main memory to synchronize it (clwb for cache line write back) and to make reading or writing from/to the main memory possible by short-circuiting the cache hierarchy. In the x86 architecture, the instruction prefetch makes it possible to load the associated cache line to an address in the way anticipated in the cache hierarchy. Instructions for invalidating a block or the whole of a cache with (wbinvd) or without (invd) prior writing in main memory (write back). To free space, the instructions clflush and clflushoptw make it possible to invalidate a line at each level of the corresponding cache hierarchy at a given linear address with a possible writing in memory if it is marked as modified. To conclude, it is possible to access the main memory (also called central or primary memory) transparently compared to caches with register transfer instructions movnti, movntq, movntdq, movntps and movntpd.

2.5.4.2. *TLB management*

Virtual addresses are translated using hardware. To avoid loss of time due to the sequential reading of several table walks, a cache called TLB is used. This handling is transparent to the programmer, but it is sometimes necessary for security reasons or obligatory because the page table hierarchy has been updated, invalidating entries in the cache corresponding to a given page. The instruction invlpg (invalidate TLB entry) invalidates the TLB entry corresponding to a given page carries out a flush operation.

2.5.5. *Hardware detection*

The instruction cpuid with Intel from 80486, if it can be executed (i.e. modifiable ID flag of the status register, *cf.* § V3-3.1.5.6), can be seen as a function whose entry parameter is passed in the EAX register, and this result is passed through several registers. It makes it possible to recover (passing in registers) many characteristics from the MPU base and to recover configuration information (extended information). This may, for example, be the reference of the family to which it belongs, the model, its series number (n = 96 bits) or information on the cache hierarchy and TLB, on energy and addressing management. For more information, see Intel (2012). Another approach to detecting a new function is to test for the presence of a flag, or a register or to try to execute a new instruction. In case of failure, an exception (*cf.* § 5.4) is generally raised.

2.5.6. *Debugging*

In the program control instructions, we can cite the instructions for entering unconditionally in debugging mode such as debug from DSP56000. The debugging aspect is addressed in Chapter V5-2.

2.5.7. *Updating*

To correct possible bugs, a manufacturer can offer FirmWare (FW, i.e. microcode) for updating, signed for security reasons. Intel offers this function from P6. It is the BIOS (Basic Input/Output System, *cf.* § V5-3.5.3) that is responsible for carrying out this operation.

2.5.8. *Verification*

Some processors provide a machine verification architecture. The MPUs involved are, for example, Pentium 4, Intel Xeon, Intel Atom and those from the P6 microarchitecture.

2.5.9. *Various*

The instruction esc from 8086 makes it possible to pass an instruction to a coprocessor (*cf.* § V3-5.4) such as 8087.

2.6. Parallelism instructions

This section summarizes the instructions that make it possible to manage parallel execution of light-weight processes (threads) or heavy-weight processes. They will be addressed in detail in future books by the author.

2.6.1. *Atomic instructions*

Instructions are executed atomically in essence, that is, they can be interrupted (*cf.* execution cycle, § V1-3.2.2 and V1-3.3.2). On the contrary, with quasi-parallelism and true parallelism (this will be covered in a future book by the author on microprocessors), it is necessary to execute sequences of code atomically, for example, to ensure mutual exclusion during multiple access to a resource. An initial solution is to forbid an interrupt request (*cf.* Chapter 5). More recently, the transactional memory mechanism (this will be covered in a future book by the author on storage) and specialized instructions gathering a classical instruction set but guaranteeing atomicity have been introduced into the instruction set.

At bit level, MPU 80386 offers specialized atomic logical instructions in testing and modifying a bit. We cote `bt` (bit test), which makes it possible to extract a bit to store it in the carry flag. The extraction can also be made by setting the bit at 0 or 1 or by bit complementation respectively done using the instructions `btr` (bit test and reset), `bts` (bit test and set) and `btc` (bit test and complement). Moreover, a search for a logical zero in one word from LSb or MSb (respectively Least and Most Significant bit) thanks respectively to the instructions `bsf` (bit scan forward) and `bsr` (bit scan reverse) makes it possible to detect a word or the first suite of consecutive logical zeros from an end of this word with, as a result, the index of the first logical 1.

At the level of a variable, MPU 80386 introduced conditional initialization of a byte with instruction `setcc` (byte set on condition) at 1 from the destination if a condition on a flag state (suffix cc) is verified (i.e. true) or else 0. MPUs MC68000 from Motorola and NS32000 from National Semiconductor (NS) with respectively the instructions `scc` and `scond` offer, with only a few details' difference, similar functions. Thus, type of instruction is useful for implementing Boolean expressions from a High-Level (programming) Language (HLL) such as Pascal.

In general, three atomic operations are needed to implement concurrent access primitives from a resource or a synchronization. These are `test-and-set`, `atomic-swap` and `compare-and-swap`. The instruction `test-and-set` makes it possible within a processor cycle to carry out the operation of writing a 1 in a memory variable and to return the former value. It is therefore an atomic operation, that is, without interruption, at execution in privileged mode (*cf.* § 3.2.2). Where there are two distinct operations, it would be possible for the associated process to be interrupted by another, which could modify the value tested. This instruction serves to implement the concept of semaphore in system programming to protect memory area from concurrent access. The instruction `atomic-swap` generalizes the previous instruction in the sense that it manipulates a value other than 0 and 1. The instruction `compare-and-swap` generalizes the previous one without changing the memory value in the memory so that there is no equality with the comparison value. We find this operation in the x86 architecture from 80486 with `cmpxchg` (compare and exchange) prefixed by `lock` in an SMP (Symmetric (shared memory) MultiProcessing) environment with MC68020 and higher versions with the instructions `cas` (compare and swap) and `cas2` (double `cas`). With an atomic test-and-branching operation, the decision is implicit, unlike the "classic" sequence with two separate instructions. To conclude, the instruction, similar to the atomic operation `xchg`, that makes it possible to exchange two operands is `bswap`, which makes it possible to reverse the byte order in a word. It makes it possible to pass little to big Endian memory storage orders (Little and Big Endian (LE and BE), *cf.* § 2.6.2 in Darche (2012)).

2.6.2. *Synchronization instructions*

Synchronization can be done in relation to the external environment. One example is the prefix instruction lock from 8086 from Intel, which makes it possible, in a multiprocessor environment, to block access to a bus to ensure unique guaranteed access to a critical section by activating its #LOCK signal. The add instruction (add) with this prefix becomes an atomic operation that operates a fetch and add (i.e. exclusively adds a constant to a memory variable) from useful concurrent programming, for example, for a mutual exclusion lock (i.e. mutex lock). The drawback with this instruction is that there can only be access to the main memory and so no storage of the result in memory. The instruction xadd (exchange and add) from MPU i486 has made this function possible.

There are other synchronization software solutions in multiprocessor environments, such as the instruction pair Load-Link and Store-Conditional (LL/SC or LLD-SCD), which makes it possible to operate an RMW atomic primitive (Read-Modify-Write), which is offered by Alpha, PowerPC, MIPS (Microprocessor without Interlocked Pipeline Stages) and Arm® architectures. These are explored in a future book by the author focusing on parallelism.

2.7. Extensions to instruction sets

This section shows sub-sets of specialized instructions in an application domain. They are added as the architecture evolves to meet a particular need. These extensions help to raise performance (*cf.* § 3.4).

2.7.1. *Multimedia extension*

An extension to the instruction set can enable a processor to adapt better to the application domain. Concerning (multi)media (signal) processing, the first specialized set was MAX-1 (Multimedia Acceleration eXtensions) from Hewlett-Packard for their PA-7100LC microprocessor, introduced in January 1994. It was followed by VIS (Visual Instruction Set) from Sun, operated for the first time with UltraSPARC from Sun (Kohn *et al.* 1995), then by Fujitsu with SPARC64 GP in 2000 (Song 1997) and described by Tremblay *et al.* (1996). The following version from HP called MAX-2 (Lee 1996; Lee and Huck 1996) concerned the 64-bit ISA PA-RISC 2.0 (Kane 1996), implemented, for example, in PA-8000 (Kumar 1997).

VIS 2.0 was implemented for the first time in UltraSPARC III (Horel and Lauterbach 1999) and in successive versions as well as in SPARC64 (Williams *et al.* 1995). VIS 3.0 was implemented for the first time with SPARC T4 (Shah *et al.* 2012). VIS 4.0 was implemented for the first time with SPARC M7 (Aingaran *et al.* 2015; Li *et al.* 2015; Konstadinidis *et al.* 2016). At Intel, the MMX (MultiMedia eXtensions) extension dedicated to multimedia was implemented for Pentium II in January 1997. Details on this are given in Peleg and Weiser (1996) and Peleg *et al.* (1997). Silicon Graphics, Inc. (SGI) and MIPS introduce their multimedia technology, called MDMX™, for MIPS Digital Media eXtensions (nickname Mad Max) in October 1996 with 32 media registers in 64-bit format and 19 new specialized instructions (Gwennap 1996). Digital added to its Alpha (Sites 1992, 1993; McLellan 1993) architecture a minimal five-instruction extension called MVI for Motion Video Instructions as well as condensed formats for integers (Rubinfeld *et al.* 1996). The announcement was made in 1996 for its MPU 21164PC (Bannon and Saito 1997) and 21264 (Kessler *et al.* 1998; Kessler 1999). Lee (1997) describes using instructions belonging to these extensions.

It should be noted that this means, in the majority of cases, more an ISA extension than just an addition to a sub-set of specialized instructions in a domain as there are, for example, register additions as for MMX with eight registers in 64-bit format MM[7:0]. The registers thus have a high format of 128 (SSEx, $x \in [1, 4]$), 256 (AVX for Advanced Vector eXtensions) or 512 bits. They contain data in the classic 8-, 16-, 32- and 64-bit formats (X_i and Y_i in Figure 2.27 with $i \in [0, 3]$) forming the components of a vector (X and Y in the same figure) on which the same operation will be carried out in parallel. These are known as (packed) or condensed numbers. This term must absolutely not be linked with "packed" in "BCD packed" representation called, for example "packed-decimal format" at IBM. Here, this means gathering several numbers from a single number set, in this case integers, and the same representation in machine. We see that a single instruction can apply to several components at the same time, hence a gain in execution speed, the other gain being specialization of the instruction, which replaces a sequence of instructions from the base. This architecture is called SIMD for Single Instruction stream/Multiple Data stream in the parallel machine classification in (Flynn 1972). But beware, unlike the packed format, the instructions for scalars are only executed for the least significant pair of operands.

Instructions of this extension type are classed in sub-families, first according to representation (whole, floating point and packed). These families include transfer, arithmetic, Boolean and advanced instructions for comparison and conversion between types. A final sub-family includes control instructions, mainly for the state and cache. Arithmetic operations are basic and others are more complex, such as the square root and its reverse (inverse square root) or the calculation of a format's minimal and maximal values.

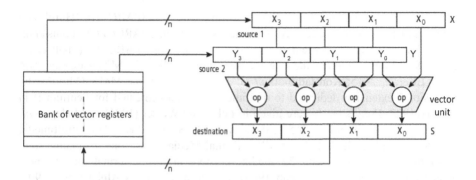

Figure 2.27. *Distribution of operations in a vector instruction in a SIMD structure*

In particular, conversion instructions can be numerous, covering all possible combinations. In the Intel 64 architecture, we cite the instructions `cvtpd2pi/cvtpd2ps/cvtpi2pd/cvtpi2ps/cvtps2dq/cvtps2pd/cv tps2pi/cvtsd2si/cvtsd2ss/cvtsi2sd/cvtsi2ss/cvtss2sd/cvts s2si/cvttpd2dq/cvttpd2pi/cvttps2dq/cvttps2pi/cvttsd2si/c vttss2si` with pi, pd and ps meaning respectively packed doubleword integer, double-precision and simple precision floating-point; dq meaning packed double word integer and si, sd and ss meaning respectively doubleword integer, scalar double-precision and single-precision floating point. These same last names also apply to basic arithmetic instructions (`addsd/adds`, etc.).

This first generation involved operations for integers. The second focused on operations in representing FP (for Floating Point) for sub-words (packed or scalar). From Intel, we cite the extension (I)SSE for (Internet) Streaming SIMD Extensions (Thakkar and Huff 1999a, 1999b) introduced with Pentium III under the code name Katmai New Instructions (KNI) and adding nearly 70 instructions. This is a simple precision version. Eight additional registers called XMM[7:0] in 128-bit format and accessible independently of the floating unit x87 are introduced for these numbers and add to the eight registers MMX[7:0], which are in 64-bit format, from the previous generation. The instructions offered for this packed format (Packed Floating-Point) are classic arithmetic and logical operations, for comparison, transfer and permutation (*cf.* § 2.3.2), summarized in Diefendorff (1999). Version SSE2 was introduced in 2000 with the Pentium 4 (Willamette microarchitecture), the first representative of Netburst microarchitecture. It extends FP representation to double-precision packed format (i.e. two numbers in n = 64 bit format in a register). The packed format for integers (packed integer) with four formats (byte, words of 16, 32 and 64 bits in a 128-bit vector) is also introduced. A total of 144 new instructions are added for the user (packed addition, subtraction, multiplication, division, compare, min, max and square root). The rival AMD with version 2 from June 2000 from its 3DNow! technology adds 25 instructions. There follow versions SSE3, codename Prescott New Instructions (PNI) with 13 new instructions, SSSE3 (Supplemental SSE3, codename: Tejas New Instructions or TNI), introduced with the Prescott version from Pentium 4 and the Merom version from MPU Core 2 respectively in 2004 and 2006. The SSE4 version (Nehalem New Instructions or NNI) with versions SSE4.1 (Penryn microarchitecture) announced in 2006 and SSE4.2 (Nehalem microarchitecture) in 2008 introduced 54 additional instructions. The SSE4.2 extension specializes in text and character chain processing (Intel 2007). It offers seven additional instructions. In particular, as the VAX mini-computer proposed speeding up its calculations, it introduced an instruction for Cyclic Redundancy Check (CRC, *cf.* § III.6.7 in Darche (2000)) called crc32 (accumulate CRC32 value) to facilitate detection (EDC for Error-Detecting Circuit/Code) or, better, error correction (ECC for Error Checking and Correcting/ Error-Correcting Code). As for the IA-64 architecture (Lee *et al.* 2001), it describes the multimedia instructions.

Additional and competing technologies to those of Intel were introduced by AMD under the references SSE4a (MPU Phenom from K10 – 2007 microarchitecture) and SSE5 (AMD 2007) with varying degrees of success.

Competing but not compatible extensions are also AltiVec (Diefendorff *et al.* 2000) from PowerPC from Motorola (other designations: VMX for Vector Multimedia Extension at IBM, Velocity Engine chez Apple) and the multimedia instruction set from the IA-64 architecture from Intel-HP (Kane 1996).

2.7.2. *Extension for signal processing*

This section could have been included in the previous one. It involves detaching a particular instruction, which is the association of two basic arithmetic instructions, such as in multiplication/addition or FMA (Fused Multiply-Accumulate) initially useful in signal processing (*cf.* § V3-5.2), multiplication/subtraction, three instructions with multiplication/addition/subtraction or multiplication/subtraction/addition, or indeed four. The FMA3 instruction group (3 being the number of operands) appeared in extension AVX2 (Advanced Vector eXtensions) from Intel announced in June 2011 and integrated into the Haswell microarchitecture in 2013, continuing SSE4. The instructions had the prefix VEX (*cf.* § 1.1). AMD had already offered this type of instruction in 2007 with the SSE5 extension, splitted in 2009 with a new coding schema in three XOP sub-sets (eXtended OPerations) and FMA4 (AMD 2009), then F16C (or CVT (ConVerT) 16).

2.7.3. *Cryptography*

A processor can offer a calculation unit that accelerates (de)cryption. So Intel offered AES NI technology (AES NI for Advanced Encryption Standard New Instructions) dating from 2010. These instructions, of which there are six, are aesdec, aesdeclast, aesenc, aesenclast, aesimc and aeskeygenassist, and the last two make it possible to manage the key.

2.7.4. *Randomization management*

The instructions rdrand (Read Random Number) and rdseed (read random seed) form part of a technology whose code name given by Intel is "Bull Mountain". They make it possible to generate a number at random.

2.7.5. *Implications*

One extension to ISA involves, at the hardware level, an impact on the chip surface and consequently extra current consumption, counterbalanced by an increase in performance. One aspect that should not be neglected is the impact on software, in particular on the SE. Adding registers, for example, may involve modifying how the execution context is handled (*cf.* § 4.2.2). MMX and 3DNOW! technologies do not add new status flags, unlike SSEx. State flags can also be added.

2.8. Various instructions

This section presents various instruction families. This may be a support for a high-level language, useful instructions for debugging or instructions for managing hardware.

2.8.1. *Instructions for handling (strings of) characters*

The 8086 microprocessor inaugurated an instruction set specialized in handling character strings. A character is coded in alphanumeric codes ASCII and EBCDIC (Extended Binary-Coded Decimal Interchange Code) respectively on 7 and 8 bits (*cf.* § III.3 in Darche (2000)), so on at most one byte. UNICODE (UNIversal CODE) and the ISO/IEC standard 10646 (ISO/IEC 2017) made it possible to move to coding using 21 bits and 32 bits, which then, thanks to the UTF transformation formats (UTF for Universal Character Set (UCS) or Unicode Transformation Format, *cf.* § III.3.9 in Darche (2000)), were transformed into a format handling respectively 8, 16 and 32 bits. The x86 family offers instructions adapted to transferring blocks of words in these different formats. We cite instructions in byte format `movsb` and `stosb` respectively for formats higher than 16 and 32 bit formats, `movsw` or `movsd` and `stosw` or `stosd`. To iterate the operation, Intel offers the prefixes `rep`, `repe`, `repne`, `repz` and `repnz`, which condition its execution with the CX register serving as counter. As for the `loop` instruction, they complexify the CU (Control Unit) and are typical of the CISC approach. It should be noted that this instruction family is reminiscent of the block displacement instructions (i.e. from memory copy) from Z80 (`ldir`, `lddr`, `cpir` and `cpdr` and for I/Os: `inir`, `indr`, `otir` and `otdr`).

2.8.2. Input/output instructions

For Input/Outputs (I/O), some microprocessors, for example, those from Intel and Zilog, have separate memory and I/O spaces (*cf.* § V3-2.1.1.1). The specific instructions `in` for reading and `out` for writing enable these processors to address this distinct I/O address space. At execution, a control signal is generated by the microprocessor to select the corresponding addressing space. These instructions such as `ind` and `outd` from Z80 can generate a pointer automatically to facilitate handling in a data block.

MCUs (MicroController Units) have instructions developed to manage parallel I/O ports. For example, those from the MCS-51 family (commonly called "8051 family" from the name of the reference circuit, hence the acronym for Micro Computer Set) offer basic logical instructions (`anl`, `orl` and `xrl`), which are executed on port P0 or P1 with an immediate value passed in operand.

2.8.3. High-level instructions

The MPU can provide high-level instructions such as `enter`, `leave` and `bound` in the x86 architecture. The instruction `enter` creates a stack frame to pass parameters of a given size. The symmetrical operation is `leave`, which frees up the frame. The instruction `bound` determines whether a value belongs to a range. This is enough to manage an array index.

2.8.4. Arithmetic instructions specific to a representation of particular numbers

The representations considered are BCD representations and fixed and floating-point representations.

2.8.4.1. *Representation in BCD*

Most MPUs offer software support for representing natural integers in useful BCD, in particular, for COBOL (COmmon Business Oriented Language) language with its computational-3 data type, as well as for representations of real numbers called "decimals", that is, using the base 10 as a support to represent the digits in machine for where there is a question of the exactitude of the coding. This exactitude of representation may be an obligation of the application domain or a legal obligation. We cite DXP (Decimal fixed-point) and DFP (Decimal Floating-Point) representations, the latter being included in IEEE Std 754-2008 (IEEE 2008). In addition to the adjustment instructions (*cf.* § 2.3.1), we cite the operations unpk (unpacked BCD) for converting a packed BCD to the unpacked version (unpacked BCD) and, conversely, pack from MPUs MC68020/30/40.

2.8.4.2. *Representation for real numbers*

For floating-point calculations, it was necessary first to use specialized software libraries, which emulated these operations. Then, hardware implementations in the form of an external component, the mathematical coprocessor (*cf.* § V3-5.4), appeared in the 1980s. They only had a single function such as, for example, the WTL 1064 multiplier or the adder WTL 1065 from WeiTek calculating in floating point. It could calculate an elementary function (GP FPP for General-Purpose Floating-Point Processor) such as 8087 from Intel, the first component of the x87 family. The latter was then integrated from a 486DX microprocessor from Intel. Instructions in floating point now form part of the instruction set for the most powerful components with a specialized integrated calculation unit. These units provide a minimum, as for whole numbers, transfer instructions, basic arithmetic operations, basic logical operations, comparison and conversion operations between number formats. For the x86 architecture, the four basic arithmetic instructions involve one number floating with another (fadd/faddp, fsubd/fsubp, fmul/fmulp and fdiv/fdivp) or with an integer (fiadd/fisub/fimul/fidiv). The latter will be converted into floating point before the operation. The destination operand will always be an FPU (Floating-Point Unit, *cf.* § V3-5.4). More particularly, the multiply-and-accumulate (mac) operation was introduced to carry out simple operations such as multiplication or the scalar or complex product such as digital filtering. It is suggested for integers and real numbers in floating or fixed point representations. One example for integers is mac for DSP TMS 320Cxx from TI. This operation is generally carried out by a specific unit called a MAC unit (MAC for Multiply-and-Accumulate, *cf.* § V3-5.2 and, in particular, Figure V3-5.4) for reasons of performance.

As indicated in the previous chapter/section § and in § 2.7.1, the floating-point numbers can be coded in packed BCD. Processors therefore provide adapted instructions. We cite as an example in Intel 64 and IA-32 architecture the instructions `addps`/`addpd` and `addsubps`/`addsubpd` respectively for single and double precision floating-point values whose numbers are expressed in packed BCD (respectively suffixes ps and pd).

Other more complex instruction families make it possible to calculate basic functions such as trigonometric or logarithmic functions (`fyl2x`, for example) or exponentiation functions (`f2xml`, for example). These calculations are generally made using a LookUp Table (LUT), that is, with the aid of values stored in a read-only memory or ROM (Read-Only Memory) which are interpolated.

2.8.5. *An unusual instruction*

To conclude, we cite the instruction `nop` for No Operation, which does nothing but increments the PC (Program Counter). One example of use is to reserve a memory area to make a patch[14] from a program, hence the term "patch zone". During a jump in this zone, the processor will irremediably reach the patch zone (NOP slide, sled or ramp). More subtly, the `nop` instruction code is generally simple, that is, only one or a few bits have an identical value. By fixing these bits electronically, by wiring or simply by leaving lines unconnected, on the data bus, an electronic system with only one processor without memory and reading any address would in fact recover the `nop` instruction code. The result was an address increment, characteristic signals from counting if they were to be observed on the screen of an oscilloscope (*cf.* exercise E2.6). (Very) long instruction word processors ((V)LIW, this will be covered in a future book by the author on microprocessors) use it to insert an execution delay in a pipeline. To conclude, it should be noted that it is equivalent to a conditional jump instruction when the logical condition is not verified (i.e. false).

2.9. Conclusion

This chapter studied a processor's instruction set. After defining and suggesting a classification for instructions in the form of classes, these different classes of a generic microprocessor as well as the possible extensions of this set are presented. Originally, this component only processed integers. Today, it is able to work with advanced types such as Boolean, BCD (Binary-Coded Decimal), fixed and floating point and character strings.

---

14 A patch replaces or adds to an existing binary code and makes it possible to avoid complete generation of an application (i.e. compilation/linking), which takes a great deal of time.

The following chapter presents additional concepts associated with instruction sets and execution. It will also deal with two subjects that are essential for actors in this domain, which are hardware and software compatibilities as well as performance measurement.

Additional Concepts

The present chapter completes the study of ISA (Instruction Set Architecture) with additional concepts linked to the instruction set and to execution. The former means the concepts of illegal, invalid, reserved and trusted instructions, instruction alignment, the instruction set's orthogonality and the symmetry and the concept of pure, re-entrant and relocatable code. The subjects of execution time, memory requirements, execution modes, portability and virtualization are then addressed. We conclude with some important aspects, which are hardware and software compatibilities, measuring execution performances and the criteria for choosing a microprocessor or MPU (MicroProcessor Unit).

3.1. Concepts associated with the instruction set and programming

This section addressed additional concepts linked to instruction sets. It completes § V1-3.5.

3.1.1. *Illegal, non-implemented, invalid, reserved and trusted instructions*

An illegal instruction is an instruction that does not exist. It has not been implemented by the designer. In general, it is the first word of the instruction that does not correspond to the instruction set. For example, the MC6802 has 72 instructions of variable size and 192 valid machine codes out of 256, and so 59 are illegal. Modern MPUs (MicroProcessor Unit) generally raise a trap (*cf.* § 5.4), which will divert execution towards a routine for processing the exception (this is the case with the Arm® family, for example). Some instructions can be considered illegal if a coprocessor (*cf.* § V3-5.4) that should process them is not present.

A non-implemented instruction is an instruction that may exist for one of a family's components but not for another. One example is an instruction from MC68020 not implemented in its forerunner, the MC68000.

An invalid instruction is an instruction from the instruction set used in a poor configuration. One example is a transfer of a register's content to an immediate value. The operation code is correct but not the rest of the instruction. In both cases, it may be a generating error from an assembler or compiler.

Some machine codes are reserved by the designer. They are not documented but it is possible to find unofficial information from reverse engineering. This involves, for example, the 8085, the Z80 or the MC6502. They are not therefore guaranteed by the designer. Another definition is to say that they are an instruction linked to an execution mode (*cf.* § 3.2.2). If it is executed in a forbidden mode, then an exception is thrown, as with the previous case.

A trusted instruction, a term used in the security domain, is an instruction that is not malicious, which can therefore be executed at a privilege level equal to or less than the one to which it belongs.

3.1.2. *Alignment or framing of instructions*

Data (i.e. instructions or information) alignment in main memory makes it possible to simplify the microprocessors' access to the data. A general case was discussed in § 2.6.1 in Darche (2012). A binary word in format $2^k \times n$ (with $k \in \mathbb{N}$) and address A is called aligned or framed in a memory in n format when the following relationship is verified:

$$A \bmod 2^k = 0 \hspace{4cm} [3.1]$$

The format n is generally a multiple of the byte and is equal to:

$$n = 2^3 \times k', k' \in \mathbb{N}^* \hspace{3cm} [3.2]$$

One example of code alignment is the MIPS (Microprocessor without Interlocked Pipeline Stages) microprocessor. The counterpart is a larger generated code than in a version with misalignment as memory locations are used for the goal of realignment. Misalignment of an operand during access may involve additional execution time just as for, originally, the x86 family from Intel. Figure 3.1 shows instruction storage in an aligned or non-aligned memory.

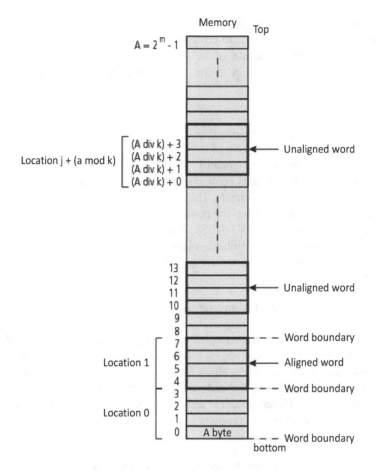

Figure 3.1. *Instruction alignment in 32-bit format*
(from Darche (2012) modified)

The word boundary is the division between two words. Considering that the memory is divided into words, we speak of access to the word boundary when it is not possible to have access with finer granularity. The architecture may not be sensitive to this constraint. If the information is between two words, the MPU will detect this. It will generate two consecutive addresses to access the complete information, which it will reconstruct internally. The management logic will be more complex than the two management logics that follow. If the alignment is imposed, the software (i.e. the compiler) will guarantee the valid instruction codes and the hardware will detect a misalignment and generally will generate a fault (*cf.* § 5.4). An intermediary solution is to use differentiated instructions in cases of misalignment to fetch the information. One example is the Arm® architecture with instructions `lwl` and `lwr` (load word left/right) for reading and, for writing, `swl` and `swr` (store word left/right). In case of accidental misalignment, an exception will be raised. Another example is the Alpha with the instruction `ldq_u` (load quadword unaligned) in addition to the instructions `extll` and `extlh` (extract longword low/high).

3.1.3. *Orthogonality and symmetry*

The instruction set's orthogonality and symmetry mainly characterize the independence of the instructions compared to the data types and format, to storage and to the addressing of the operands. They also express the fact that the instructions do not show any specificity from the point of view of the registers, data formats or the upgrading of flags (*cf.* § V3-3.1.5). These two characteristics are sometimes interchangeable, and indeed confused, in the literature. Also, these are the precise definitions from Hunter (1987) and Levy and Eckhouse, Jr. (1989) which will be retained.

Orthogonality, also called completeness, characterizes the fact that each type of data that can be processed by the processor hardware has a complete instruction set (addition, subtraction, multiplication, division, logical operations, etc.). We also speak about regularity. A data type is, for example, an integer in all its formats (8, 16, 32 bits, etc.), a real number in all its formats, a character, etc. Orthogonality has a role in the compactness of the code and so in the generality of the code. The programmer is also better able to understand the program. The principle of orthogonality also applies to exceptions (*cf.* § 5.4). Orthogonality makes it possible to simplify the hardware.

Symmetry refers to operand specification. It characterizes the fact that each instruction can use any addressing mode to access the operands. Registers are general purpose and interchangeable. A transfer instruction will be able to carry out its operation in both directions. The code is made symmetrical by separating the instruction code from the addressing mode. The absence of symmetry complicates Assembly Language (AL) and code generation by translation tools such as compilers or assemblers (*cf.* § V5-1.2) by multiplying specific cases.

In the world of MPUs, we cite the MC68000 family from Motorola and the 32000 series from National Semiconductor (NS), which introduced an orthogonal and symmetrical architecture. It was possible to link any of its instructions with an addressing mode and a data format (8, 16 and 32 bits). The instruction set of the PDP-11 mini-computer from Digital Equipment Corporation (DEC), then that of the VAX (Virtual Addressed eXtended) were a benchmark for symmetry. The 8080/8085 family was well known for its programming, complicated by the asymmetry of the instruction set. The x86 family inherited this. One example is the instruction stos, which uses specific indexing records and transfers in only one direction. A microprocessor such as MC6800 had two transfer instructions for (down)loading the accumulator.

3.1.4. *Pure, re-entrant and relocatable codes and code for read-only memory*

A pure code is a code that contains only invariant (i.e. constant) instructions data. In particular, it should not self-modify (this is the case, for example, for some IT viruses called polymorphic). It allows re-entry.

A re-entrant code enables several tasks, from one or more users, to use it without losing data coherence. To do this, the code should be invariant (pure code), and each user has their own data zone. The x86 family with separate segments of code and data enables that. For example, the TMS320C31 allows re-entry.

A relocatable code is position-independent. It is the opposite of an absolute code. The benefit of a Position-Independent Code (PIC) or Position-Independent Executable (PIE) code is that the program (i.e. instructions and data) can be stored in any place in the memory. Managing the main memory, a task that falls to the Operating System (OS), is simplified. To do this, the programmer should not use absolute (i.e. fixed) addresses but relative addresses (*cf.* § 1.2.3.2) or symbolic addresses that will be resolved during the assembling and link editing (*cf.* § V5-1.2). Adapted addressing modes are based on relative addressing (i.e. at the Program Counter). The manufacturer DEC used four addressing modes using the Program Counter (PC immediate, absolute, relative and relative deferred addressing modes, *cf.* § 1.2). The absence of an MMU (Memory Management Unit, this will be covered in a future book by the author on memories) can be palliated by this approach, but it is obsolete today as modern processors use the virtual address. Segmentation uses them for the programmer in a transparent manner.

A "ROM-able" code is a program intended for implementation in read-only memory[1]. This means that the instructions and constants will go to ROM (Read-Only Memory) while the variables, which are therefore modifiable, will be stored in volatile memory. This contrasts with the "von Neumann" arrangement that stored everything in a single memory, called "unified". This responds particularly to demand from embedded systems. It justifies the concept of specialized sections in programs in assembly language for instructions, data and constants.

---

1 This will therefore be FirmWare or FW (i.e. software stored in read-only memory).

3.1.5. *Levels of programming languages*

The instructions the microprocessor executes present in the form of binary words in a set, fixed or variable format. This is what we call machine language. Since it is not easy to use them in this form for programming, since it is a natural binary, a symbolic High-Level (programming) Language has been invented to move closer to natural language. This is Assembly Language (AL). Formed mainly of mnemonics (*cf.* § 2.1), that is, of symbolic instruction names, it comes close to human language. To each mnemonic and, if this is applicable depending on the addressing mode of the operand(s), there will correspond a binary instruction. The two major defects are a lack of readability for a large programme and an absence of advanced control structures. Also, to respond to these limitations, high-level or advanced languages have been invented. To move from one language to another, it is necessary to use software tools that translate such as the assembler or, at a higher level, the compiler. The assembler moves from a symbolic language to machine language. Figure 3.2 illustrates the hierarchy that exists between these different languages.

The linker makes it possible to add other object[2] modules (or object codes), the results of compiling a source program not necessarily written in the same language as that of the direct chain and stored in a static library. It should be noted that the editing of links also makes it possible to refer to object modules shared in a DLL (for Dynamic Link Library in Windows®). Each instruction is, depending on its architecture, either executed by a wired micromachine or interpreted internally by a microprogrammed micromachine. This aspect will be developed in a future book by the author on microprocessors.

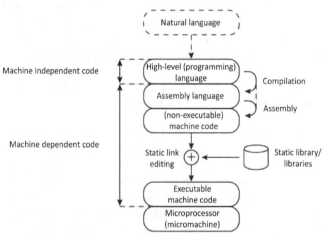

Figure 3.2. *Levels of programming language*

---

2 Not to be confused with the object languages concept of the same name.

The development chain and, more particularly, assembly language are detailed in the following volume.

3.2. Concepts linked to execution

This section develops some concepts linked to execution. These are variation of execution and memory space, the concept of internal states, execution modes, code portability and virtualization.

3.2.1. *Consequences for execution time and memory requirements*

Addressing modes and their possible combinations have consequences for the number of machine cycles and the instruction format. Table 3.1 shows the details of time costs and costs in memory space for the indexed addressing mode from MC6809, which may be substantial.

Type	Forms	Non Indirect				Indirect			
		Assembler Form	Postbyte OP Code	$\overset{+}{\underset{\sim}{x}}$	$\overset{+}{\#}$	Assembler Form	Postbyte OP Code	$\overset{+}{\sim}$	$\overset{+}{\#}$
Constant Offset From R (twos complement offset)	No Offset	,R	1RR00100	0	0	[,R]	1RR10100	3	0
	5 Bit Offset	n, R	0RRnnnnn	1	0	defaults to 8-bit			
	8 Bit Offset	n, R	1RR01000	1	1	[n, R]	1RR11000	4	1
	16 Bit Offset	n, R	1RR01001	4	2	[n, R]	1RR11001	7	2
Accumulator Offset From R (twos complement offset)	A — Register Offset	A, R	1RR00110	1	0	[A, R]	1RR10110	4	0
	B — Register Offset	B, R	1RR00101	1	0	[B, R]	1RR10101	4	0
	D — Register Offset	D, R	1RR01011	4	0	[D, R]	1RR11011	7	0
Auto Increment/Decrement R	Increment By 1	,R+	1RR00000	2	0	not allowed			
	Increment By 2	,R++	1RR00001	3	0	[,R++]	1RR10001	6	0
	Decrement By 1	,-R	1RR00010	2	0	not allowed			
	Decrement By 2	,--R	1RR00011	3	0	[,--R]	1RR10011	6	0
Constant Offset From PC (twos complement offset)	8 Bit Offset	n, PCR	1XX01100	1	1	[n, PCR]	1XX11100	4	1
	16 Bit Offset	n, PCR	1XX01101	5	2	[n, PCR]	1XX11101	8	2
Extended Indirect	16 Bit Address	—	—	—	—	[n]	10011111	5	2
	R = X, Y, U or S	X = 00	Y = 01						
	X = Don't Care	U = 10	S = 11						

$\overset{+}{\sim}$ and $\overset{+}{\#}$ Indicate the number of additional cycles and bytes for the particular variation.

Table 3.1. *Additional cost in the number of cycles and memory clutter for the MC6809 indexed addressing mode (Motorola 1981, 1983)*

Table 3.2 specifies the calculation time for addressing modes for the 8086 microprocessor from Intel. Two clock cycles are added to the given value set during a segment override. It should be noted that the complexity of the addressing modes increases the machine's number of cycles. This information is specified in each instruction's explanatory notes. For an instruction, there are a number of basic (i.e. constant) cycles to which we must add a variable value depending on the complexity of the addressing. In this table, DISP (DISPlacement) meaning offset is a value (in bytes) to be added algebraically.

Addressing modes	Calculating the effective address	Number of clock periods
Offset only	PC	6
Based or index only	(BX, BP, SI, DI)	5
(Based or index) + offset	(BX, BP, SI, DI) + DISP	9
Based + index	BP + DI, BX + SI	7
	BP + SI, BX + DI	8
Based + index + offset	BP + DI + DISP	11
	BX + SI + DISP	
	BP + SI + DISP	12
	BX + DI + DISP	

Table 3.2. *Effective address calculation time (8086)*

Chow *et al.* (1987) have shown that a simple addressing mode, base register plus offset, makes it possible to implement High-Level (programming) Language (HLL) functionalities. By optimizing its calculation time, the implantation of other complex modes can be considered and the Control Unit (CU) is thus simplified. This is one of the reasons for the RISC (Reduced Instruction Set Computer) approach whose main aim was to rationalize the instruction set to diminish its cardinality (this will be covered in a future book by the author on microprocessors).

3.2.2. Execution modes

The notion of an execution mode has been introduced to ensure that the user's, or another user's, programs can access unauthorized resources (processor, memories, Input–Output (I/O), etc.). The number of execution modes is historically two for the Cray Y-MP supercomputer. These are supervisor execution modes, called privileged modes, administrator, system (root), kernel, protected or monitor, and user, also called non-privileged mode, real or normal (Z8000). The user mode is the normal mode for executing applications. The kernel of the operating system runs in privileged mode. This number may be higher. An initial example is R4000, which has three modes, user, supervisor and kernel. Kernel mode is comparable to the supervisor mode in other microprocessors. The new mode called supervisor is an intermediary mode for promoting the operation of systems organized in layers. Intel microprocessors from the x86 family from i286 are a second example. They have a hierarchy of four levels (hierarchical protection domains) generally represented by a ring protection system as Figure 3.3 illustrates. Level 0 is reserved for the operating system kernel. Level 1 is used for services offered to I/O controller pilots and to user programs. Level 2 is assigned to pilots, and the final level is for user programs.

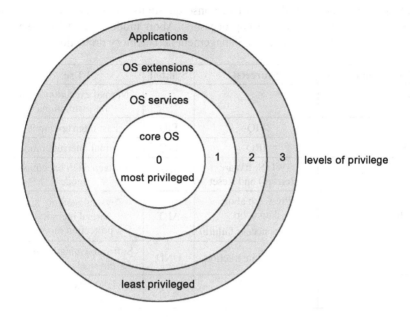

Figure 3.3. *Hierarchy of protected execution modes*
from the x86 family from Intel (from MPU 80286)

Modern operating systems require management of the virtual memory, which offers a (logical) address space that is larger than the physical address space and introduces memory protection and address translation. It also requires an execution mode known as privileged mode compared to user mode and, in a multiprocessor environment, synchronization primitives. The concept of execution mode reinforces security. A program with protection level n can execute instructions at level n or higher. Below this, a system call is needed in the form of a software interruption (i.e. trap). The reverse occurs, either by a specialized instruction such as rte for MC68010 or by manipulating a supervisor bit in a status register. An attempt at executing a privileged instruction or one with particular privileges in a mode with less privilege causes an exception (*cf.* § 5.4).

Another benefit of this hierarchization is that it creates grades of protection. Thus, OS services such as I/O controller pilots and peripheral devices have an intermediary privilege level. Those from Arm® decline the privileged mode into system mode, supervisor mode, Interrupt ReQuest (IRQ) mode or Fast Interrupt (FIQ) mode, undefined mode and abort mode, which brings the total to 7 (Table 3.3). System mode is used by the OS to execute its tasks in privileged mode. Supervisor mode is a protected mode in the OS. IRQ mode is the mode traditionally used by interrupt handlers. FIQ mode is used for fast response questions. Undefined mode involves software emulation of hardware coprocessors. Abort mode is used by the virtual memory mechanism for its internal management and memory protection.

Execution modes	Source(s)	Symbol	Use
User	–	USR	Normal execution mode for instructions
Fast IRQ	FIQ	FIQ	Fast interrupt mode
IRQ	IRQ	IRQ	Normal interrupt mode
Supervisor	SWI (SoftWare Interrupt) and Reset	SVC	Protected OS execution mode
Abort	Pre-fetch abort data abort (memory access failure)	ABT	Physical memory and virtual memory protection modes
Undefined	Undefined instruction	UND	Software emulation mode for physical coprocessors
System	–	SYS	Privileged execution mode for OS processes

Table 3.3. *Arm® architecture execution modes*

Flags can be assigned to indicate the mode as for the ARM11 family with binary indicators (i.e. mode bit) M[4:0] from the CPSR (Current Program Status Register) register. The mode's indication can be in hardware form. MC68000 has three outputs FC_i (FC for Function Code, $i \in [0, 2]$) for external controllers that encode the execution mode (supervisor or user) and the type of address space (program, data and CPU or Central Processing Unit) during access to the main memory. It makes it possible to, for example, control access. In x86 architecture, the level of privilege for I/Os or IOPL (I/O Privilege Level) is stored in the status register. When access to I/O is requested, the MPU compares this level to the CPL (Current Privilege Level) of the task being executed. This should be less than or equal to the IOPL for authorization to be granted.

With several execution modes, there should be multiple stacks. But beware, just because it has two stack pointers, this does not mean that the MPU has two execution modes, one example being the MC6809 (*cf.* § V3-3.1.8).

From the integration of virtualization technologies (*cf.* § 3.2.4) VT-x and AMD-V, the designers respectively Intel and AMD have added an additional level, hypervisor mode (= -1) to support virtualization of higher levels using hardware.

Figure 3.4 shows the different operating modes of a modern MPU. We must distinguish real addressing modes, protected modes, virtual-8086 modes and system management. Protection modes do not exist in real(-address) mode to be able, after material initialization, to initialize protected mode. One curiosity with the 80286 was that once in protected mode; this MPU could only return to real mode via initialization (reset). To enter System Management Mode (SMM), the interrupt pin SMI# should be activated. The associated handler is executed in real mode. It is the rsm (Resume from System Management Mode) instruction that takes the MPU out of this mode. This mode is useful for low-level system management such as energy and temperature management, and potentially, for debugging. These execution and operating modes are needed to ensure security of execution but are not sufficient with regard to new flaws like Spectre (Kocher *et al.* 2018) and Meltdown (Lipp *et al.* 2018). Moreover, SMM mode may also become a security flaw (Embleton *et al.* 2008).

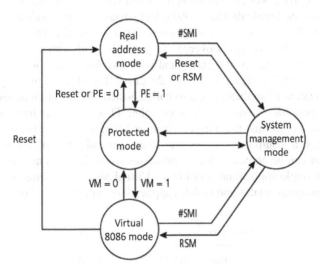

Figure 3.4. *Operating modes of an MPU from IA-32[3] architecture from Intel® (Intel 2003)*

Further technical details (hardware and software) are summarized in Intel (1984, 1986a, 1987a, 1987b) and, for information on protected mode, Shanley (1996, 2009) also in a future book by the author on microprocessors.

---

3 IA for Intel Architecture.

3.2.3. *Portability*

(Trans)portability is a system's, product's or component's ability to be transferred from one hardware or software environment to another (definition adapted from (ISO/IEC/IEEE 2017)). At software level, portability represents its ability to adapt to several execution environments. This adaptation may be more or less easy to achieve depending on whether it is a real execution or an interpretation. In the context of generating an executable, the associated terms "porting" or "portage" refer at least to targeted operation of recompiling or editing links.

3.2.4. *Virtualization*

Modern machines use virtualization, an approach from the 1970s to 1980s represented by IBM System/370 computers and IBM's OS VM/370 (Creasy 1981) and for languages, Smalltalk (Kay 1993). Virtualization was abandoned in the 1980s in favor of the less costly environment offered by the microprocessor and microcomputers. It was "rediscovered" in particular with virtualization in a server environment at the start of the 2000s and with java language (Gosling *et al.* 2018; Lindholm *et al.* 2018). Figure 3.5 shows the possibility of a virtual computer system with virtualization of applications, also called hosted virtualization above a host OS. It makes it possible to encapsulate a complete IT system (i.e. hardware, OS and applications). To do this, the Virtual Machine Monitor (VMM) is a software layer that emulates a computer's hardware layer. Instead of virtualizing a system, virtualization can be achieved during processes where it offers an execution above the OS for a single application. JVM (Java Virtual Machine) is one example of this. Virtualization encapsulates and isolates applications, in particular from faults.

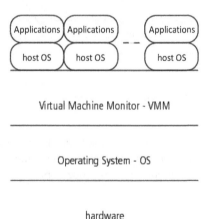

Figure 3.5. *Virtualization in an application*

The hypervisor approach is another declension where a monitor between the hardware and the OS makes it possible to manage the different virtual machines (Figure 3.6). The current trend (2018) moves towards ever-greater factorization of layers.

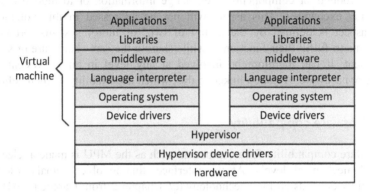

Figure 3.6. *Hypervision of virtual machines*

Containers (Figure 3.7(a)) and the "serverless" approach (Figure 3.7(b)) allow for lighter applications by taking advantage of the number of cores in current MPUs. Containers share a common OS. The "serverless" approach provides a standard interface in the application.

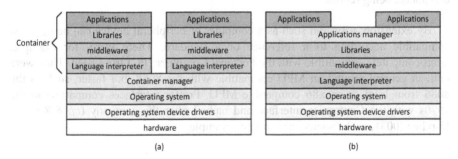

Figure 3.7. *Differences between container (a) and serverless (b) (from Wong (2016, 2017) modified)*

An excellent book on virtualization is Smith and Nair (2005).

3.3. Hardware and software compatibilities

A system's compatibility can be seen from two angles, which are interoperability and coexistence (ISO/IEC 2014). Interoperability is the ability of two (or more) systems, products or components to exchange information or to mutually use the information exchanged. This aspect will not be addressed in this volume. The second aspect is defined by the ability of two (or more) systems, products or components to fulfill their function(s) while sharing the same hardware or software environment. It can therefore be involved at any level in an IT system, either software or hardware. A notion linked to this, which is portability, is then defined.

3.3.1. *Hardware compatibility*

Hardware compatibility for a component such as the MPU is made at electronic, time and mechanical levels. At the interface, this involves signals. Electronic compatibility depends on logic technology (*cf.* Chapter 2 from Darche (2004)). This can also involve their time characteristics. The type and pinout of the component package may also be identical.

Pushed too far, hardware compatibility may also result in conflict between manufacturing competitors. One example is MCS6501, which was compatible with the MC6800 at pinout level and the signals from the bus, which resulted for MOS Technology in an industrial legal challenge from Motorola, which led to the component being retired.

By extension, a system such as a computer or peripheral device can be declared compatible according to a reference or a standard. There were, for example, microcomputers compatible with the Personal Computer (PC) from IBM. They were built in general around an MPU compatible with the 8088, but faster, such as the 8086 from Intel or an x86 compatible MPU. Printer interfaces compatible in the 1970s with the Centronics interface and named after the company (*cf.* § 8.1.1 in Darche (2003)) or the society are another example.

3.3.2. *Software compatibility*

An MPU can have a sub-set of the instruction set, or indeed the whole set, compatible with another component. One example is the 8085 microprocessor from Intel that was 100% software compatible with the 8080A. From the same manufacturer, it is the same with Pentium and the previous MPUs from the x86 family.

But the MPU is not only an IT system. Software portability with computer architectures and operating systems is a growing demand from software developers and computer manufacturers. It is motivated for technical and economic reasons to improve the efficiency of software and hardware development. To do this, it is necessary to ensure software compatibility at source code (or program), object code and computer code level. Software compatibility requires an adaptation called portage (*cf.* § 3.2.3) as a recompilation, re-assembly or a new edition of links. This aspect is developed in § V5-1.2.

3.3.3. *Upward and downward compatibilities*

Generally speaking, backward compatibility is a digital system's ability to interact with an older system or, for software, to operate correctly in a more recent environment. We also speak of upward[4] compatibility (on this, *cf.* Leonard and Kluth (1989)) or also downward compatibility. This is common in IT. It will be able, for example, to execute an old program without modifying it (i.e. without recompiling it) on a new version of OS for which it was developed or on more recent hardware. This ability is used particularly, commercially, in video games. Each new-generation MPU sees its instruction set enriched by new instructions to meet, for example, a specific need in a domain such as multimedia. Instructions of components from older generations are thus recognized. Each new generation is thus backward compatible. The benefit lies in the fact that older software can be executed by new microprocessors. There is thus binary compatibility in a family. The major drawback is growing hardware complexity, which old instructions have to master.

An initial example is the x86 family where the instruction set is formed of a hierarchy (Figure 3.8). It retains backward compatibility at each level. We must distinguish between base, extended and system sets. The base set comprises the most up-to-date instructions (arithmetic and logical calculations, data transfer, control and I/O transfer). The extended set is suggested for a particular application domain such as multimedia or a particular execution mode (186, 286, etc.). This latter type makes it possible to control a sub-set such as managing and protecting memory. One of the first extensions is the MMX set (*cf.* § 2.7.1) from Intel.

A second example is the ISA from the MIPS I processor (Kane 1988) which was extended forwards four times, from MIPs II to MIPS V (Figure 3.9) to then end with MIPS 32/64. Each extension is therefore backward compatible with the previous. Therefore, an MIPS IV component can execute a binary program using the instruction set of a previous ISA. Another example is the MC6809, which is upward compatible with the MC6800 at the source code, that is, for the instruction set and

---

4 The corresponding pairs backward = downward and forward = upward can be found (see Wikipedia article on compatibility) but will not be used in this book.

addressing modes. It is therefore possible to assemble the MC6800 source using an MC6809 assembler.

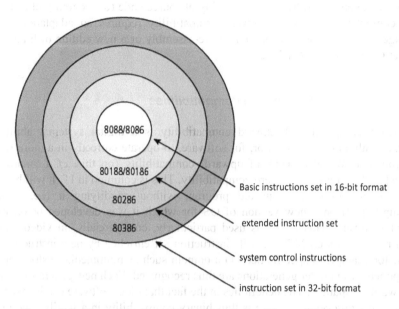

Figure 3.8. *Hierarchization of the instruction set from x86 architecture*

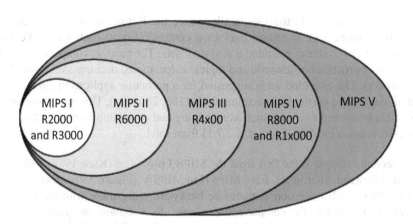

Figure 3.9. *Backward compatibility of the instruction set architecture by enriching the instruction set*

At data level, there is upward compatibility between versions of a software if the new version can use files created using the older version. One example is the most recent version of Word text processing from Microsoft whose text file extension is ".docx", which can always read the old format ".doc". A final example, from hardware, is the USB 3.0 whose upward compatibility is ensured with plug connectors.

Generally speaking, downward compatibility is a digital system's ability to interact with a more recent or future system or, for software, to operate correctly in an older environment. This compatibility is important at data level. Since it is more difficult to implement, it is encountered more rarely. One example is when a more recent software can be executed using an older OS version for which it has been developed or on older hardware. A degradation in performance is accepted. At data level, there is downward compatibility between versions of a software if the files created by the new version can equally be used by the older version. By returning to the previous example of text processing, Word 2013 is capable of opening a ".docx" file from the more recent generation but with reduced function. A converter is generally used. For additional reading from the perspective of development, read Ponomarenko and Rubanov (2012). We also speak of forward compatibility (*cf.* note at the bottom of page no. 5) or of post-compatibility or downward compatibility. Figure 3.10 summarizes the two types of compatibility.

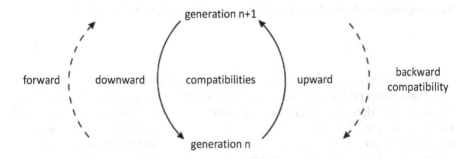

Figure 3.10. *Types of compatibility of a digital system*

Compatibility exists at register level. A processor can manipulate the same data register but with different formats. For example, Intel64 architecture uses its A register in 16- and 8-bit (respectively called AX and AH/AL from 8086), 32-bit or 64-bit formats (respectively called EAX and RAX).

3.4. Measuring processor performances

Performance is a key characteristic of a microprocessor, as too may be its power dissipation P_D (*cf.* § V3-6.1.2) or its architecture. Methods for evaluating performances are divided into three areas, measurement, performance modeling, analytics and simulation (Heidelberger and Lavenberg 1984); both models can be summarized in a hybrid model. But how do we measure the performance of an architecture, a mainframe computer or, in particular, a microprocessor or the performance of a whole computer? The less complex the architecture of a microprocessor, the easier it is to evaluate its calculating power. Today, with the multiplication of operating units (this will be covered in a future book by the author on microprocessors) and because they are combined, comparison becomes difficult. In addition, performance measurement also involves other sub-sets such as those belonging to the memory hierarchy (caches and main memory) with, for example, evaluation of its bandwidth (*cf.* below).

3.4.1. *Clock rate*

Metrics involve calculating speed and, in addition, transfer speed. A microprocessor in its most up-to-date version, that is, a synchronous microprocessor, is timed using a clock signal (*cf.* § V3-2.4.1). The initial indicator is therefore the clock rate f_{clock} of the CU (Control Unit; clock rate or speed) in hertz. The equivalent unit is the number of clock cycles per second. The higher its frequency, the faster the component will calculate. Its period T_{clock} (s) is deduced by the relationship:

$$T_{clock} = \frac{1}{f_{clock}} \hspace{3cm} [3.3]$$

The frequency is a performance indicator for the microprocessor's electronics and organization (in the sense of § V1-3.1.4), and it is a design choice. For example, the designers Alpha (Compaq) chose to increase frequency while Hewlett-Packard (HP) with the PA-RISC (PA for Precision Architecture) optimized its microarchitecture (Agarwal *et al.* 2000). This improvement has a direct impact on energy consumption, especially on MOS (Metal-Oxide Semiconductor, *cf.* § 2.4 in Darche (2004)) technology because of its dynamic power P_D (*cf.* § V3-6.1.2 and § 3.7 in Darche (2004)) which depends on it. On the contrary, this indicator should be handled with caution since, from one microprocessor to another, an instruction with the same functionality (i.e. operation and addressing) can require a different number of cycles for its execution. The causes of this are both internal (due to its microarchitecture) and external. A program is only written with a single instruction, and the addressing modes have an impact on an instruction's execution. Moreover, a microprocessor can also divide the internal clock rate (*cf.* § V3-2.4.1). An old example is the MC6802 with a division factor of 4. The processor's environment is also involved, in particular the memory hierarchy with, in the first place, the different cache levels and the I/O controllers. Today, these are (i.e. 2000) integrated into the southbridge chipset (*cf.* § V5-3.3). Moreover, for technical reasons, manufacturers have chosen to favor increasing the number of kernels to the detriment of the clock rate (*cf.* § V3-2.4.1).

3.4.2. *Number of instructions per cycle*

A second indicator [is] the average number of Instructions (executed) Per Cycle or IPC (Instructions Per Cycle). The IPC is generally calculated according to the formula at program level [3.4] from the total number of instructions executed I and the number of clock cycles C needed to execute them. The number of cycles considered here is the number of instructions executed, that is, terminated, and it can include stall cycles when the processor is stopped (the case with pipelined architecture).

$$IPC = \frac{I}{C} \qquad [3.4]$$

This unit of measurement is generally used to evaluate the Instruction-Level Parallelism or ILP (this will be covered in a future book by the author on microprocessors). A value lower than the unit indicates parallelization of execution. It is linked to the average number of (clock) Cycles Per Instruction (CPI) by the relationship:

$$CPI = \frac{1}{IPC} \qquad [3.5]$$

This indicator can be declined per instruction family i, whether arithmetic and logic, transfer (loading-storing) and (de)branching instructions. For a given program, it is then possible to calculate the CPI by considering the number of instructions C_i of a class i and the usage frequency F_i (%) of n instruction families. It is equal to the sum of the results of all classes taking account of their importance:

$$CPI = \frac{\sum_{i=1}^{n}(CPI_i \times C_i)}{I} = \sum_{i=1}^{n}(CPI_i \times F_i) \qquad [3.6]$$

The number of Instructions Per Second or IPS is calculated from the average number of cycles per instruction using the formula [3.7]. The influence of the clock rate is perceptible directly in this equation since it acts on the cycle time. Increasing it makes it possible to decrease the instruction execution time. This can be done by improving or changing the technology or by intervening at the microarchitecture level. For the CPI, it must act as before on the organization, the ISA and, to a lesser degree measure, on the compiler and programming. Finally, to decrease the number of instructions in a program, it must intervene at the level of the ISA, the compiler and the programming.

$$IPS = \frac{f_{clock}}{CPI} = f_{clock} \times IPC \qquad [3.7]$$

A current multiple is the MIPS or Million (10^6) IPS. If the processor includes additional operating units such as the Floating-Point Unit (FPU) or a coprocessor, their performance should be integrated. Figure 3.11 shows the evolution of the calculating performance of the first MPUs from Intel expressed in this unit. The MIPS (Million Instructions Per Second) does not take account of the instructions used. The value obtained will therefore vary depending on the program used. An MPU manufacturer could easily show a favorable result. The comparison becomes difficult with different instruction sets. The same goes for MFLOPS, which is, also, dependant on the program used. It can sometimes be distinguished between peak or sustained rates, to emphasize the computing power of a particular sub-set such as a calculation unit. With the emergence of RISC microprocessors, the MIPS is no longer sufficient to compare different architectures. The instruction set is simplified so it can accelerate operation of the CU (Control Unit), but the compilers generate more instructions.

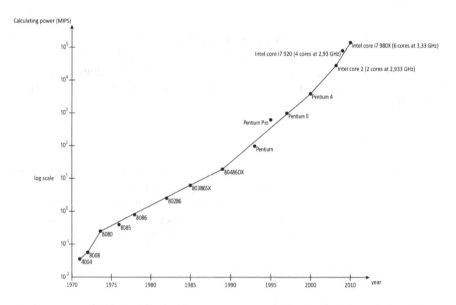

Figure 3.11. *Evolution of the calculating performance (MIPS) of the first MPUs from Intel*

For floating points, there is the number of floating-point operations per second and its multiple, the MFLOPS[5] or megaFLOPS (= Million FLoating point Operations Per Second). For the Digital Signal Processor (DSP, *cf.* § V3-5.2), we measure the number of multiplications-additions per second or MACS (Multiply-ACcumulates Per Second), with MACs being the operations currently (but not solely) used in digital filtering (*cf.* § V3-5.2).

---

5 For an evaluation, consult Giladi (1996).

3.4.3. *Execution time*

The program's execution time t_{exec} formed of I instructions is given by the formula [3.8] called "iron law" by Shen and Lipasti (2005). It depends on the compiler, which generates low-level instructions and the ISA. CPI is a function of the microarchitecture and its implementation. To conclude, the clock rate depends on the micro-electronic technology and implementation:

$$t_{exec} = I \times CPI \times T_{clock} = \frac{instructions}{program} \times \frac{cycles}{instruction} \times \frac{seconds}{cycle} \qquad [3.8]$$

A performance index P can be defined for a given program as follows:

$$P = \frac{1}{execution\ time} = \frac{IPC \times frequency}{number\ of\ instructions} \qquad [3.9]$$

A relative performance can then be defined by comparing the execution of a given program on two computers A and B:

$$P_{relative} = \frac{P_A}{P_B} = \frac{t_{exec\,B}}{t_{exec\,A}} \qquad [3.10]$$

Particular points of the architecture can then be evaluated, such as, for example, the branching prediction failure rate (this will be covered in a future book by the author on microprocessors). For the embedded systems domain where energy autonomy is vital, the MIPS (Million Instructions Per Second)/mW ratio should be preferred (*cf.* § V3-6.1.4 and Figure V3-6.6). The metrics at the MPU should consider its immediate environment, that is, the top of the memory hierarchy and, more particularly, the caches and main memory, as well as the compiler's performances since all these characteristics are intricated and difficult to dissociate from one another. So performances at data cache and instruction levels (hit ratio), Virtual Address (VA) translation performances with TLBs (Translation Lookaside Buffer), for example, memory alignment (*cf.* § V1-2.2.2) as well as the main memory bandwidth will have to be considered. The metrics of modern MPUs is complex. It should also consider its software environment (Toong and Gupta 1982). As an example, Lua (1989) compares the different performances of the first MPUs from the x86 family.

3.4.4. *Benchmark suites*

The metrics for a computer should consider the overall environment, both hardware and software. Thus, it may be necessary to consider the performance of the chipset (*cf.* § V5-3.3) or that of the I/Os such as the secondary memory data rate, for example. It is therefore necessary to use programs to evaluate performances. According to Hennessy and Patterson (2003, 2003b), this may be the targeted application, a suite of performance test programs ((synthetic) benchmark suites) as part of a suite (kernel benchmark), for example, calculation of a Fast Fourier Transform (FFT) or just a specific program to test, for example, only the floating-point division (microbenchmark). We can also list the toy benchmark, a small program of less than 100 lines of code such as QuickSort, the sieve of Eratosthenes or the towers of Hanoi and real programs representative of a domain such as a game.

Benchmark suites are programs, most of the time written in high-level language, representing an application domain (a database, for example) or which are generalists or represent a family of computers (a microcomputer or server for example) by making it possible to measure the CPU (Central Processing Unit) rate or, based on this, by calculating an indicator (arithmetical average or weighted sum of individual results), to evaluate the calculating power of a CPU (Central Processing Unit) or a computer compared to a benchmark.

An initial category is the synthetic suite. In this category, we cite the Whetstone and Dhrystone programs. The Whetstone program (Curnow and Wichman 1976) bears the name of the firm that wrote an ALGOL (ALGOrithmic Language) compiler (Randell and Russell 1964). It was written in 1972 in this language at the National Physical Laboratory (NPL) in the UK, published in 1976 then translated into FORTRAN (FORmula TRANslation). It is a simple or double precision mathematical calculation in floating point. Its unit of measurement and multiple are respectively the kWIPS (kiloWhetstone Instructions Per Second) and the million Whetstone instructions per second (MWIPS). Dhrystone is a program written originally in C by Reinhold Weicker in 1984 (Weicker 1984). Its name is a wordplay on the name of the previous test program (w(h)and - d(h)ry). It is a mathematical calculation for integers that gives the number of instructions executed per second. The unit is the DMIPS (Dhrystone MIPS[6]).

Another category is the application suite currently used. One example is the SPEC suite (for System Performance Evaluation Corporation[7]) (Dixit 1991) with SPECint (int for *integer*) and SPECflop (SPEC floating point). The first SPEC suite, SPECmark89, included 10 programs (4 for integers and 6 for numbers in floating-point). After executing each program, it provided a number (SPECmark) that made

---

6 The MIPS should not be confused with a "classic" MIPS. A MIPS here means 1.75 DEC VAX MIPS!

7 Non-profit society originally called System Performance Evaluation Cooperative, founded by IT manufacturers.

it possible to compare the element being tested with a reference computer, as it happens the VAX 11/780 (SPEC 1989). Suites SPEC92 (SPECint92 and SPECfp92), SPEC95 (SPECint95 and SPECfp95) and SPEC CPU2000 (1999) followed. Today, the SPEC2006 suite includes two programs for integers and 17 programs for numbers in floating-point. The influence of the language, its compiler and runtime library is evident (Weicker 1990). For more information, see the site of the non-profit SPEC society (URL: www.spec.org). Figure 3.12 shows the development over time of performances of microprocessor systems measured in SPECint.

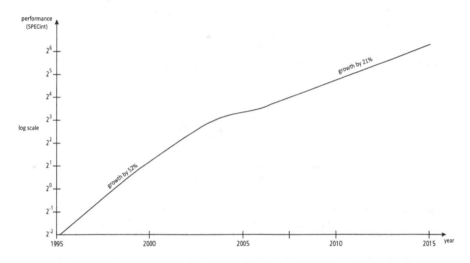

Figure 3.12. *Development of MPU systems'*
performance over time (SPECint)

Two other categories are the toy benchmark, which is a set of small pieces of code such as Hanoi Towers, and kernel benchmarks, which are extracts of real application code. For the latter, LINPACK (Dongarra *et al.* 2003), an acronym for LINear Algebra PACKage, and supplanted by LAPACK (Anderson *et al.* 1990), an acronym for Linear Algebra PACKage, are suites of subroutine written respectively originally in FORTRAN66 and FORTRAN90 to solve linear equation systems. The first was used to classify the first 500 supercalculators (TOP500). Figure 3.13 shows a comparative development of performances between supercalculators and microprocessors, mainly the RISC type.

MPU manufacturers may have their own index. We cite iCOMP (Intel COmparative Microprocessor Performance) (Intel 1996, 1999), which has had three versions respectively released in 1990, 1992 and 1999. It involves a weighted average (Table 3.4) of several synthetic benchmark suites compared to a benchmark MPU, 486SX/25, Pentium 120 and Pentium II and III respectively for versions 1.0, 2.0 and 3.0.

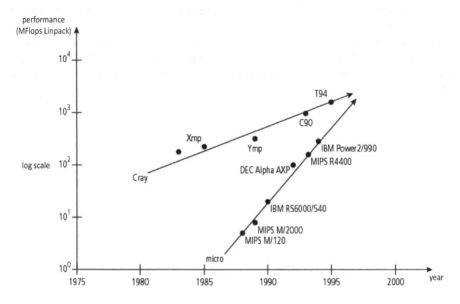

Figure 3.13. *Comparison of uniprocessor performances between supercomputers and microprocessor systems (from Culler and Singh (1998))*

iCOMP		iCOMP 2.0	
Suites	**Weight (%)**	**Suites**	**Weight (%)**
PC Bench 7.0.1	68	Norton SI32	15
SPECint92	25	CPUmark32	40
SPECfp92	5	SPECint_base95	20
Whetstone	2	SPECfp_base95	5
–	–	Intel Media Benchmark	20

Table 3.4. *List of iCOMP benchmarks*

To conclude, there are commercial benchmarks. As an example, we cite PCMark from UL Benchmarks (e.g. Futuremark® Corporation) for measuring the performance of a professional PC (Personal Computer) type microcomputer (office or otherwise) or even, 3DMark for gaming PCs. Others are suggested by magazines, for example, those suggested by PC Magazine.

3.4.5. Development of performances over time

Reducing the etching fineness has reduced transistor size. This has made it possible to increase circuit density. This increase makes it possible implement more logic gates and so more functional blocks. The consequence was a growing complexity in microarchitectures. The pipeline is one example of this, multiplying stages by decreasing levels of logic with each cycle. Moreover, the gate length makes it possible to reduce transistor switching time and so its operating frequency increases. The increase in functions and in the clock rate and the progress in compilation made it possible to double performances every three years before 1986, which is a growth factor of 1.26 per year, then every 1.5 years (52%) before stagnating finally (by considering only a core) from 2006 after an increase of 20% as Figure 3.14 shows. It is also useful to compare this first trace considering the MPU environment, in particular that of the main memory. Two measures are latency and the bandwidth (or throughput), definitions of which were recapped in § V1-2.1. These two characteristics apply to three memory categories, main, secondary and tertiary, as well as to the I/O domain as in network domains, as well as to the microprocessor. Its performance has only developed by 7% per year for main memory. Another case study is MacGregor and Rubinstein (1985), which compares the performances of MC68020-based systems. McCalpin (1995) proposes the STREAM benchmark (URL: https://www.cs.virginia.edu/stream/) to evaluate the sustained memory bandwidth for vector calculations.

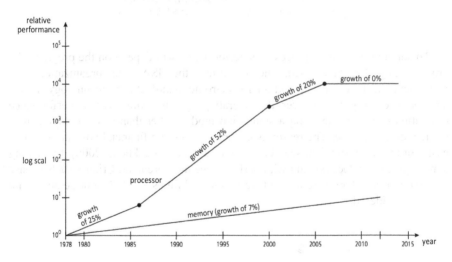

Figure 3.14. *Comparing (single-core) MPU performances with DRAM[8] performances (from Hennessy and Patterson (2011))*

---

8 DRAM for Dynamic Random Access Memory.

A final comparison is the performance of different categories of computer (*cf.* § V1-1.2) as Figure 3.15 illustrates. It shows in particular the moment where microprocessors "killed off" mini-computers (dotted circle in the figure) and, later, mainframe computers when they became competitive (killer micro, *cf.* § V1-1.2).

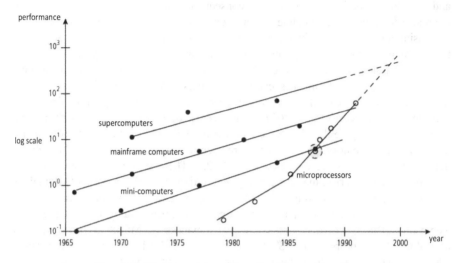

Figure 3.15. *Comparison of performances between computer classes (from Hennessy and Jouppi (1991))*

To summarize, a microprocessor's performance will depend on the program, the programming language used, the compiler, the ISA, the organization that implements it, the clock rate and microelectronic manufacturing technology. It will also be necessary to consider the operating system. Moreover, a performance estimation can be made using a simulation model rather than a real component to guide a design choice. The reason is economic, both the financial cost and the time cost. For more information, see, for example, John and Eeckhout (2006). Evaluating a microprocessor does not end with performance measurement. Criteria such as ease of programming, hardware and software compatibilities (*cf.* § 3.3) or setup should also be considered.

3.5. Criteria for choosing

Classic criteria for choosing a microprocessor are first of all classical technical criteria such as the performances desired (i.e. calculating power, transfer rate, etc.) and the characteristics of its ISA. This specifies the type of architecture (register-oriented, stack-oriented, etc.), memory addressing characteristics (alignment or not, storage order, access format, addressing capacity), the available addressing modes, operand characteristics (number, type, format and representation (i.e. encoding) and, of course, instructions (family, mnemonic, syntax, semantics, authorized addressing modes and encoding) and, finally, data and address path formats. The application domain makes it possible to make a preliminary selection by choosing an adapted architecture. A DSP will be more appropriate for processing digital signals than a GPP (General-Purpose Processor, *cf.* § V3-1.1). Economic criteria of course involve the costs of the component and of peripheral components, software development tools (compiler, assembler, linker and debugger) and hardware and hardware and software testing tools among others. The code's upward compatibility (*cf.* § 3.3.3) is also important for a family of microprocessors as it limits future investments. There are also criteria that are not non-technical but are nonetheless important, for example, supply issues such as the availability and existence (strongly advised) of secondary manufacturing sources.

3.6. Conclusion

This chapter focused on additional concepts linked to instruction sets and to execution. It first explored what illegal, invalid, reserved and trusted instructions are. It then introduced notions of memory alignment, orthogonality and the symmetry of the instruction set and the concepts of pure, re-entrant and relocatable code. Then, the subjects of execution time, memory requirements, modes of execution, portability and virtualization were addressed. The important aspects of hardware and software compatibilities, execution performance measurement and criteria for choosing a microprocessor were completed this chapter.

The chapter that follows will focus on the concept of a subroutine.

Subroutine

After studying the principles of basic microprocessor operation and programming in previous chapters, we present here the concept of the subroutine. Thanks to the subroutine, it is possible to implement the concepts of function and procedure of High-Level (programming) Language (HLL) such as C or PASCAL. To be able to do this, a memory called a stack is required. Its operation, as well as that of its subroutine, are studied. This concept has been derived from that of interruption, invented to accelerate I/O (for Input/Output) handling and presented in the chapter that follows for teaching purposes.

NB. The context of this study is a mono-processor unless otherwise indicated.

4.1. Stack memory

Stack memory simply means the stack as well as the LIFO (Last-In/First-Out) buffer to indicate the order of data circulation. Figure 4.1 shows the graph symbol of a stack S of a size s words.

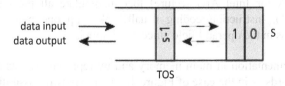

Figure 4.1. *Suggested visual representation of a stack S*

The word "stack" is an analogy with a stack of plates where the last plate stacked is later the first to be picked up. In our context, the information represents the stack. The location that will be accessed is the top of the stack or TOS (Top-Of-Stack). For information, the data that precedes it takes the name NOS for Next-On-Stack. Two primitives are needed to manage the stack: stack() and destack(). The place occupied by this memory is zero or one word at initialization. The location is a writing action on the stack, and the stack therefore increases in size. Unstacking is a reading action on the stack, and the stack therefore reduces in size. Reading is destructive in the sense that access to the data occurs only once but the information will persist in memory at least until the next stacking action and if there have not been any other unstacking actions between the two operations. These two primitives classically translate for many microprocessors (MPU for MicroProcessor Unit) through instructions respectively push and pop (or pul – pull data from stack from MC6800, for example), hence its other names push-in/pop-out or push-down/pop-up memory. But other MPUs such as the Arm® family offer two generalist transfer instructions ldm and stm (load and store multiple registers). The processor, to manage this memory, should have two to three pieces of data, which are the stack start address, the address of the location stored in the stack pointer and, eventually, the maximum size for detecting a possible overflow. A memory area of maximum size can be reserved for it such as a segment (a concept explained in the next volume). The stack pointer is implemented in the form of a specialized register called, for example, SP (Stack Pointer) in the x86 family. Other registers can be used as a stack pointer. We list, for example, the a7 (address register) from MC68000, r13 for the Arm® family and GPR1 (General-Purpose Register) in PowerPC (Performance Optimization With Enhanced RISC Performance Computing) architecture with an adapted addressing mode such as auto-increment and auto-decrement (cf. § 1.2.3). For Arm®, there are two synonyms, push and pop respectively for instructions ldm and stm that specialize the transfer using the r13 register as a base register and by automatically managing its following access. The benefit of using a general-purpose register[1] makes it possible to access the stack at random with, for example, an indexed addressing mode (cf. § 1.2.3.4), which is useful for working with local variables or the parameters of a function/procedure. The registers to be stacked or unstacked can be specified as an operand or are implicit, one example being the instructions pusha (push all) and popa (pop all) from IA-32 (IA for Intel Architecture) that manipulate all the General-Purpose Registers (GPR). Instruction coding usually takes up one byte as there is no specified address in the operand field since it is implicit.

At an implementation in main memory and by representing this with addresses ascending upwards as in the case of Figure 4.5, there are two possibilities: either the stack ascends towards the upper addresses or its ascent moves towards lower addresses (which creates an image of the stack of plates being glued to the ceiling!),

---

1 Historic note: the PDP-11 mini-computer used a general-purpose register, R6, as a stack pointer. The stack was managed with auto-decrement addressing modes with R6 for a stacking and auto-increment, still with R6 for an unstacking.

hence the final name of push-down or push-down storage (JEDEC 2002, 2013). In the first case, it is called an ascending stack, in the second, a descending stack. In this last case, which is the most classical, a stacking action is linked to a decrement and respectively an unstacking action is linked to an increment of the stack pointer. Depending on the implementations, the action of stacking or unstacking can be made before or after the increment/decrement of the stack pointer. When the stack pointer points the last element stacked or the one that will be the first to be unstacked, the stack is called full. In the case where it points the next free location for a stack, it is called empty. There are therefore four possible solutions for implementation, as listed in Table 4.1. It should be noted that Arm® architecture offers these four possibilities.

Stack names	Push	Pop	Examples of implementation
FD for Full Descending	Pre-decrement	Post-increment	MC6809, x86, Arm®
ED for Empty Descending	Post-decrement	Pre-increment	MC6800, Arm®
FA for Full Ascending	Pre-increment	Post-decrement	Arm®
EA for Empty Ascending	Post-increment	Pre-decrement	Arm®

Table 4.1. *Solutions for managing a stack in main memory*

Figure 4.2 shows the pseudo-code of the two main stack manipulation instructions for the x86 family. The stack pointer here points the last stacked element or the next to be unstacked and the pile ascends downward from the memory (full descending stack). The descent value here is 2 as the memory is managed in byte format while the stack is managed in 16-bit word format (= 2 bytes) for reasons of alignment (*cf.* § 2.6.1 from Darche (2012)) in relation to the processing format for integers of this MPU. It should be noted that, in rare cases, a processor cannot offer this implicit management of the stack pointer. In contrast, one benefit of an explicit management of the stack is choosing its ascent at the price of software cost.

push   pop

SP ← SP - 2   source operand ← [SP]
[SP] ← source operand   SP ← SP + 2

(a)   (b)

Figure 4.2. *Pseudo-code for stacking (a) and unstacking (b)*
in the format n = 16 bits for the x86 family (Intel)

The TMS320C31 runs the stack system in an upward direction! This means that a push instruction carries out a pre-increment and, pop, a post-decrement of the stack pointer SP. We can also deduce from this that the SP points the last element stacked. In contrast, the other stacks can be managed in two directions. Figure 4.3 summarizes these operations in a writing inspired by C language.

Push

*++SP ← operand   ; pre-increment

(a)

Pop

operand ← *SP-- ; post-decrement

(b)

Figure 4.3. *Operations of stacking and unstacking for TMS320C31*

During operation, two errors can happen, stack overflow[2] and stack underflow. Over- and under-flow are caused respectively by excess stacking or unstacking. We consider the pushup stack from Figure 4.4. To detect them, one possibility is to add a stack boundary limit register. Registers B and L make it possible to define the stack boundaries (shaded in the figure). Linked to the SP, they make it possible to detect the errors in its management. The conditions are the following:

if SP > L then (over-)flow;

if SP < B then under-flow.

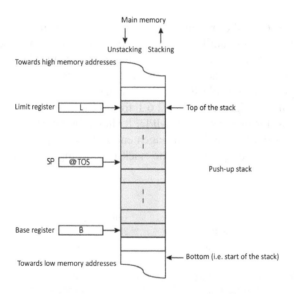

Figure 4.4. *Managing an ascending stack*

---

2 To be coherent with floating-point representation, it would have been good to choose the terms "positive and negative overflows".

The role of the stack is to store information temporarily. In addition to the return address, the stack may contain other information on the subroutine, hence the name of the execution or run-time stack. It classically contains the ingoing and outgoing parameters also called input and output parameters respectively, as well as local variables belonging to each function being executed (*cf.* § 4.2.3), as Figure 4.5 illustrates (no nested calls in the example). During execution, a (sub)routine can use the stack to save temporarily the content of a register. To make (*cf.* § 3.1.4) a subroutine re-entrant or for it to be callable recursively, an area for its local variables is allocated to it on the stack each time it is called. This area is called the stack frame, also called the call frame, activation record or activation frame. The stack frame is dependent on the computer and the ABI (Application Binary Interface, *cf.* § V5-1.1.4). To manage it, it is necessary to have a pointer on this area, local to the subroutine, here the indirection register BP (Frame Base Pointer, *cf.* § 1.2.3.4) from the 8086 microprocessor. It may be necessary to have other pointers of the same type towards frames of higher lexical position in the case of nested calls. This organization is explained in the following section.

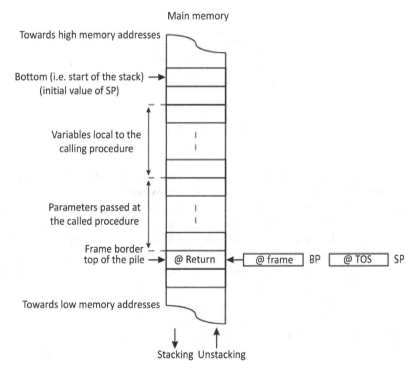

Figure 4.5. *Classical structure of an execution stack (x86 family from Intel)*

It may seem strange from the perspective of implementation to have an operation of the stack "in reverse", since the bottom of the stack is situated at the top of the main memory and data stacking increases the stack from the top. But from the perspective of managing the memory, there is none since the programs are stored at the bottom and the stack at the top for optimal management of space, as Figure 4.6 illustrates. Its maximum size is set in programming in assembly language (i.e. declaration of a stack segment[3] in x86 architecture, for example) or automatically by the compiler. For information and without going into detail, the other specialized areas that appear in the figure are intended as dynamic and static allocations for, for example, variables such as the BSS (Block Started by Symbol) area or for the instructions.

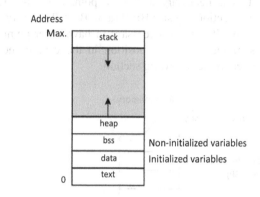

Figure 4.6. *Classic main memory mapping*

A stack can be managed with software or hardware. With software management, a Random Access Memory (RAM) area, for example, the main memory, is transformed for each program into LIFO. Because it requires using a management program, this solution is necessarily slower than in hardware management of microprocessors. Implantation in a memory stack makes it possible to have a large space, but the problem of protecting access in a multi-task environment is posed. With segmented main memory, a segment is naturally given to it, which moreover limits its maximum size to the size of the segment. The stack can also be implemented in the form of a finite stack register inside the MPU (integrated stack). We speak of a hardware stack, also called a stack cache or stack register file. Each stack shifts the values in the registers, the last element being lost. During unstacking, either the last element is doubled or the null value is injected. In

---

3 Concept linked to the concept of Virtual Memory (VM), both detailed in a future book by the author on memories.

the second case, the accumulator communicates with the top of the stack. At each stacking, the data registered is shifted downward, hence the two other names "cascade stack" or "push-down stack". This form is faster since it is integrated into the MPU and does not require a stack pointer. In contrast, its number of registers is limited and it shows the drawback of losing data when the structure is full. The reading is then called destructive, unlike the same operation on a memory stack where the data can remain, at least (i.e. if there are no other unstacking operations) until the next stacking. One example is that of the 8087 coprocessor (*cf.* § V3-5.4) for floating-point calculation, which integrates a stack in the form of 8 registers ST[7:0] in the format n = 80 bits, these also playing the role of a flat register file. In contrast, this component manages its registers in two ways (Figure 4.7). Access can be made as for a stack or by random addressing with classic load (ld) and unload (st) instructions. This mixed management provides suppleness of use.

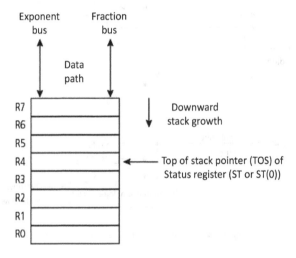

Figure 4.7. *Stack register of a mathematical coprocessor in floating point from 8087 (Intel)*

A bank of registers can be run as a stack. O'Connor and Tremblay (1997) describe such a structure from the front of a processing unit in the context of a hardware implementation of a virtual Java machine. This stack register file or stack cache is run as a circular memory buffer.

A variant of implementation is a stack whose upper part is located in the processor and the rest in main memory to obtain faster access as with the B5000 mainframe from Burroughs. A final variant, which is not very fast, is implementation with the help of Shift Registers (SR), as illustrated on Figure 4.8. Each bit of the word is managed by an SR. A combinatorial circuit, aided by a modulo maximum size counter, manages positive and negative overflows. It should be noted that elements of the hardware stack shift and the top of the stack is fixed. However, in a software stack, the opposite happens, that is, the elements are static, and the stack pointer is dynamic.

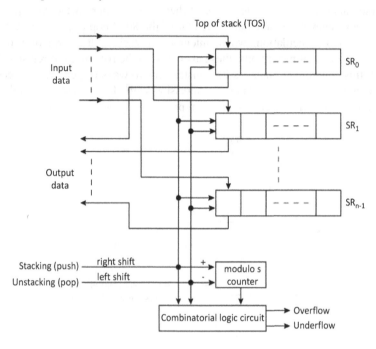

Figure 4.8. *Stack in shift-register version*

Address alignment (*cf.* § 2.6.1 in Darche (2012)) at the stack may be necessary for higher-generation 8-bit microprocessors when the memory is run in byte format. This is the case with the Intel x86 family whose transfers are made only in 16- or 32-bit format depending on the component's working format. Moreover, there is no dynamic control of this alignment, but the assembler controls the operand format during stacking or unstacking. The introduction of a misalignment would introduce serious dysfunction in the system. For ascending compatibility (*cf.* § 3.3.3) in a family of microprocessors, there may be an address-size attribute that specifies the transfer format of 16, 32 or 64 bits.

4.2. Subroutine

This concept came from the EDSAC (Electronic Delay Storage Automatic Calculator) project under the term "closed subroutine" (Wilkes *et al.* 1951). A subroutine is a block of instructions that is executed following a call from a calling subroutine. This block is a factorization of a fragment of code that can be used in different places in the application. The call is made by a specialized instruction such as `call` (x86), `bsr` (branch to subroutine) or `jsr` (jump to subroutine). In the same way, the return is made using a specialized instruction such as `ret` (return, x86) or `rts` (return from subroutine). This code is duplicated no more than necessary, that is, it is present only once. Instead, it is the number of jumps that is multiplied. The subroutine should not be confused with the macro-instruction (*cf.* § V5-1.3.4), possibly parametered, each of the expansions adding the corresponding code. Figure 4.9 shows a processor's single-task activity. Following a call and until a return, the execution flow is passed to the subroutine instructions.

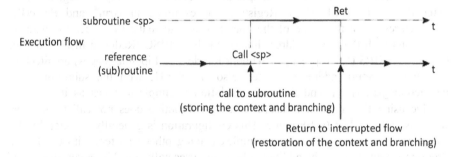

Figure 4.9. *Unfolding execution of a program with a call to sub-program*

Debranching can take place simply by initializing the Program Counter (PC) with the subroutine start address. To return to the calling program, it is necessary to have the return address. Its value is in fact the instruction address following the one corresponding to the call, that is, the value of the PC after decoding the call instruction but before its effective execution (*cf.* execution cycle, § V1-3.2.2.4 and V1-3.3.2). It should be saved by the call instruction before initialization of the PC with the branching address and restored on return by the return instruction. There are several methods or places for saving this return address. The most current is the one that uses the stack (Figure 4.10). The stack pointer is run automatically by the call and return instructions, which involves a complex execution. Moreover, once the stack is implanted in main memory (*cf.* § 4.1), the overhead is higher. The major benefit is proper management of recursivity.

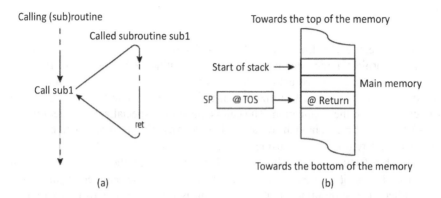

Figure 4.10. *Subroutine call and return and stack content (x86 architecture)*

The second method is to use a specialized, and thus an implicit register. This latter is called an LR (Link Register), for example, in Arm® and PowerPC architectures, from the name of the operation and to make the execution address correspond with the return address linking method. RISC (Reduced Instruction Set Computer) MIPS (Microprocessor without Interlocked Pipeline Stages) architecture uses the ra (return address) register, also called r31, with the subroutine call instruction `jal` (jump and link). This solution is simple and fast as it does not involve using the stack. It is useful when a subroutine does not call to another, which is called a leaf (sub)routine. This configuration is generally detected by the compilers. If the context is more complex (saving other registers with the PC or Program Counter), then the additional handling uses software. Moreover, in case of interruption, this can be problematic. The last solution is to use an explicit register for saving. Still using MIPS architecture, the instruction `jalr` (jump and link register) saves the return address in any register specified in the operand field.

To facilitate implementation of the compilers, high-level instructions can be proposed, such as `enter` and `leave` from Intel. Motorola used the equivalent instructions `link` and `unlk` for its MC68000. Moreover, it offers up to 10 stack frame formats.

One subroutine call that is not classical is the CDP1802 (also called COSMAC for Complementary Symmetry Monolithic Array Computer). It has its register bank of 16 registers in 16-bit format, each of which could be a PC (Program Counter). Register switching has made it possible to carry out branching to a block of instructions such as a subroutine.

4.2.1. *Nested calls*

The mechanism is cascadable and potentially recursive, as Figure 4.11 illustrates.

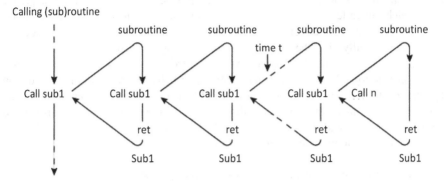

Figure 4.11. *Recursive calls and returns from a subroutine (nested calls)*

At each call, the return address is saved on the stack. Figure 4.12 shows the state of the stack at instant t. Unstacking, thanks to the LIFO access policy, is carried out in the reverse direction to that of stacking. The call depth will be the number of nested calls carried out. Knowing its maximum value makes it possible to dimension the stack size. If the stack is poorly dimensioned, then there will be a stack overflow. The condition for the recursivity to be passed correctly is that the subroutine's code should be re-entrant (*cf.* § 3.1.4). This means that it should not use global or static variables, like a high-level programming language, such as C.

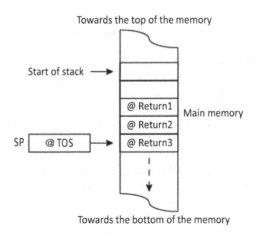

Figure 4.12. *Recursive calls and returns from a subroutine (nested calls)*

4.2.2. *Execution context*

It is necessary to save on the stack a set of data needed to make the debranching transparent, that is, to make it as if there had not been any break in the sequence with which the caller is executed. To do this, this set, which is called the execution context, will be restored on the return. It contains at least the return address contained initially in the microprocessor's program counter to make this debranching transparent. Also, a call instruction from a subroutine can be seen as a macro-instruction (Blaauw and Brooks 1997) as it behaves like a normal instruction by making transparent the execution of the block of instructions representing the subroutine. At most, this involves all the MPU's registers. Work is distributed between the caller and the called. The backup location is either internal within the registers or external in main memory in a stack.

There are three approaches for carrying out this processor state backup/restoration[4]. One is for this operation to be implicitly carried out by an instruction. The call instruction and the return instruction save/restore the internal state. One example is the complex instruction `calls` from the mini-computer's processor VAX (Virtual Addressed eXtended), which made it possible to choose the registers to be saved. In another approach involving software, instructions are explicitly responsible for carrying out the work. Only the return address is saved automatically. The remainder of the context is the responsibility of the caller or the called depending on the call convention (see the following section). The final approach is an implicit hardware management, one example being register windowing (*cf.* § V3-3.1.11.3) from the RISC SPARC family (Scalable Processor ARchitecture).

4.2.3. *Passing parameters and call conventions*

To implement a function or procedure, it is necessary to pass parameters and define who or what will manage them, the caller or the called. We recall that there are ingoing and outgoing parameters, since the function can only have an outgoing parameter, unlike the procedure in PASCAL language, for example. The type of passing defines whether the parameter is passed by the value or by the address, by

---

4 Several types of state can be distinguished in an IT system. The state of the processor or internal state refers to the content of registers that are or are not accessible (i.e. "architecture", *cf.* § V3-3.1). The external state is that of the system without the processor. It covers the state of the memory hierarchy (for the concept, *cf.* § V1-2.3 and § 1.2 in Darche (2012)) with, in particular, the caches and main and secondary memories. The state of a process refers to all the information affecting it. It can cover the states of the processor and the operating system if it is in the processing of being executed.

pointer or by reference[5]. The mode of passing defines the storage location of the parameter: register, global variable or stack. The MPU 2650 from Signetics has an interesting characteristic: it has two banks of three registers selectable by the RS (Register Select) bit from the state register. These make it possible to pass arguments easily from one process to another by switching the banks, since the accumulator is common to both. The passing can be done explicitly using classical data movement instructions (cf. § 2.2.1) or automatically while executing the call instruction. One example is the MC68020, which, as well as the classic call instruction to a subroutine, has two specialized instructions for modular programming called callm and rtm.

RISC microprocessors have optimized the passing of registers using a mechanism called register file windowing. The hardware implicitly manages the passing of parameters. To do this, a Register File (RF, cf. § V3-3.1.11.1) is subdivided into sub-sections called windows. A window is formed of three parts, which are the block communicating with the lower level, the block for local variables and the block communicating with the higher level. One example is register windowing from the RISC SPARC family (Figure 4.13 (a)). This solution was espoused for calls of low depth (i.e. < 4). The windows overlap at the communication blocks (overlap registers or overlapping register-window). The passage of outgoing and ingoing parameters between the caller and the called occurs between the intermediary of the same registers, which coincide in the windows. In particular, the return address is found in the outgoing parameter area. Only a single window is active at any one time. By using only registers, this approach makes it possible to avoid CPU (Central Processing Unit) time consuming access to the main memory. Moreover, there is a non-windowed area reserved for general-purpose registers. Figure 4.13 (b) shows a linear view of these same registers. This mechanism will be detailed in a future book by the author on the RISC philosophy.

This set of rules defining, among other aspects, what is responsible for backup in the execution context (apart from the PC or Program Counter), is called the calling convention. It is possible to have two backup conventions, caller saving and callee saving. Manufacturers provide a reference document. From Arm®, for example, we list in any order AAPCS (Procedure Call Standard for the Arm® Architecture), APCS (Arm® Procedure Call Standard), TPCS (Thumb® Procedure Call Standard) and ATPCS (Arm® TPCS).

---

5 There is a fourth form of passing called "pass by name" where the name of the argument is passed during the call as in ALGOL 60 (ALGOrithmic Language). This is an address on the variable that is accessed via indirection. This type of passing was used in prefix machines (cf. Meinadier (1971, 1988) on this subject).

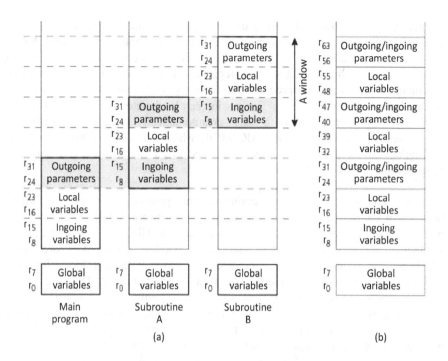

Figure 4.13. *Windowing registers (from Scott (2016))*

To summarize, we need to distinguish three types of call. The first is the subroutine call where there is, as a minimum, only storage of the return address (in fact, the address present in the PC or Program Counter before the jump) to win time when changing the context. Other registers, depending on the instructions, can be backed up. The second is the function call where two other things must be saved: the parameters to be passed and the local variables. The last is the system call, which occurs without interruption, and is the subject of the following chapter (*cf.* § 5.4 and 5.8).

4.3. Conclusion

After introducing how the stack and LIFO memory access operates, we studied the concept of the subroutine. This makes it possible to implement a higher-level language function or procedure. A similar mechanism is interruption, which is, like the first mechanism, a re-routing of the execution flow, but one particular direct towards I/O handling. It is studied in the following chapter.

Interrupt Mechanism

Execution flow (*cf.* § V1-3.1.2) can also be altered by an interrupt mechanism. We will first introduce the basic mechanism used in the first microprocessors (generations with 4 and 8 bits, *cf.* Chapter V3-1). Then, we will enrich our model with the concept of exception, present in second-generation microprocessors. This chapter enriches the section dedicated to this in Chapter 4 in Darche (2003) and § 3.2.2. It will be complemented in other books; processor architecture is becoming increasingly complex. The study will be made using different associated aspects such as nested requests, priority requests and vectorization to finish with execution modes and advanced architectures.

5.1. Origin, definition and classification

The concept of software interrupt was implemented for the first time[1] in the UNIVAC (Universal Automatic Computer) 1103A (Rojas and Hashagen 2000) at the start of the 1950s (1953 according to Mersel (1956)) to prevent potential overflow (*cf.* § II-3.1.1. and II-3.3.3. in Darche (2000)) during an arithmetical calculation (Hennessy and Patterson 1994). It was then used for the first time in I/O (Input/Output) in the DYSEAC (Second Standards Electronic Automatic Computer) (Leiner 54) from NBS (National Bureau of Standards) (Smotherman 1989a b). With the development of 16-bit generation microprocessors and the start of the use of Operating Systems (OS) in microcomputers, the concept of interrupt[2] encapsulated that of exception (Schlansker and Rau 2000). The interrupt sometimes takes the

---

1 Kuck (1978) dates the concept to Babbage's analytical engine (*cf.* § V1-1.1), which stopped by requesting human intervention using a bell (the routine!) when the wrong program card is inserted.

2 In some works such as Dumas II (2006), Harris and Harris (2007) and Hamacher (2012), it is the reverse.

name of the sub-set that generated the interrupt request, for example, "I/O interrupt" or it bears the name of the cause such as "page fault".

The general term "interrupt" or IT refers to a class of low-level hardware or software events that forces MicroProcessor Units (MPUs) to interrupt a (sub-)program's normal execution flow, as a jump instruction would do (cf. § 2.4), to re-route to a routine called an interrupt handler (or Interrupt Service Routine, giving the acronym ISR). For its protagonists, whatever generates the request (an I/O controller, an instruction, etc.) is called the "the signaler" and the processing routine is called "the processor". The processor is responsible for processing the event, ideally in a privileged mode in the case of a processor with several execution levels (cf. § 3.2.2) to then return to a normal execution of the interrupted program or to restart another if it is abandoned. The processing routine should be as fast as possible so as not to slow the main processing or not to lose requests. As Figure 5.1 illustrates, interrupts can be classified by their cause, external or internal to the MPU or linked to management of the memory. What distinguishes the two branches is their (a)synchronous character. The external cause, and so the hardware origin, is always the state of an electrical signal or its variation. It is necessary to distinguish the hardware interrupt and the hardware exception triggered by a malfunction. The internal cause is always linked to the execution of an instruction. For interrupts with an internal cause, the request is always synchronous with the clock since it is linked to the instruction's execution cycle, which generates the request explicitly, and so where it is wanted (software interrupt) or implicitly software exception. But beware, they generally appear at random. The exception is an interrupt category. In this volume[3], it is an unprogrammed event, one that is abnormal, unusual and rare[4], linked perhaps to a breakdown or an execution error[5] which will alter the sequential execution flow. But beware, an error is an exception, but the reverse is not always true. Exceptions the processor is able to detect are of two types, which are faults and aborts. A special operating mode is the step-by-step mode (cf. § 5.5 and 5.6). Inspired by the classification from Intel for its IA-64 (IA for Intel Architecture) and OSs, it is necessary to distinguish four classes of interrupt[6], which are distributed in the proposed hierarchy. These are hardware and software interrupts (or trap) and the exception that can be broken down in cases of faults and aborts in both the previous classes.

Criteria other than the origin of the cause can be used to classify interrupts. (Hennessy and Patterson 1990; Walker 1992) and thus suggest criteria that are

---

3 The meaning of this term varies depending on the authors and designers.

4 This name for an exceptional event is relative, quite clearly, to the context in which it is situated.

5 An error indicates the part of a state that is not correct (Melliar-Smith and Randell 1977).

6 Intel calls this an "exception".

asynchronous/synchronous, voluntary/forced, masked/unmasked, between or internal to the instruction, precise/imprecise or simple/multi-level, which Tables 5.12 (a) and (b) show at the end of the chapter (*cf.* § 5.11) after they have been explained.

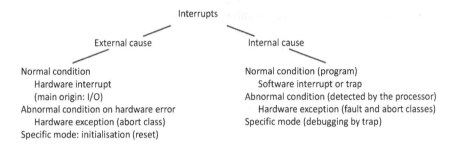

Interrupts

External cause   Internal cause

Normal condition   Normal condition (program)
  Hardware interrupt   Software interrupt or trap
  (main origin: I/O)   Abnormal condition (detected by the processor)
Abnormal condition on hardware error   Hardware exception (fault and abort classes)
  Hardware exception (abort class)   Specific mode (debugging by trap)
Specific mode: initialisation (reset)

Figure 5.1. *Origins of an interrupt request (Darche 2003)*

5.2. External causes

The external interrupt originates in hardware and is asynchronous in nature. It is therefore an unprogrammed event, that is, one not triggered by an instruction (i.e. an unscheduled event). It is therefore more difficult to handle than internal requests, and this is even more true in a multiprocessor environment. Interrupt requests mainly provide I/O controllers, which thus signal a request or indicate an end to the I/O. This is a predicted event. A hardware exception is caused by a hardware malfunction external to the processor, generally coming from the memory, the bus or the power supply, which leads for the most part to a system shutdown. This is an unpredicted and catastrophic event such as an imminent power shutdown. It leads to an abort of the execution, then to this major error, which originates in hardware. Control of the memory or transfer sub-sets in a bus relies on logical parity (*cf.* § III.6.6 in Darche (2000) and § 2.6.4 in Darche (2012)) in the case of a simple approach. It can also be a temporal error (no response in the time allotted for the access cycle). Another example is the earliest possible detection of an imminent power fault, which makes it possible to save the context. It should be noted that a machine check that indicates a dysfunction is a type of abort. An MPU can have an input for hardware exceptions of the fault type as with the 65C816 from MOS Technology and the IT ABORTB that made it possible to signal a page fault or a memory access violation.

The interrupt request is made via a binary electrical signal (Figure 5.2) applied on a dedicated pin of the processor. The request can therefore be level-triggered on a logical level (0 or 1) or on a (ascending/rising or descending/falling) signal edge (edge-triggered). The type of trigger is either fixed by the hardware (the case of the microprocessor) or programmable (in general, in the interrupt controller). The main fault with a level trigger is the risk of resetting if a later request is authorized, one example being the management of IT from the ISA (Industry Standard Architecture, *cf.* § V2-4.5) bus. Hence, most signals are edge-triggered. The main defect with edge-triggering is the risk of losing requests while an interrupt is processed. The source of interrupt can be synchronous (i.e. periodical) or asynchronous.

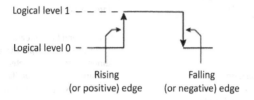

Figure 5.2. *Ideal forms of external interrupt request*

As Figure 5.3 (a) shows, the interrupt request has not immediately been taken into account. There is an interrupt latency (*cf.* the study by Macauley (1998) on the MPU 8086) between the request and its consideration, that is, the launch of the associated routine. This time corresponds at least to the end of the execution of the instruction underway or it can be higher in the case where the request is masked. The execution context is saved on the stack (Figure 5.3 (b)), and branching takes place. Once supplied externally, for example, by an interrupt controller (*cf.* § 4.1.1 in Darche (2003)), the jump address at the ISR is provided in the form of an interrupt vector (*cf.* § 5.7). After execution of this routine, on execution of the interrupt return instruction `iret`, the context is restored (stacking) to resume the execution of the program earlier suspended at the instruction following the interrupt. This re-routing is similar to a subroutine call (*cf.* § 4.2).

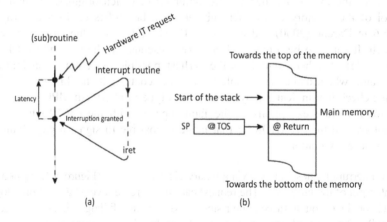

Figure 5.3. *Call and return of a non-nested hardware interrupt*

By taking Figure 4.9 as a model, it is possible to describe the execution of an interrupt with Figure 5.4. At the moment when it is considered, the mechanism resembles the execution of a subroutine described in the previous chapter if an instruction iret ends the execution of the interrupt routine. The fourth step requires identification of the handler (i.e. their start address) and its launch. Re-launching the interrupted program is achieved by restoring the context.

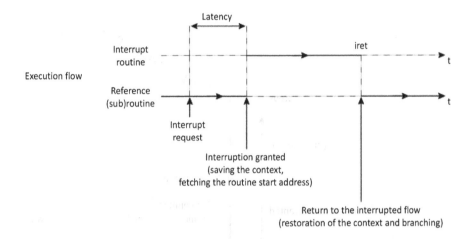

Figure 5.4. *Execution flow of a program during a hardware interrupt request*

Therefore, we can define five steps in the handling of an interrupt request (Figure 5.5). They are its detection, its consideration, saving the context, execution of the associated handler and re-launching the interrupted program[7]. When the IT is recognized, a return-receipt in the form of an electrical signal can be re-sent to the requester, generally the IT controller. The IT is called delivered when the corresponding handling routine is executed; it is called terminated when the control flow returns to the caller.

The interrupt storm is an expression to characterize the fact that an unusual number of requests are made and that the system cannot satisfy them or can satisfy them only poorly. We should remember the 1202 alarm from the on-board computer (LGC for LEM (Lunar Excursion Module) Guidance Computer) on Apollo 11 during the first moon landing, indicating a processing overflow linked indirectly to this problem. If requests occur too close together, there is then a risk of losing the request as the request is made on an edge. In the case of a request on a level, the problem no longer occurs, as it will be maintained so long as it is not considered.

7 In a multi-programming context, we would speak about a process or task.

Moreover, in a multi-task environment and in real time, interrupt routines should have a very short execution time so as not to monopolize the processor. As a last remark, in a multi-task environment, the designer should ask the question of how to determine the type of software processing appropriate to the interrupt. Does it require a function (or a procedure), a task (i.e. heavy-weight process) or a thread (i.e. light-weight process)?

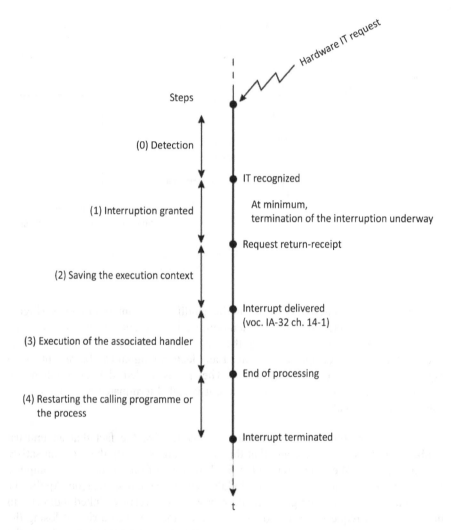

Figure 5.5. *Stages in handling an interrupt*

5.2.1. *Execution context*

We recall that the execution context is the data set needed to make the branching transparent (*cf.* § 4.2.2). It comprises all or some of the registers internal to the microprocessor. The minimal context is the program counter containing the address of the next instruction to be executed and the status register. Depending on the processors, only this minimal context is saved, such as the x86 architecture, or indeed all the registers are saved. The choice can also be left to the programmer. So the MC6809 microprocessor from Motorola had a hardware interrupt called FIRQ (Fast IRQ) that saved only this minimal context, that is, the value of the PC (Program Counter) at the moment when it was considered. Recall that the reason this IT exists is that it is executed rapidly from context switching, to meet an external demand as quickly as possible, hence its name. Its other interrupts, on the other hand, save all its registers. This microprocessor's state indicator (E for Entire flag) makes it possible to know whether all the registers had been saved or not. The vector's value (*cf.* § 5.7) is either fixed once and for all in hardware or can be modified by the program, if the vector is implanted in volatile memory, for example, in a table (*cf.* below).

The location options for saving the context are the two main ones cited for the call function (*cf.* § 4.2.2), that is, the stack or the registers. Shadow registers make it possible to have several sets from one, some or all of the registers; bank switching is achieved by passing the flow of control. Arm® architecture has several execution modes for interrupts (*cf.* Table 3.3). For FIQ (Fast Interrupt reQuest) mode, seven registers (r8 to r14) are replicated compared to two (r13 and r14) for the other modes. MC88100 and PIC32 use it. A third solution is to replicate the stacks (to make shadow stacks); this means that a stack is substituted by a replicated register. Its successive values are stacked there. MC88100 uses this mechanism under the acronym PCS for Program Counter Stack (Grohoski 1990). Two other options cited by Walker and Cragon (1995) are checkpointing hardware (Hwu and Patt 1987a, 1987b)) and the auxiliary processor that is responsible for processing the interrupt (*cf.*, for example, Keller (1975)).

It should be noted that if the saved context includes the status register and that if this contains an IT (in)validation flag, the ITs will then be automatically restored on return to the associated service routine thanks to a return instruction, such as `iret`.

5.2.2. *Sources*

The MPU in most cases has several interrupt request inputs (Figure 5.6 (a)). We call these multi-level interrupts. This solution was costly for the first generations of MPUs, as the number of DIP pins (Dual-In-Line (DIL) Package, *cf.* § 3.3 in Darche (2004)) was limited at that time. If the number of sources exceeds the number of inputs, it is possible to share an input, as Figure 5.6 (b) shows, with the help of a simple external element such as a logical OR (e.g. a wired OR based on a collector or open drain from an output transistor) or more complex ones such as an interrupt controller. These demands therefore involve only a single type of IT. This is an interrupt called a "simple level" interrupt, and there is no priority if its input is shared. Microcontrollers (*cf.* § V3-5.3), because of their application domains, offer many interrupt possibilities. One example is the 16-bit microcontroller SAB-C167 from Siemens (now Infineon) which has 56 sources of interrupt request.

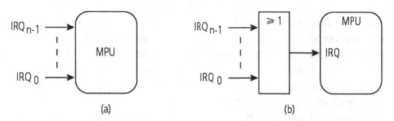

Figure 5.6. *Different sources of external interrupts*

We cite the traditional names for a hardware interrupt, which are IRQ or INTR (Interrupt Request) and its variant FIRQ (see above), NMI (Non-Maskable Interrupt) or Reset (*cf.* the following section). NMI is generally reserved to avoid serious or critical hardware error such as an error on a bus (*cf.* § V2-3.2), a memory error (*cf.* § 2.6.4 in Darche (2012)) as was originally the case with the PC (Personal Computer) from IBM (1981) or to indicate an imminent power failure. The IRQ is generally used by I/O controllers. We cite a final example, the #Halt signal from MPU (MC6809), which required it to halt. This same component possesses the instruction `cwai` (Clear CC bits and Wait for Interrupt), which alerts the latter to a possible interrupt. As these requests are external, they are intrinsically asynchronous with the processor's operation, although it is possible to synchronize them with external electronics. It should be noted that the INTR signal from 8086 should be kept active (latched) as the interrupt is not served since the request is not stored internally. We again cite ABORT from MPU WDC 65C816, which was an edge-triggered, unmaskable IT aimed at hardware exceptions such as a page fault or memory access violation. The recovery point after a return instruction (`rti` for return from interrupt as it happens) was the original instruction and not the following one. For example, a virtual memory handler or MMU (Memory Management Unit) such as the z8010 component from Zilog generates an interrupt request via its output #SEGT (SEGment Trap request) when there is an access or right violation (in writing).

A particular interrupt is a hardware reset of abort type. The hardware aspect was addressed in § V3-6.2. The microprocessor, when it is switched on, is found in an undetermined state. When the supply voltage is stabilized and is found in a value allowed by the electrical specifications, it is necessary to initialize the microprocessor using hardware for its state to be known. This operation is carried out by activating a pin of the microprocessor using a specialist control responsible for, among other tasks, monitoring power supplied, or a "watch dog" (*cf.* § 3.3.1 in Darche (2003)). Clearly not maskable and the highest priority, it is the only one to be considered within an instruction's execution cycle for a non-parallel MPU. It is level-triggered, but it is blocked in the initialization state so long as the active level continues. It sets the interrupt mask to prevent the maskable interrupts and disarm the unmaskable interrupts. The user can trigger an initialization by relying on the dedicated button. Unlike other interrupts, no specific instruction for processing is linked and the routine finishes implicitly with continuation or, if it exists, by an explicit branching to a configuration or boot program. The signal that is applied to the microprocessor is generally applied also to the whole system including the I/O controllers. Finally, it should be noted that the instruction `restart` from MC6809 makes it possible to reboot the system as during a hardware initialization (i.e. reset) using the RESET vector.

5.2.3. *Masking*

Generally, routines that process interrupt requests of the same priority level mutually forbid one another from being interrupted. So, the MC6800 microprocessor of those from the x86 architecture, when considering an IRQ, masks requests from input into the corresponding management routine. Two possible strategies are to reinitialize the pending IT flip-flop either as early as possible or at the end.

Meinadier (1971, 1988) distinguishes seven states for a hardware interrupt request handler. The first is the disarmed state. The logic cannot take any other request into consideration. Once armed, the system is ready to accept a request. The firing state means that a request has arrived, been stored and it is being processed. This request can be forbidden, also called masked (4th state) or inhibited for a postponement of treatment. The "authorized" state means that no other request from a higher level has arrived and that it can be processed. The state before the last is to wait for a state that accepts the control unit (to finish execution of an instruction in general). The last, active state corresponds to execution of the associated processing routine. A request can be lost if it is not seen by the system (a missing interrupt). Figure 5.7 shows an IT processing logic.

If an input is shared by several sources, there may be an interrupt flag belonging to a special register (individual masking) or a global flag that invalidates all the maskable interrupt requests. These individual or global masking possibilities have a role in an ISA's (Instruction Set Architecture, *cf.* § V1-3.5) power. This generalist decision chain will only have a single maskable IT input, while a microcontroller may have several. Figure 5.8 provides an example of the COP8 microcontroller from

National Semiconductor (NS). Another example of the same philosophy is the MPU PACE (Fox and Reyling 1975) with an INT EN (master INTerrupt ENable) validation flag and five IE_i ($i \in [1, 5]$, individual Interrupt Enable) flags belonging to the classical status register and control flags.

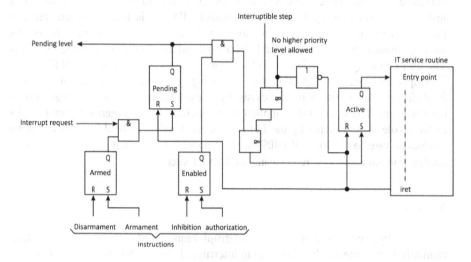

Figure 5.7. *Example of management logic for IT requests (Meinadier 1971, 1988)*

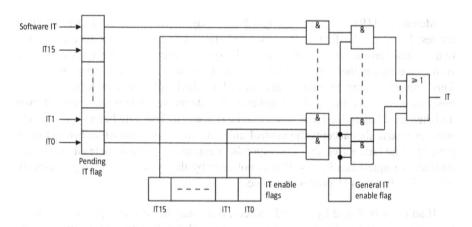

Figure 5.8. *Processing chain for several sources of interrupt sharing a single internal input (microcontroller COP8 from NS)*

Table 5.1 summarizes interrupts that are maskable and those that are not. Those from an internal source are explained in § 5.4.

Sources	Interrupts	
	Unmaskable	**Maskable**
External	Hardware interrupt (NMI)	Hardware interrupts Classic (IRQ) Fast (FIRQ)
	Hardware error (memory, bus, etc.)	
	Specific mode (reset)	
Internal	Software interrupts (instructions swi, trap, etc.)	-
	Software exception (reserved instruction, cache fault, page fault, etc.)	

Table 5.1. *Maskable and non-maskable interrupts*

Specialist instructions such as `cli` (Clear Interrupt Mask) and `sei` (Set Interrupt Mask) for the AVR microcontroller family make it possible, by manipulating the IT, validation flag to mask these. It is necessary, on the other hand, to take care that this masking does not last too long or the requests will be lost. Moreover, when an IT processing routine is executed, it has generally masked the ITs, which can be masked, and the previous remark on the duration, here applied to processing, applies. It should be noted that the instruction `iret` from 8086 re-authorizes maskable IT (IF = 1).

5.2.4. *Consideration and priority*

In the von Neumann computer model, the processor executes instructions sequentially. Before beginning an instruction, it verifies the absence of interrupt requests (Figure 5.9). The hardware interrupt request therefore has priority over execution of an instruction. We recall, on the other hand, that execution of an instruction is atomic and cannot be interrupted except during a hardware initialization reset. Interrupts are therefore interruptible instruction "at the boundary" (*cf.* § 1.1 and 3.1.2). It should nonetheless be noted that a microarchitecture can consider an IT request at the level of micro-instructions for speed of processing, one example being the sliced microprocessor (*cf.* § V3-5.1).

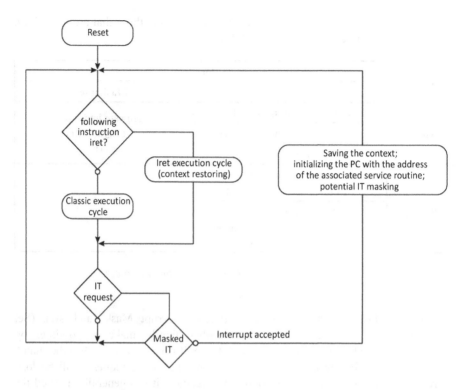

Figure 5.9. *Simplified decision organigram
for considering a hardware interrupt*

In the context of multi-level interrupts, during simultaneous requests, it is difficult to decide which request should be considered first. It is therefore necessary to arbitrate. To a source of interrupt, there is therefore allocated a priority, generally fixed for a microprocessor, which leads to a hierarchy of interrupts depending on their priority (0 is generally the highest priority level). We speak of a prioritized interrupt. Figure 5.10 shows the order for taking account of ITs from the MC6809 microprocessor. We note that after initialization, NMI takes priority, IRQ (which is maskable) comes next. According to the implementations, when an NMI routine is being executed, the input for this interrupt can be invalidated automatically during its processing (the most common case, since it is preferable). Therefore, the 80386 does not manage nested NMIs. It waits for the first to be terminated before considering the second. The software interrupt (*cf.* § 5.4) is the last to be considered, as it is an instruction that should be decoded to know its function. For modern microprocessors, interrupt classes that combine interrupts of the same priority have then been created, then sub-classes that define priorities within a single class. On the contrary, the hardware interrupt RESET takes priority. It can interrupt the execution cycle at any moment.

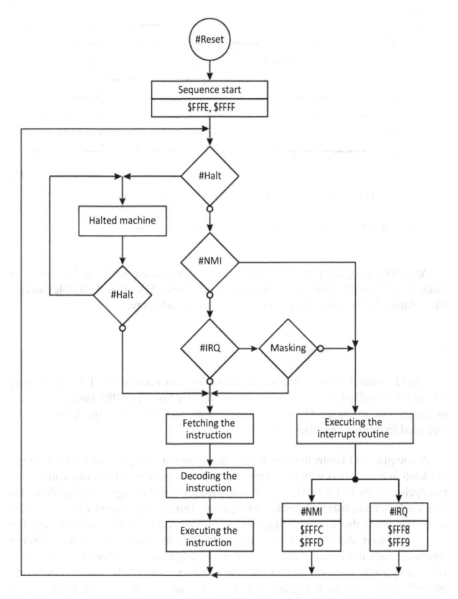

Figure 5.10. *Execution organigram of a simple MPU: the MC6802 (Motorola 1984)*

Figure 5.11 shows an example of pre-emption during execution of IT routines.

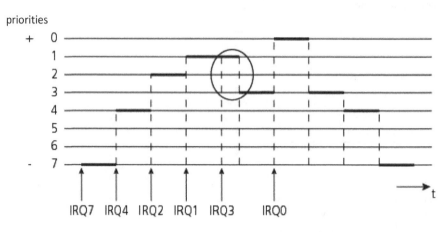

Figure 5.11. *Pre-emptive execution in a system of hierarchized interrupts*

An acknowledgment is generally sent to a requester when it is seen. One example is MC6809, which indicates using the signals BA (Bus Available) and BS (Bus Status) that reading of a hardware interrupt is underway.

5.2.5. *Interrupt controller*

The IT controller was initially an external logic or component (EIC for External Interrupt Controller), one example being the 8259A from the 8086 family. This type of component manages ITs in a vectorized manner. We thus speak of VIC for Vectored Interrupt Controller in the Arm® family.

A complex I/O controller can have a dialogue with its processor. For example, the 8086 in association with its external 8259A controller generates two consecutive bus cycles via its INTA (INTerrupt Acknowledge) signal to signify recognition. The first cycle accomplishes the acknowledgment. During the second cycle, the 8259 controller sends the number of the corresponding vector. In the inactive state, this signal can alert the controller to its availability to receive a request. When a controller does not respond during the acknowledgment stage, then the interrupt is called a spurious interrupt and an internal exception is generally raised (case of the MC68000, for example). Figure 5.12 shows the internal logic for considering the request from this controller.

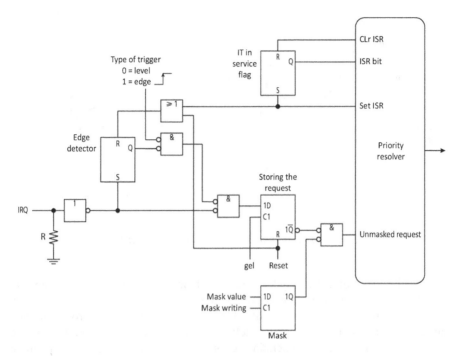

Figure 5.12. *Simplified processing logigram of an interrupt from the IT 8259A controller (Intel 1988)*

It was first integrated into the southbridge chipset (*cf.* Chapter 1 in Darche (2003)) and now into advanced MPUs (IIC for Internal Interrupt Controller) as well as in microcontrollers (AVR or PIC (Peripheral Interface Controller/Programmable Intelligent Computer) family, for example). At Intel, it is called APIC for Advanced Programmable Interrupt Controller (*cf.* § 5.11).

5.3. Nested interrupts

In the case where another request arrives during processing of an interrupt, the same context saving and branching process will be executed. There is no state incoherence since access to the stack is "Last-In, First-Out" (LIFO). The only problem is the size of the stack that stores contexts (of limited depth) and the coherence of the sub-program execution state (possible side-effect if the program is not re-entrant). Interrupts are called nested interrupts or stacked interrupts. Figure 5.13 illustrates an interrupt nesting.

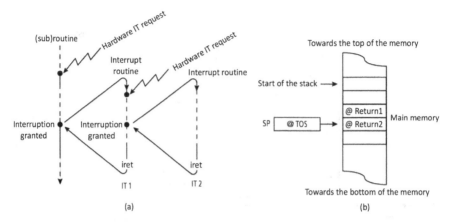

Figure 5.13. *Mechanism of nested hardware interrupts*

Nested calls should be avoided because of problems with reaction time and starvation. They cumulate the handling times of the execution context (i.e. saving/restoration) and, in the case of a blockage in one of the sub-programs, they can cause starvation, that is, an indefinite waiting time. They complicate the software, are a source of operating errors and do not, in general, improve performances (*cf.* § 3.4). Fortunately, it is possible to forbid consideration of an IT using the mask interrupt mechanism. Masking the request can delay its acknowledgment. If interrupts are hierarchized, lower ranking requests are masked. Masked does not necessarily mean lost. In the microprocessor status register, there is an indicator (Interrupt Flag or IF) that controls its consideration using programming (authorization or invalidation at state 1 according to implementations). The new request is then registered, but the re-routing is reported until the flag is updated. The interrupt is then called maskable. Internally, a flip-flop then registers the interrupt request. If the sensitivity is of edge type, a loss of request can occur. On the other hand, when the flag is re-initialized, the flip-flop re-enregisters the request that follows. If the interrupt is not maskable, the designer automatically invalidates the interrupt input with or without the possibility of modifying this behavior depending on the implementation. The MPU can also lose an interrupt request if the processing is not fast enough. On the contrary, a critical application in real time cannot accept the loss of an interrupt without the penalty of serious problems in managing the procedure, for example, the destruction of an embedded system such as a rocket.

Another way of processing requests is to queue interrupts. This technique is addressed in § 5.8.

5.4. Internal causes

Interrupt requests (Figure 5.1) originate in specialized instructions (trap), or they come from an execution error (software exception). Hence, we speak respectively of synchronous and exception interrupts. It should be noted that interrupts due to internal causes can always be reproduced, which is not the case with external interrupts, because of their nature.

A software interrupt or trap, occasionally called an internal interrupt, is an event triggered explicitly by a specialized instruction (programmed interrupt). It is therefore a deliberate act by the programmer, which wishes to raise a trap. An instruction such as swi (microprocessor MC6809 (Motorola 1984)), as Figure 5.14 illustrates, explicitly requires a re-routing. This instruction masks IRQs during its execution. There can be a passing of parameters such as the operand with the instructions int (x86 architecture) and trap (MC68000). Interrupt return instructions are the classical iret (interrupt return, x86 architecture, for example) and eret (exception return, MIPS (Microprocessor without Interlocked Pipeline Stages) architecture, for example). These specialized instructions are therefore well adapted to call on an OS' services (system or supervisor call) as the associated routine will be executed in a privileged mode (*cf.* § 3.2.2) if the MPU offers it, which was not the case with 8-bit generations of that era. It should be noted that Arm® has an instruction swi whose operand format is formed of three bytes, so 2^{24} ISR possible!

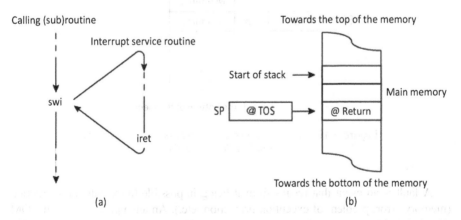

Figure 5.14. *Call and return of a non-nested software interrupt (example with MC6809)*

We find the same concept of nesting requests for external IT (*cf.* § 5.2), as Figure 5.15 illustrates.

calling (sub)routine

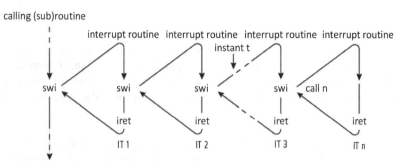

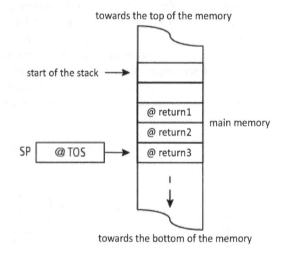

Figure 5.15. *Call and return of nested software interrupts (example with MC6809)*

Figure 5.16 details the development of the stack following these nested requests.

Figure 5.16. *Call and return of nested software interrupts (example with MC6809)*

A fault is an event that results from it being impossible to execute an instruction (memory error, problem of execution protection, etc.). An attempt at writing in ROM (Read-Only Memory), an absence of memory at this address (i.e. access in the void), an illegal address or a page fault in physical memory are examples of memory error. It is generally correctable and corrected, for example, by a re-execution of one or more instructions (retries) in the case, for example, from an OS service. As this happens during execution of an instruction, it is possible to define three sub-classes of fault linked to the execution stages (*cf.* § V1-3.3.2). These are raised after an instruction fetch, at its decoding and at its execution. A software exception can fall into the "fault" class (the most common) or the "abort" class. The abort results from a string of two faults. Intel calls it a "double fault". It announces a serious problem at the kernel. Table 5.2 classes interrupts in three categories to decide whether there is a double fault or not. It should be noted that the tendency towards integration has meant that external requests that were hardware exceptions of the "abort" type are transformed into software faults. One example is the abort called "coprocessor segment Overrun", uniquely for the 386, which then became a fault.

Categories	no.	Description
Benign exceptions	1	Step-by-step (debugging)
	2	NMI
	3	Breakpoint
	4	Overflow (relative integer)
	5	Boundary control
	6	Invalid operation code
	7	Coprocessor unavailable
	16	Coprocessor error
Contributing exceptions	0	Division error
	9	Coprocessor segment overflow
	10	Invalid TSS
	11	Segment not present
	12	Stack exception
	13	General protection
Page faults	14	Page fault

Table 5.2. *Categories of interrupt to qualify a double fault in 80386 (Intel 1986)*

Table 5.3 allows us to decide if there is a double fault, considering the causality of IT requests.

		Second exception		
		Benign exception	**Contributing exception**	**Page fault**
First exception	**Benign exception**	No	No	No
	Contributing exception	No	Double	No
	Page fault	No	Double	Double

Table 5.3. *Decision criteria for qualifying a double fault in 80386 (Intel 1986)*

A fault is automatically generated (we say it is raised) on an abnormal condition during execution of an instruction. A fallible instruction is an instruction that causes an exception. It can result from programming errors or abnormal conditions. It can be a forbidden instruction, one that is impossible to execute or non-existent (undefined operation code). One example is the page or segmentation fault, which is an abnormal and unusual event caused by execution of an instruction. Resuming consists of loading the faulty page or segment and re-executing the instruction. Calculation exceptions involve whole and relative integers or fixed and floating-point numbers. For integers, there is the overflow or division by zero. For example, at Intel, overflow is a trap-raised by the instruction into (interrupt on overflow), and so it is wanted by the programmer and is not a fault. For floating point, the R4000 microprocessor has, for example, five exceptions, which are an invalid operation, underflow, overflow, division by zero and inexact result (rounding-off problem). It should be noted that a division by zero that calls an ISR raising the same exception creates an infinite loop.

The difference between a trap and a fault lies at the point of recovery. For the first, it lies in the instruction following the branching, while for the second, it will be situated at the faulty instruction. A TLB failure (Translation Lookaside Buffer, this will be covered in a future book by the author on memories) is a fault. An exception on overflow is a trap. There is no resumption of the program, or the task follows an abort since it involves a serious error.

5.5. Debugging

Debugging an ISR is difficult, since the insertion of a debugging code can influence the system's operation, by slowing it, for example. One particular software interrupt is trace or step-by-step mode where a trap is raised at the end of each execution of an instruction, which will launch a specific debugging routine. To do this, it is necessary that the processor is in a particular execution mode (cf. § 3.2.2). The routine is in fact the debugging program (cf. § V1-2.2.4), which makes it possible among other things to visualize the different memory areas (instructions, data, stack, etc.) and the registers. For 8086, as Figure 5.18 shows, the IF and TF (Trap Flag) flags are set at zero during its execution. This means that it is executed in normal mode and not in step-by-step mode. With this same processor, the breakpoint uses the instruction int 3, which replaces the right instruction placed after the one stopping the execution (patch) and is saved provisionally. The associated routine should save the context, call the debugging program and, at the end, execute the replaced instruction and restore the context to make this break transparent. A hardware aide is often available, either an elementary one such as a Light-Emitting Diode (LED) or a more elaborate one such as a JTAG (Joint Test Action Group) hardware probe (cf. § V5-2.2.5), for example. A final function that the MIPS (Microprocessor without Interlocked Pipeline Stages) microprocessor offers is its EPC register (for Exception Program Counter), which contains the address of the instruction that generated the trap.

5.6. Priority between internal and external interrupts

It is desirable to be able to receive requests from different sources. It is necessary to be able to serve them to define a priority between them. There is a priority between hardware and software interrupts. Figure 5.17 shows the decision organigram. The consideration is called "at the instruction boundary". Hardware interrupt requests are evaluated before the start of an instruction's execution. They are therefore a priority. The trap is evaluated during its execution. On the contrary, we see here that a trap underway masks future maskable hardware interrupt requests.

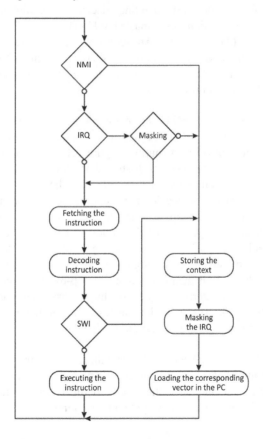

Figure 5.17. *Decision process from MC6809 (simplified organigram without HALT and Reset modes in particular) from Motorola (1984)*

A counter-example is 8086 where software interrupts are priority. Raising them means that the associated ISR is launched at the following cycle. Table 5.4 gives the priorities for different interrupts.

Interrupts	Order of priority
Division error, int, into	From high
NMI	
INTR	
Step-by-step	To low

Table 5.4. *Priorities of different interrupts from 8086*

Figure 5.18 shows the corresponding decision organigram. Each request acceptance leads to invalidation of the maskable ITs (IF flag = 0) and of the step-by-step execution mode (TF flag = 0). An additional test is inserted just before the execution of the routine body, so as to know if there has been an NMI request (more priority) since the first test. The variable TEMP makes it possible to save the state of the execution mode, either normal or step-by-step.

The priority chosen for the MPU step-by-step mode leads to an unwanted effect in IT processing that means that the debugging routine is called just before the first instruction of the most prioritized routine. Figure 5.19 gives an example with the processing of a non-maskable interrupt. It should be noted that the unstacking of the CS and IP registers is symbolized in this figure by the word "return". This side effect can be inconvenient for development since an execution delay or worse, a break, is introduced in the interrupt routine. Hence, in the following generation (i.e. 80286), Intel increased the priority of this mode just behind the division by zero exception (*cf.* Table 5.5), so before the external interrupts. Processing routines invalidating the step-by-step mode during re-routing are no longer disrupted in their execution. The hardware thus guarantees that the step-by-step execution mode stops when there is a hardware interrupt request so that the associated handling routine is not executed in this mode. If this mode is necessary, it is then necessary to execute an instruction int to execute the corresponding handler.

Figure 5.20 shows the instance of two simultaneous interrupt requests, one internal and non-maskable, and the other external and maskable. This latter is processed after the first and once the return to the main program is made. The drawback cited in the previous case is applied to each interrupt routine.

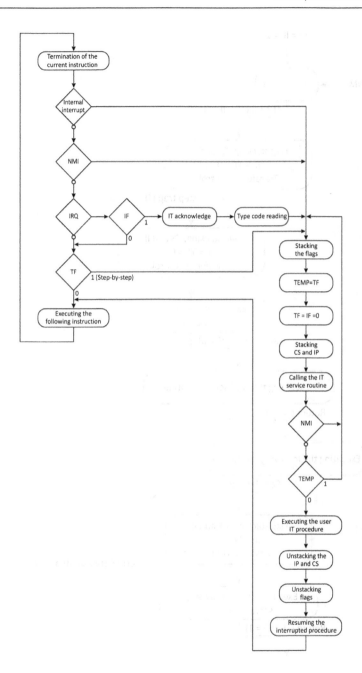

Figure 5.18. *Processing sequence for interrupt requests from 8086 (Intel 1989)*

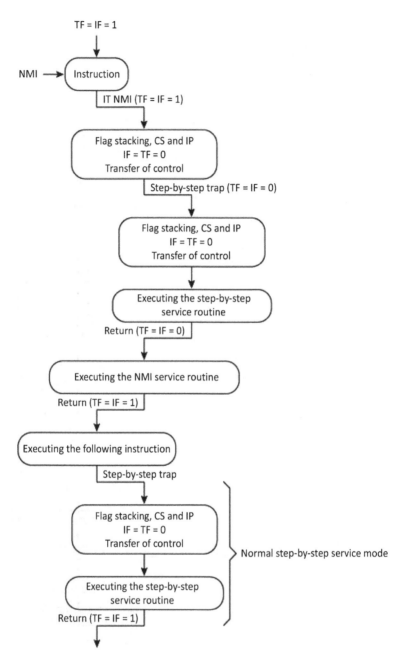

Figure 5.19. *Step-by-step execution modes with NMI and normal (Intel 1989)*

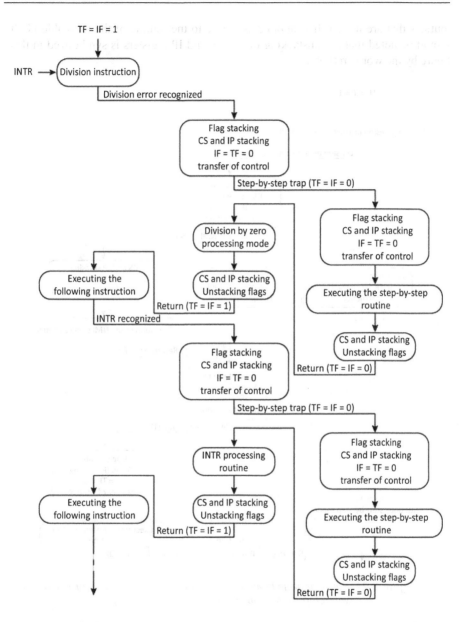

Figure 5.20. *Simultaneous software exception and maskable external interrupt interacting with the step-by-step execution mode (Intel 1989)*

One exception to all these priorities is the case of three simultaneous requests (Figure 5.21). In this case, the step-by-step mode is not applied to unmaskable routines that are nested. It is applied as before to the routine of the maskable IT. It should be noted that the unstacking of the CS and IP registers is symbolized in this figure by the word "return".

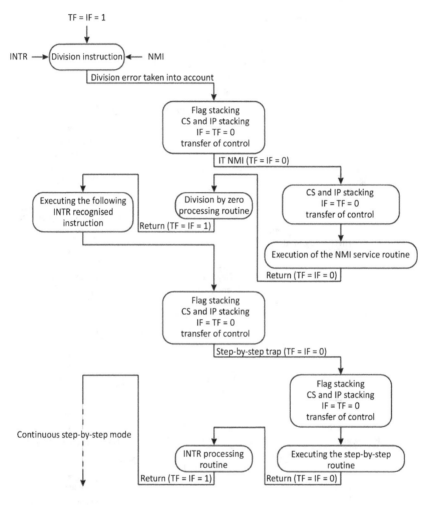

Figure 5.21. *Simultaneous NMI, INTR and division by zero in interaction with step-by-step execution mode (Intel 1989)*

To summarize, Figure 5.22 shows an organigram for processing IT programs representative of the first decades of MPUs, that is, the 8-bit generation, which is the MC6809 from Motorola.

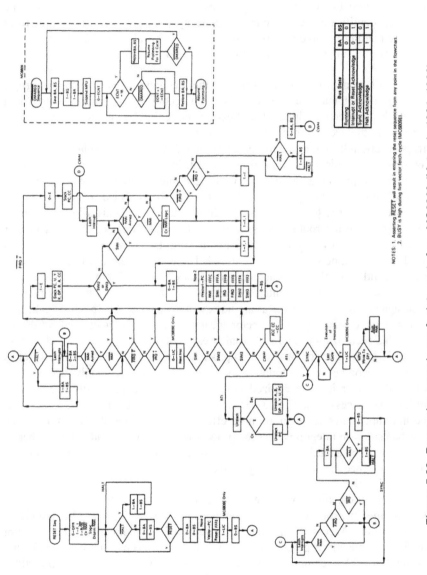

Figure 5.22. *Processing organigram for interrupts from MC6809 (Motorola 1981, 1983)*

5.7. Identification of the source and vectorization

One difficult case is identification of the interrupt source when the line of requests is shared by several interrupt sources. We saw in § 4.1.1 from Darche (2003) that identification could only be done by polling from possible interrupt sources by reading the interrupt request register. It can also be done by hardware polling or daisy chain, by diffusion or by multi-level interrupts.

Almost all modern microprocessors use the technique of vectorizing interrupts that gather all automatic interrupt recognition techniques to be considered and branching by indirection (indirect addressing, *cf.* § 1.2.3.3) at the routine. With vectorization, the execution flow is directed towards a start address for each interrupt except in the case of auto-vectorization (*cf.* § above for the latter case). The vectorization mechanism relies on an indirection. Information, making it possible to locate the interrupt routine, is sent to a vectorized interrupt request. It may be an IT address or number. When it is an address (first case) provided in general by the interrupt controller (*cf.* § 4.1.1 in Darche (2003)), the MPU loads it in the program counter to execute the routine. It is a number (second case), an unsigned integer (format n = 8 bits, for example, for x86 architecture) that serves as a cell index in a table where the routine start address is stored. There are therefore two definitions of a vector depending on the manufacturers or authors. A vector is either the processing routine start address[8] called an interrupt (address) vector or also an interrupt pointer, or an unsigned integer that serves as an index in a table (Intel 2003b, 2005) called an ISR lookup table. Each interrupt vector location (i.e. cell) is addressed by the IT number. This vectorization can be internal or external. In the first case, which is rare, this table is in the interior of the microprocessor and the content of the vector is fixed. In the second case, it is found in the random access or read-only memory (i.e. RAM or ROM) or in a specialized controller, and it is modifiable under some conditions (i.e. access rights). As a vector corresponds to each interrupt, recognition of the interrupt source is therefore more effective than sharing the line alone since the mechanism is an integral part of the processor. On the other hand, the number of inputs is limited by a hardware that is costly in the number of pins and this approach is not flexible since the priority policy is fixed.

At consideration, after saving the context, the program counter is loaded with the content of the interrupt vector that contains the start address of the associated interrupt routine. Access to the routine is achieved by indirection. The interrupt vector is consequently a pointer (Figure 5.23). This concept was operated for the first time in the TX-2 computer from MIT Lincoln Labs (Clark 1957). 8-bit MPUs that supported vectorization are the 8085 and the Z80. In the 16-bit version, we list

---

8 The definition was retained for this book.

the 80x86. Software interrupts from 8085 are vectorized. Among hardware interrupts (trap, RST 5.5, 6.5 and 7.5), only INTR is not vectorized.

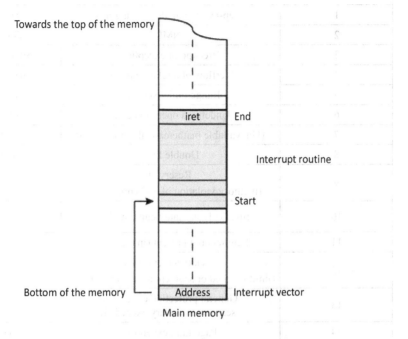

Figure 5.23. *Vectorization of the interrupt*

The address of the table is specific to each (family of) component(s). The MC680x family has its table of four vectors placed at the top of its address space. Table 5.5 shows the IVT (Interrupt Vector Table) from IA-32 architecture (i.e. x86 architecture in 32-bit version) situated in the memory area, the start address 0000:0000 (Intel 2003a). Each interrupt has a priority called a "type" and an associated vector. The priority defines the order of processing. The table has been completed as new generations appear. The 8086 (Intel 1989), for example, designated vectors no. 5 to 31 as reserved. The 80286 adds seven new interrupts, four for the 80386. Since this MPU's memory is segmented and acts on the real mode (i.e. unprotected), the size of a vector is 4 bytes, including two for the segment (this will be covered in a future book by the author on memories) and two for offset. It should be noted that the Reset vector does not appear in the table as it is placed for most processors generally high in the memory space in a non-volatile memory with start and initialization FirmWare (FW) (*cf.* § V5-3.5.3). A counter-example is MicroBlaze from Xilinx, which is a "soft processor core" implanted in an FPGA (Field-Programmable Gate Array, *cf.* § 4.3.2 in Darche (2004)).

Type (vector no.)	Designation	Origins
0	Division by 0	8086/8088
1	Step-by-step mode (debugging)	8086/8088
2	NMI	8086/8088
3	Breakpoint exception	8086/8088
4	Overflow of a relative integer	8086/8088
5	Range limit exceeded	80286
6	Undefined operation code	80286
7	(Unavailable mathematical) coprocessor	80286
8	Double fault	80286
9	Reserved (memory violation of 387 coprocessor)	80286
10	Invalid Task State Segment (TSS)	80386
11	Segment not present (in memory)	80386
12	Stack (segment) fault (limit reached or segment absent in memory)	80386
13	General protection exception (segment boundary exceeded)	80286
14	Page fault exception	80386
15	Reserved	–
16	Floating-point calculation error (x87)	80286
17	Alignment-checking exception (memory)	80486
18	Computer control exception	Pentium Pro
19	SIMD floating-point calculation error (instructions SSE and SSE2)	IA-32
20–31	Reserved	–
32–255	Available for the user	8086/8088

Table 5.5. *Table of 256 interrupt vectors from IA-32 architecture*

Note that for the first microprocessors or for some interrupts such as IntR, automatic presentation of the IRQ vector happens via an external module (Figure 5.24), the IT controller and not by reading the table of vectors, according to a defined protocol.

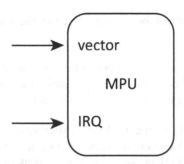

Figure 5.24. *External vectorization*

One variant is the presentation of an operational code instead of a vector. For example, we cite the MPU Z80 from Zilog, which has three maskable IT management modes for compatibility reasons and because of the possibilities offered. The first (no. 0) is Intel 8080 mode where an external controller provides an instruction code of one byte, generally `rst` (restart, that is, the equivalent of a `call`) making it possible to branch at one of eight locations (8 bytes long) starting from the memory address space (page 0) where the corresponding ISR is found. Mode no. 1 executes an instruction `rst` with 0038h as a start address, which is equivalent to an NMI processing but at a different address from the one normally linked to it (= 0066h). The last, the most powerful mode, makes it possible to make an indirect call to a routine placed anywhere in the memory space from a vector formed from 8 bits provided by the controller (LSB for Least Significant Byte) and from the content of a register named I (MSB for Most Significant Byte) that addresses a table's cell in 16-bit format containing the ISR address (starting location).

There is a table variant that does not contain the vector but contains the routine code directly (PowerPC [9] and Arm® approaches). Since the available size is small (8 bytes for the (MCU for MicroController Unit) 8051 microcontroller from Intel, RESET aside), the cell generally only contains one jump instruction to an associated routine, since it is constrained by memory space (size of one jump instruction or an instruction from the routine itself). The table was called a jump table. One advantage is that the cell can contain the instructions `nop` or a jump to the following cell, enabling a fall-through approach. A second advantage is a faster handling since there is no indirection.

MC68000 has many useful functionalities such as auto-vectorization. This term means that an IT controller too simple or old to provide a vector can benefit from vectorization. To do this, the MPU itself generates a vector depending on the priority of the given request on its inputs, called an Interrupt Priority Level or IPL[2:0], the

9 PowerPC for Performance Optimization With Enhanced RISC Performance Computing.

number of the basic vector and their number fixed by the manufacturer (respectively = 19_{16} and 8).

In the first microprocessors, which positioned indicators at the end of execution, the state of these latter should be explicitly tested so as to be able to process the exception. Others can raise the exception automatically.

One original approach is that of MIPS (Microprocessor without Interlocked Pipeline Stages), which does not use vectorization. It stores the type of interrupt pending in a cause register (Hennessy *et al.* 1982), speaking of the surprise register, containing an identification code for the origin of the interrupt in the format n = 4 bits. Table 5.6 shows its different values for MPUs R2000, R3000, R4000 and R6000. The benefit is that it makes handling of interrupts orthogonal to handling of instructions. It becomes uniform regardless of its type. Requests can be processed by a centralized routine, which can make the vector table useless. The drawback is that the processing is slower than with the solution that uses a vector table. It should be noted that this MPU's status register does not have classical status flags (NZVC, *cf.* § V3-3.1.5.1). A counter-example is the COP8 microcontroller (from NS), which uses a general fixed address management routine (i.e. 00FFh), of which the first instruction is `vis` (1-byte format). The latter determines the cause of the interrupt, making it possible to address a cell from a 16-vector table, and then makes an indirect jump to the corresponding management routine.

Number	Mnemonic	Description
0	Int	External interrupt (i.e. hardware)
1	Mod	TLB modification exception (cache)
2	TLBL	TLB reading failure exception (reading or fetching an instruction)
3	TLBS	TLB writing failure exception
4	AdEL	Address error exception (reading or fetching an instruction)
5	AdES	Address error exception (writing)
6	IBE	Bus error exception for fetching an instruction
7	DBE	Bus error exception for a data reading or writing
8	Syscall	Call system exception
9	Bp	Breakpoint exception
10	RI	Reserved instruction exception
11	CpU	Unusable coprocessor exception
12	Ov	Arithmetical overflow exception
13	Tr	Trap (R4000 and R6000 only)

Number	Mnemonic	Description
14	NCD	LDCz/SDCz (writing/reading in/of the processor) towards an un-cached address (R6000 only)
14	VCEI	Virtual coherence exception instruction (R4000 only)
15	MC	Computer control exception (R6000 only)
15	FPE	Floating-point exception (R4000 only)
16–22	-	Reserved for future use
23	WATCH	Reference to the address stored in the registers WatchHi/WatchLo (R4000 only)
19–30	-	Reserved for future use
31	VCED	Virtual coherence exception data (R4000 only)

Table 5.6. *List of exception codes (ExcCode) for MIPS architecture (Kane 1988; Kane and Heinrich 1992)*

Figure 5.25 shows two possible implantations of an IT system (vector table at the start of the address space). The vectors in the table are initialized by initializing the system in the case of storage in Random Access Memory (RAM). If the system has a monitor (*cf.* § V5-2.2.4.1), the IT table will be with it.

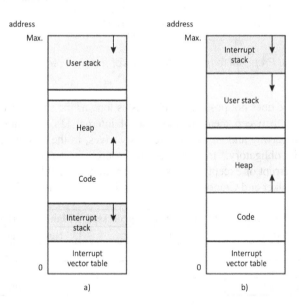

Figure 5.25. *Two typical implantations of different memory areas of an IT system*

5.8. Nested and queued interrupts

Simultaneous processing can generate many problems. One example is a division by zero that triggers a routine that, itself, executes a division by zero, therefore triggering an infinite loop. System programmers avoid having to process these cases by raising the double fault exception for example, which will halt the program or the faulty process, and by signaling the error. Externally, apart from critical hardware exceptions that require halting the machine, requests are generally masked during an IT processing. However, they should not be lost.

Simultaneous requests can be made using nested interrupts (*cf.* § 5.3). When the number of IT sources is high, it becomes difficult to assign a vector and a routine to each of them. Moreover, if requests are not processed fast enough, there is a risk that requests will be lost. One solution is to put in place a message queue, each message encapsulating a request (queued interrupts). It is useful to put requests in a queue as it serializes requests and their associated processing. The drawback is that it is impossible to raise another interrupt if one is being handled; it will be queued like the others. As Figure 5.26 illustrates, the IT service routine manages the role of transmitting messages and a process manages them.

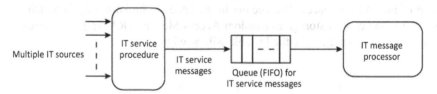

Figure 5.26. *Proposal for processing flow for many IT requests (Intel 1980)*

This technique does not pose any problems as long as the source is external. There is no causal link between them. In the case of internal ITs, the same is true if an internal IT is underway and an external request arrives. In the two other cases, nested management is obligatory. In fact, as the source is an instruction execution, programmed interrupt or exception, it is necessary to process it before returning to the previous one. Walker and Cragon (1995) summarized all the cases using Table 5.7.

Interrupt underway	IT request to be processed	Management options
External	External	Nesting, queueing
External	Internal	Nesting
Internal	External	Nesting, queueing
Internal	interne	Nesting

Table 5.7. *Management options in the case of multiple IT processing*

5.9. Uses

Hardware interrupts were first used mainly for I/Os as they mean the microprocessor does not lose time (i.e. active waiting) to detect possible external events, for example, end of I/O transfer, using the polling technique (*cf.* § 4.2.1 in Darche (2003)). It is the I/O controllers that generate these maskable requests, and they are processed by OS drivers. But beware, the interrupt mechanism is not always the best solution for handling I/Os. Polling or a hybrid solution can give better performances (*cf.* Pajari 1989; Yang *et al.* 2012) studied this subject in the framework respectively of a serial interface and of block mode transfers in the (mass) storage domain. The interrupt is also used to indicate a major hardware error. The MPU is generally put in halt mode while waiting for a hardware initialization (reset).

Modern OSs make massive use of software interrupt request instructions to call their services and exceptions to manage faults and aborts. Software interrupts are usually encapsulated in a function of a High-Level programming Language (HLL). Calls to operating system services are made by a trap, making it possible to change from execution (user/supervisor) mode. Within the OS, the exceptions are transformed into signals that are sent to processes, for example, by calling on the "kill()" function in UNIX OSs. Task switching is triggered according to the rhythm of the interrupt requests from the timer. We recall that this controller has a (de)counter/timer that generates interrupt requests. For a presentation of the latter, see § 3.3.1 in Darche (2003). The exceptions make it possible to detect execution errors, in particular calculation errors (overflow, division by zero, etc.). Modern MPUs detect illegal or invalid instructions (*cf.* § 3.1.1) and generally raise a trap that will reroute the execution towards an exception handling routine (the case of the Arm® family, for example). The MC68000 detects an instruction machine code that has not been implemented by raising exceptions named line A and line F, the latter being the hexadecimal figure corresponding to the binary words detected (first byte of the operational code). Misuse involves setting a breakpoint (*cf.* § V5-2.2.2) and emulating an instruction of an absent mathematical coprocessor. More details are given in Clements (1997). Table 5.8 summarizes the resolution.

In microcomputers before 2010, interrupt management routines belonged to a BIOS (Basic Input Output System, *cf.* § V5-3.5.3) that was stored in a read-only memory (FirmWare or FW). The concept of interrupt is essential today in the domain of embedded systems. In its absence, development of this type of application would be excessively complex.

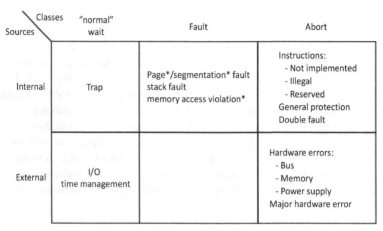

Classes Sources	"normal" wait	Fault	Abort
Internal	Trap	Page*/segmentation* fault stack fault memory access violation*	Instructions: - Not implemented - Illegal - Reserved General protection Double fault
External	I/O time management		Hardware errors: - Bus - Memory - Power supply Major hardware error

* : from an external source, before the MMU was integrated into the MPU

Table 5.8. *Table summarizing interrupts*

5.10. Interrupts and execution modes

Microprocessors, since the 16-bit generation, have considered execution mode (*cf.* § 3.2.2) in handling the interrupt request. Therefore, interrupts are executed classically in three modes, privileged (or protected), user and real (address). Table 3.3 shows execution modes from Arm® architecture. It integrates the classic interrupt modes IRQ and fast FIQ as well as abort mode. There is in fact an execution mode for a type of interrupt. On consideration, control transfer is effected at the same priority level or at a higher level of privilege but never at a lower level. An attempt at execution of a privileged instruction or one with a particular privilege in a mode with less privilege causes an exception.

It is necessary to protect the IT Vector Table (IVT) since an interrupt can be diverted from its processing routine by a malicious program such as a virus, for example, as was possible, for example, with the 8086. At Intel, there is an IVT in protected mode named Interrupt Descriptor Table (IDT) where each vector is supplemented by flags. Unlike its counterpart, it can be implanted anywhere in the address space thanks to the IDTR (IDT Register) that contains its start address that is modifiable thanks to the `lidt` instruction (load interrupt descriptor table register). Each input (8 bytes in IA-32 architecture) contains a gate descriptor, either of a task, and interrupt or a trap.

5.11. Interrupts and advanced architectures

Modern architectures, to improve execution time, integrate processing units that operate in series (pipeline) and in parallel (superscalar architecture). These microarchitectural approaches are described in detail in the second volume. Also, this section is only an introduction, which will be completed later.

In a monoprocessor architecture without a pipeline, considering only internal interrupts and supposing that the interrupt handlers (ISR) cannot generate interrupt requests (i.e. fault-free handler), managing the context is simple and there is at most only a single instruction to re-execute (in case of fault). Table 5.9 shows recovery points for the classic ITs of a classic MPU. One serious error is a hardware breakdown or an erroneous system table. There is therefore no recovery. Some errors provide an error code, useful for a potential retry or for a debugging.

Interrupt names	Classes	IT no.	Instructions involved	Restart points	Error on the stack
Division by zero	Fault	0	div, idiv	At the instruction in question	No
Step-by-step	Hardware trap (!)	1	All	Following instruction	No
NMI	IT hardware	2	int 2, all	Following instruction	No
Breakpoint	Trap	3	int 3	Following instruction	No
Overflow (integers)	Trap	4	int 4, into	Following instruction	No
Extent boundary exceeded (boundary control)	Fault	5	int 5, bound	At the instruction in question	No
Invalid operation code	Fault	6	Undefined	At the instruction in question	No
MPU extension of (coprocessor) unavailable	Fault	7	esc, wait	At the instruction in question	No
Reserved (Intel)	–	8–15	–	–	–
MPU extension error	Fault	16	esc, wait	–	–
Reserved (Intel)	–	17–31	–	–	–
Defined by the user (i.e. available for)	Trap	32–255	int	Following instruction	–

Table 5.9. *Interrupt recovery points for the 80286*

Table 5.10 shows the restart points in real mode for the same MPU.

Interrupt name	Classes	IT no.	Instructions involved	Restart points
Limit of an interrupt table that is too small	Abort	8	–	At the instruction in question
Segment overflow from the coprocessor	Fault	9	esc with a too high operand address	At the following instruction
Segment overflow	Fault	13	With a too high memory address	At the instruction in question

Table 5.10. *Recovery point for ITs for the 80286 (real mode)*

Table 5.11, following the two previous tables, does this for protected mode. The column called "restart" indicates whether the program/process can continue or should be stopped.

Interrupt names	Classes	IT no.	Possible restart	Restart points	Error code on the stack
Double fault	Abort	8	No	At the instruction in question	Yes (= 0)
Segment overflow of the coprocessor	Abort	9	No	Following instruction	No
Invalid task state segment	Fault	10	Yes	At the instruction in question	Yes (= TSS at fault or selector)
Segment not present	Fault	11	Yes	At the instruction in question	Yes (= descriptor selector)
Stack segment overflow or stack segment not present	Fault	12	Yes	At the instruction in question	Yes (= segment selector or 0)
General protection	Abort	13	No	At the instruction in question	Yes (= descriptor selector)

Table 5.11. *Recovery point for ITs for the 80286 (protected mode)*

It is not the same with parallel architectures. Several instructions are issued in parallel and can also be executed in parallel. First, it is necessary to define what sequential and serial executions are. An execution is called sequential if each instruction is executed completely before execution of the next is launched. This was true for the first MPUs. A serial instruction execution is an execution that respects their order of arrival. The MPU's state change follows the same order. This is the case with a pipeline processor. But such a processor does not carry out a sequential execution.

Several interrupt requests can therefore be generated internally, to which several external requests can be added. Except for an external interrupt and RESET aside, consideration does not only occur at the instruction boundary but can be done between the different sub-steps in the execution cycle. During interrupts, these architectures generate additional execution time costs that may be prohibitive. For example, in a pipeline, when an interrupt request is effective, it may be necessary to terminate execution of instructions engaged in the pipeline to facilitate recovery of the interrupted thread. Walker (1992) thus defines six stages in managing interrupts for pipelined architectures. These are detection, termination of the instruction underway, cancelation of the execution (pipelined architecture), saving the context, execution of the handler and restarting of the interrupted process. It is then necessary to define the concepts of precise and imprecise interrupts.

Interrupts as they were described previously, that is, for a single processor without an accelerator mechanism, are called precise. For them to be so, three conditions should be met for the execution to continue correctly (Smith and Pleszkun 1988). First of all, all the instructions preceding the instruction being executed at the moment of the interrupt request should be executed and they should have modified the state of the process correctly. Those that should follow should not be executed and should not modify the state of the process. To finish, if the interrupt request is caused by an instruction, this should be executed completely, for example, during an overflow, or it should not or cannot be executed at all (e.g. in the case of a page fault). The state of the process before a precise interrupt is called serially correct, that is, identical to a sequential execution (Walker and Cragon 1995). This state can be the one before or after the execution in question. It will not be sequentially correct during a precise interrupt. The precise interrupt is used if the state of the processor should be rebuilt, for example, in the case where the software should repair the error that caused the interrupt request and should allow recovery of execution. If the cause is external, recovery is easy. For an internal cause, this may be costly in terms of time in the case of a parallel hardware environment (pipeline and superscalar architecture). But this type of interrupt is needed in mechanisms such as the memory page fault (this will be covered in a future book by the author on memory) or requested by the IEEE 754 standard (Hennessy and Patterson 2017) that concerns calculation in floating point in base 2 (IEEE 1985, 2008) (for the associated representation, cf. § II.4.2 in Darche (2000)). Therefore, the interrupt model for floating-point calculation units (FPU for Floating-Point Unit) is most of the time of a precise type. A counter-example is the PowerPC family (Motorola 1996). With this family, the programmer can choose the exception mode from among four for calculation in floating point. An imprecise interrupt means that the instruction following the one that produced the exception may be terminated or in the process of being executed. The state at this instant is fragmented but recoverable (Grohoski 1990), that is, restorable albeit with a time cost. The choice of this type of interrupt is therefore guided by a gain in performances. A microprocessor such as Alpha from Digital Equipment Corporation (DEC) may have some precise interrupts and others that are not precise (Compaq 2002). Samadzadeh and Garanabi (2001) study five management strategies for this type of execution. For more information on this subject, see also Moudgill and Vassiliadis (1996) and Rudd (1997).

The serialization of interrupt requests in parallel environment will consist of ensuring that they are processed sequentially. This is one of the roles of the interrupt controller (cf. § 4.1.1 in Darche (2003)).

In a superscalar architecture, the processor is capable of launching and withdrawing (i.e. end of execution) several scalar instructions per cycle (multiple-issue processor). The result is that they can be executed in parallel. Hence, they were first called look-ahead processors (Rau and Fisher 1992, 1993), that is, a processor with anticipated execution. The instructions are provided sequentially, and it is the internal hardware that is responsible for their distribution on different functional units. Other than the IT software already mentioned, the generation of requests and consideration of exceptions can only be done during speculative execution of an instruction. Consideration should therefore be deferred. One solution is to carry out speculative execution only for instructions that do not raise an exception (safe speculation). Another approach is boosting (Smith et al. 1992; Smith 1992), which consists of labeling the instruction to "boost" with a bit called a reservation enabling the MPU to decide whether an instruction should be re-executed. A state information is saved until execution of another path. Another solution is the poison bit (Hennessy et al. 1982). The schema of the poison bit consists of attaching the aforementioned bit to the result register of destination register with the idea of reporting an event. When a trap is raised following an execution, the poison bit of the register is positioned, but the exception does not take place. On the contrary, if, afterwards, an instruction reads this register, then this exception takes place. Walker and Cragon (1995) study ITs in pipelined and superscalar environments.

To succeed to monoprocessor architecture and the classic 8259A controller from Intel, in a multiprocessor environment, interrupt control functions were distributed between the microprocessors and I/O controllers. In the case of Pentium, a specialized bus called ICC (Interrupt Controller Communications) makes it possible to make different APIC (Advanced Programmable Interrupt Controller) controllers communicate with one another. Each controller receives interrupt requests linked to its node (LINT for Local INT) and, via the bus (APIC or ICC bus), transmits and receives, in particular, requests from other UCs to be able to handle the IT (Figure 5.27, and *cf.* § 4.1.1 in Darche (2003)). The local controller was integrated for the first time in the Pentium P54C (1954). The architecture includes an external controller called I/O APIC (IOAPIC) under the reference 82489DX. In this architecture, it is necessary to distinguish two types of processor, which are the starting microprocessor (BSP for BootStrap Processor) and the application processor (AP). Other versions followed, such as 82093AA and the xAPIC architectures and its extension, x2APIC respectively appeared with the Pentium 4 MPU (microarchitecture NetBurst – 2000) and the Nehalem microarchitecture (2008). Interrupts in a multicore environment will be studied in a future book by the author.

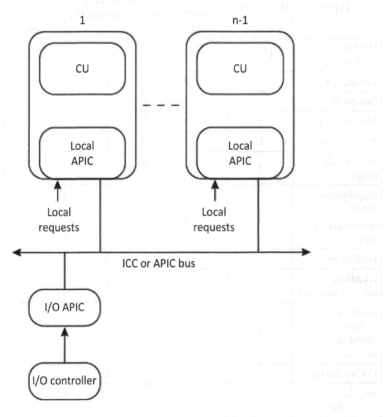

Figure 5.27. *Organization of different APICs*

To summarize, Tables 5.12 (a) and (b) show a list of the most common interrupts by specifying their properties. The term "voluntary" means choosing a programmer. This is an explicit request by instruction, which is different from unwanted requests, that is, constrained or submitted requests. An additional column would have been one that indicated a program stop, or indeed a stopping of the machine or a continuation or recovery, at the level of the instruction or the following one. The term is terminate/restartable–resume–continue. Instances of breaks are cases of serious problems such as, at hardware level, a major failure or an imminent power cut, or at software level, a double fault or an undefined instruction. A final criterion may also be whether the IT request can be nested (*cf.* § 5.3) and/or placed in a queue (*cf.* § 5.8).

Types	External (E)/internal (I)	Synchronous (S) /asynchronous (A)	Voluntary(V) /constraint (C)	Between instructions (E) /internal to the instruction (I)
Hardware malfunction	E or I	A	C	I
I/O request	E	A	C	E
Bus error	E	A	C	E
Memory error	E	A	C	E
Power failure	E	A	C	I
System call (trap)	I	S	V	E
Step-by-step mode (execution trace mode)	I	S	V	E
Breakpoint	I	S	V	E
Overflow (integer number)	I	S	C	I
Over- and under-flow (floating number)	I	S	C	I
Formatting error	I	S	C	I
Invalid instruction	I	S	C	I

Types	External (E)/internal (I)	Synchronous (S) /asynchronous (A)	Voluntary(V) /constraint (C)	Between instructions (E) /internal to the instruction (I)
Undefined instruction	I	S	C	I
Memory protection violation	I	S	C	I
Misaligned memory access	I	S	C	I
Page fault	I	S	C	I
Segment fault	I	S	C	I
Privilege violation	I	S	C	I
Stack fault	I	S	C	I
Double fault	I	S	C	I

Table 5.12a. *Suggestion for classification criteria according to Hennessy and Patterson (1990) and Walker (1992)*

The following table continues this presentation of classification criteria.

Types	Precise (P)/ imprecise (I)	Simple level(S) /multi-level (M)	Maskable (M) or not (NM)
Hardware dysfunction	I	S	NM
I/O request	P	M or S	NM/M
Bus error	I	S	NM
Memory error	I	S	NM
Power failure	I	S	NM
System call (trap)	P	M or S	NM
Step-by-step mode (execution trace mode)	P	M or S	M
Breakpoint	P	M or S	M
Overflow (whole number)	P or I	M or S	M

Types	Precise (P)/ imprecise (I)	Simple level(S) /multi-level (M)	Maskable (M) or not (NM)
Over- and under-flow (floating number)	P/I	M or S	M
Formatting error	I	S	NM
Invalid instruction	P or I	S	NM
Undefined instruction	I	S	NM
Memory protection violation	I	S	NM
Unaligned memory access	I	S	M
Page fault	P	M or S	NM
Segmentation fault	P	M or S	NM
Privilege violation	I	S	NM
Stack fault	I	S	NM
Double fault	I	S	NM

Table 5.12b. *Suggestion of classification criteria according to Hennessy and Patterson (1990) and Walker (1992)*

5.12. Conclusion

This chapter took the subject of interrupt mechanisms. It was first invented to process an overflow problem. It was then used to optimally manage I/Os by avoiding the polling technique.

Interrupts internal to the MPU are either requested explicitly by an instruction (trap) or linked to a problem during the execution (exception). A classification was suggested, and the operation of these hardware and software interrupts has been detailed. The causes of internal then external interrupts have been detailed. The study was pursued with the presentation of different associated aspects such as nested requests, request priority and vectorization.

This chapter ended with execution modes and advanced architectures. In fact, the interrupt mechanism is used in a general way in modern OSs and embedded systems. Having first addressed instruction parallelism or ILP (Instruction-Level Parallelism) and the virtual memory mechanism, this IT concept will be completed in the following volumes by following the development of architectures.

Conclusion of Volume 4

The MicroProcessor Unit (MPU) lies at the heart of modern digital systems. This programmable logic component executes instructions sequentially from a program stored in the main memory. The previous volume presented the hardware aspects of this component.

This fourth volume presented the software aspects of how a microprocessor operates. The programmer will refer to Instruction Set Architecture (ISA, see § V1-3.5), which specifies the type of architecture (General-Purpose Registers (GPR), stack, etc.), the memory addressing characteristics (alignment or not, storage order, access format, addressing capacity), available address modes, operand characteristics (number, type, format and representation (i.e. encoding) and, of course, instructions (family, mnemonic, syntax, semantics, authorized and encoding address modes)) and, finally, data and address path formats.

The first two chapters studied the three main characteristics of an ISA. We then presented instruction coding and format, addressing modes and the instruction set in the form of classes with, in particular, the multimedia extension to modern microprocessors.

The third chapter focused on additional concepts associated with instruction sets and execution. It first of all studied what illegal, invalid, reserved and trusted instructions were. It then presented the concepts of memory alignment, the orthogonality and symmetry of the instruction set and pure, relocatable and re-entrant code. It then discussed the subjects of execution time, memory occupation, execution modes, portability and virtualization. This chapter ended with the important aspects of hardware and software compatibilities, execution performance measurement and the criteria for choosing a microprocessor.

Subroutine call mechanisms and interrupt mechanisms were then studied respectively in the last two chapters. The first made it possible to implement a function or procedure in high-level languages. The interrupt is a similar mechanism. It was originally invented to process an overflow problem. It was then used to manage Input/Output (I/O) in an optimized way by avoiding the polling technique. A classification was proposed following the original request criteria, external or internal, and the operation of these hardware and software interrupts was detailed. The interrupt mechanism is used in a generalized way in modern Operating System (OS) and embedded systems.

As we can therefore see with these last two volumes, the design of the microprocessor requires the competency of multiple domains ranging from micro-electronic technology to functional architecture via Boolean algebra and the design of logic circuits. For the software designer in relation to the hardware aspect, an equilibrium will exist between the different logical sub-sets depending on the applications targeted. For scientific calculation applications, some mathematical instructions could be used. For database applications, complex addressing modes will be used. Two trends have therefore clashed, in design and manufacturing, from the beginning of the 1980s. These are the CISC and RISC approaches (respectively Complex/Reduced Instruction Set Computer, this will be covered in a future book by the author on microprocessors). The CISC architecture favored complexity of the instruction set and therefore of the Control Unit (CU), while the RISC architecture favored registers and simplified the internal structure of the CU (Control Unit) and the Integer Unit (IU).

For more information on this component, a special set of *Proceedings of the IEEE* is dedicated to it (Patt 1995). See also IEEE (1996).

The following volume will present the software tools for low-level development, as well as hardware and software aspects of debugging applications. It will end with a study of the architectures of the first microcomputers.

NOTE.– The concepts presented in this book will be complemented as new ones are introduced. The second book will focus on the modern aspects of processors from 1980 to 1990, in particular virtual memory and parallelism of execution. The third book will focus on multicore parallelism.

Exercises

Here are some exercises that complement the concepts presented in this book. Their numbering refers to the chapter with which they are associated.

Chapter 1. Exercises

E1.1. Recall the definition of a register.

Answer. A register is a memory with one-word capacity in the format n bits, which operates at the speed of the component that integrates it. This means that a microprocessor's register does not slow down its operation when it is accessed.

E1.2. Cite some elements (logic components or logic sub-sets) that are involved in the implicit addressing of a microprocessor.

Answer. The registers and the stack (so the main memory for modern MicroProcessor Units (MPU)).

E1.3. Calculate the maximum number of I_{max} instructions if the function field of the instruction word has a format f fixed at 5 bits.

Answer. $I_{max} = 2^{format} = 2^5 = 32$ instructions.

E1.4. If the addressing mode field has a format a = 3 bits and the instruction set is symmetrical (*cf.* § 3.1.3), calculate the number of possibilities for coding one instruction, also taking the previous question into account.

Answer. There are 2^3 possible addressing modes. This makes $2^5 \times 2^3 = 2^8$ possibilities for coding one instruction.

E1.5. Inverse problem. The MCS6502 MPU has 151 legal operation codes. What is the minimal format c of this word of code?

Answer. You have to go through the logarithm function. This will give:

$$c_{min} = \lfloor \log_2(151) \rfloor + 1 = 8$$

Chapter 2. Exercises

E2.1. Specify the correction algorithm for an addition in packed Binary-Coded Decimal (BCD) and in ASCII.

Answer. The format n of a digit in packed BCD (*cf.* § II.1.2 in Darche (2000)) is 4 bits. With a binary addition of two digits in BCD, the result is false in this representation when it is greater than 9. To correct the result, it is then necessary to add the constant 0110_2 and move the carry to a higher order to obtain a fair result. This is what we call a decimal adjust. Most MPUs have a specialized instruction that should be executed behind a classic binary addition (instruction daa for Decimal Adjust AL after Addition from 8086, for example, on a byte, i.e. two decimal figures). The drawback is that it must carry out this operation after each addition. One interesting peculiarity of the MCS6502 is that it is possible to configure the adder so that it operates in binary or decimal mode (i.e. BCD mode) by setting the decimal mode flag (patented concept, *cf.* § V3-3.1.5.2) using the instructions cld and sed to respectively the clear and set decimal flag. One drawback is that it is necessary to properly manage the positioning of this flag to avoid a calculation error. In ASCII (i.e. a decimal figure coded on a byte with the least significant weight quartet which is equal to 3), this is the instruction aaa (ASCII adjusted after addition) from 8086 that must be used, which renders a result in a packed BCD. To finish, the adjustment can be made on the three other arithmetical operations (i.e. subtraction, multiplication and division) with the associated instructions.

E2.2. Specify the correction algorithm for a subtraction in packed BCD and ASCII.

Answer. The step is identical to that in the previous exercise. With a binary subtraction of two figures in BCD, the result is false in this representation when the figure to be subtracted is smaller than the one that is subtracted. To correct the result, it is then necessary to remove the constant 0110_2 and move the borrow to a higher order to obtain a fair result. This is always a decimal adjust. Most MPUs have a specialized instruction that should be executed behind a classic binary subtraction (instruction das for Decimal Adjust AL after Subtraction from 8086, for example).

The decimal mode from MCS6502 is controlled by positioning the corresponding flag using the instructions cld and sed for respectively the clear and set decimal flag. For the 8086, the correction in ASCII is made using the instruction aas (ASCII adjusted after subtraction), which renders a result in unpacked BCD. To finish, the adjustment can be made on three other arithmetical operations (i.e. addition, multiplication and division) with associated instructions.

E2.3. Give the indicators that are involved during a test for superiority, inferiority and equality.

Answer. Any comparison is first reduced to a subtraction that positions the different binary indicators, then compared to zero (*cf.* exercise E2.2). This can be confirmed by consulting the programming manual or the datasheet (*cf.* Chapter V3-6) of a MPU. Table 2.2 gave the logical expressions corresponding to the desired test operation, which is associated with the conditional jump instruction.

E2.4. Propose a method to initialize a bit at 1 or 0, whatever may be its value.

Answer. It is necessary to use the Boolean operators, in this case the presence of a neutral element and an absorbent, and use a binary value called a mask. To set at zero a bit of position i ($0 \leq i \leq n-1$) in a word in format n, the rank bit i of the mask should be at 0 (absorbing element of logical AND), the others being at 1 (neutral element of the logical AND), and it is necessary to make a logical AND between the value and the mask. This is the same step for setting at 1 using the absorbing element from logical OR, which is 1.

E2.5. Propose a method to isolate and test or extract the value of a bit.

Answer. To test or extract a bit of rank i, we must set all the other bits at 0 by masking using the properties of the Boolean operators (see the previous exercise) and test the value obtained compared to 0. It is not necessary to shift the bit being tested to the Least Significant bit (LSb).

E2.6. Draw the signals of the address bus if the MPU is continuously reading a set of instructions nop (*cf.* § 2.8.5).

Answer: The instruction nop for no operation does nothing operational other than to increment the PC. Considering that the first is located at the address 0 and that the size of its machine code amounts to a byte, execution of this set will lead to the appearance of a modulo-2^m count on the address bus, as Figure E2.28 illustrates.

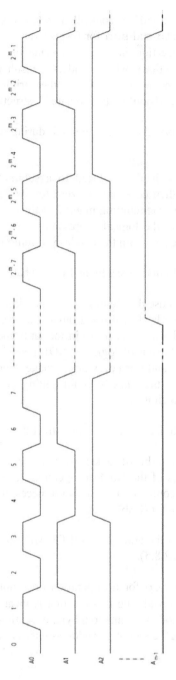

Figure E2.28. *Generation of address signals corresponding to an execution of a set of instructions nop*

Chapter 5. Exercises

E5.1. What is an interruption vector?

Answer. An interruption vector is, depending on the definitions, the start address of the IT management routine considered (ISR for Interrupt Service Routine), or a natural integer serving as an index to a table containing these addresses (see the following question); the former is the one used in this book series.

E5.2. What is an interrupt vector table?

Answer. A vector table is a data structure, in this case a table, linked to an interrupt mechanism. Each post is indexed by an interrupt number, making it possible to identify the source. Each post contains a vector that is the start address of the corresponding IT management routine. Its address for implantation in memory is fixed for MPU running in real(-address) mode (*cf.* § 3.2.2). An alternative is to order the code in the ISR in one post of the table to avoid indirection.

Appendix

Tables for Encoding and Decoding Instructions

The four documents are from Motorola (1984). The first table gives information on the designer, the memory space occupied and the number of cycles of each instruction depending on the addressing mode used. The other tables concern instruction coding depending on the addressing mode chosen. We also find the same information as in the first table. The last table concerns branching.

TABLE 9 — HEXADECIMAL VALUES OF MACHINE CODES

OP	Mnem	Mode	~	#	OP	Mnem	Mode	~	#	OP	Mnem	Mode	~	#
00	NEG	Direct	6	2	30	LEAX	Indexed	4+	2+	60	NEG	Indexed	6+	2+
01	*				31	LEAY		4+	2+	61	*			
02	*				32	LEAS		4+	2+	62	*			
03	COM		6	2	33	LEAU	Indexed	4+	2+	63	COM		6+	2+
04	LSR		6	2	34	PSHS	Immed	5+	2	64	LSR		6+	2+
05	*				35	PULS	Immed	5+	2	65	*			
06	ROR		6	2	36	PSHU	Immed	5+	2	66	ROR		6+	2+
07	ASR		6	2	37	PULU	Immed	5+	2	67	ASR		6+	2+
08	ASL, LSL		6	2	38	*	—			68	ASL, LSL		6+	2+
09	ROL		6	2	39	RTS	Inherent	5	1	69	ROL		6+	2+
0A	DEC		6	2	3A	ABX		3	1	6A	DEC		6+	2+
0B	*				3B	RTI		6/15	1	6B	*			
0C	INC		6	2	3C	CWAI		≥20	2	6C	INC		6+	2+
0D	TST		6	2	3D	MUL	Inherent	11	1	6D	TST		6+	2+
0E	JMP		3	2	3E	*	—			6E	JMP		3+	2+
0F	CLR	Direct	6	2	3F	SWI	Inherent	19	1	6F	CLR	Indexed	6+	2+
10	Page 2	—	—	—	40	NEGA	Inherent	2	1	70	NEG	Extended	7	3
11	Page 3	—	—	—	41	*				71	*			
12	NOP	Inherent	2	1	42	*				72	*			
13	SYNC	Inherent	≥4	1	43	COMA		2	1	73	COM		7	3
14	*				44	LSRA		2	1	74	LSR		7	3
15	*				45	*				75	*			
16	LBRA	Relative	5	3	46	RORA		2	1	76	ROR		7	3
17	LBSR	Relative	9	3	47	ASRA		2	1	77	ASR		7	3
18	*				48	ASLA, LSLA		2	1	78	ASL, LSL		7	3
19	DAA	Inherent	2	1	49	ROLA		2	1	79	ROL		7	3
1A	ORCC	Immed	3	2	4A	DECA		2	1	7A	DEC		7	3
1B	*	—			4B	*				7B	*			
1C	ANDCC	Immed	3	2	4C	INCA		2	1	7C	INC		7	3
1D	SEX	Inherent	2	1	4D	TSTA		2	1	7D	TST		7	3
1E	EXG	Immed	8	2	4E	*				7E	JMP		4	3
1F	TFR	Immed	6	2	4F	CLRA	Inherent	2	1	7F	CLR	Extended	7	3
20	BRA	Relative	3	2	50	NEGB	Inherent	2	1	80	SUBA	Immed	2	2
21	BRN		3	2	51	*				81	CMPA		2	2
22	BHI		3	2	52	*				82	SBCA		2	2
23	BLS		3	2	53	COMB		2	1	83	SUBD		4	3
24	BHS, BCC		3	2	54	LSRB		2	1	84	ANDA		2	2
25	BLO, BCS		3	2	55	*				85	BITA		2	2
26	BNE		3	2	56	RORB		2	1	86	LDA		2	2
27	BEQ		3	2	57	ASRB		2	1	87	*			
28	BVC		3	2	58	ASLB, LSLB		2	1	88	EORA		2	2
29	BVS		3	2	59	ROLB		2	1	89	ADCA		2	2
2A	BPL		3	2	5A	DECB		2	1	8A	ORA		2	2
2B	BMI		3	2	5B	*				8B	ADDA		2	2
2C	BGE		3	2	5C	INCB		2	1	8C	CMPX	Immed	4	3
2D	BLT		3	2	5D	TSTB		2	1	8D	BSR	Relative	7	2
2E	BGT		3	2	5E	*				8E	LDX	Immed	3	3
2F	BLE	Relative	3	2	5F	CLRB	Inherent	2	1	8F	*			

LEGEND:
~ Number of MPU cycles (less possible push pull or indexed-mode cycles)
# Number of program bytes
* Denotes unused opcode

 MOTOROLA Semiconductor Products Inc.

Table A.1a. *Hexadecimal values of machine codes*

TABLE 9 — HEXADECIMAL VALUES OF MACHINE CODES (CONTINUED)

OP	Mnem	Mode	~	#
90	SUBA	Direct	4	2
91	CMPA		4	2
92	SBCA		4	2
93	SUBD		6	2
94	ANDA		4	2
95	BITA		4	2
96	LDA		4	2
97	STA		4	2
98	EORA		4	2
99	ADCA		4	2
9A	ORA		4	2
9B	ADDA		4	2
9C	CMPX		6	2
9D	JSR		7	2
9E	LDX		5	2
9F	STX	Direct	5	2
A0	SUBA	Indexed	4+	2+
A1	CMPA		4+	2+
A2	SBCA		4+	2+
A3	SUBD		6+	2+
A4	ANDA		4+	2+
A5	BITA		4+	2+
A6	LDA		4+	2+
A7	STA		4+	2+
A8	EORA		4+	2+
A9	ADCA		4+	2+
AA	ORA		4+	2+
AB	ADDA		4+	2+
AC	CMPX		6+	2+
AD	JSR		7+	2+
AE	LDX		5+	2+
AF	STX	Indexed	5+	2+
B0	SUBA	Extended	5	3
B1	CMPA		5	3
B2	SBCA		5	3
B3	SUBD		7	3
B4	ANDA		5	3
B5	BITA		5	3
B6	LDA		5	3
B7	STA		5	3
B8	EORA		5	3
B9	ADCA		5	3
BA	ORA		5	3
BB	ADDA		5	3
BC	CMPX		7	3
BD	JSR		8	3
BE	LDX		6	3
BF	STX	Extended	6	3

NOTE: All unused opcodes are both undefined and illegal

OP	Mnem	Mode	~	#
C0	SUBB	Immed	2	2
C1	CMPB		2	2
C2	SBCB		2	2
C3	ADDD		4	3
C4	ANDB		2	2
C5	BITB	Immed	2	2
C6	LDB	Immed	2	2
C7	*			
C8	EORB		2	2
C9	ADCB		2	2
CA	ORB		2	2
CB	ADDB		2	2
CC	LDD		3	3
CD	*			
CE	LDU	Immed	3	3
CF	*			
D0	SUBB	Direct	4	2
D1	CMPB		4	2
D2	SBCB		4	2
D3	ADDD		6	2
D4	ANDB		4	2
D5	BITB		4	2
D6	LDB		4	2
D7	STB		4	2
D8	EORB		4	2
D9	ADCB		4	2
DA	ORB		4	2
DB	ADDB		4	2
DC	LDD		5	2
DD	STD		5	2
DE	LDU		5	2
DF	STU	Direct	5	2
E0	SUBB	Indexed	4+	2+
E1	CMPB		4+	2+
E2	SBCB		4+	2+
E3	ADDD		6+	2+
E4	ANDB		4+	2+
E5	BITB		4+	2+
E6	LDB		4+	2+
E7	STB		4+	2+
E8	EORB		4+	2+
E9	ADCB		4+	2+
EA	ORB		4+	2+
EB	ADDB		4+	2+
EC	LDD		5+	2+
ED	STD		5+	2+
EE	LDU		5+	2+
EF	STU	Indexed	5+	2+
F0	SUBB	Extended	5	3
F1	CMPB		5	3
F2	SBCB		5	3
F3	ADDD		7	3
F4	ANDB		5	3
F5	BITB		5	3
F6	LDB		5	3
F7	STB		5	3
F8	EORB		5	3
F9	ADCB		5	3
FA	ORB		5	3
FB	ADDB	Extended	5	3
FC	LDD	Extended	6	3
FD	STD		6	3
FE	LDU		6	3
FF	STU	Extended	6	3

Page 2 and 3 Machine Codes

OP	Mnem	Mode	~	#
1021	LBRN	Relative	5	4
1022	LBHI		5(6)	4
1023	LBLS		5(6)	4
1024	LBHS, LBCC		5(6)	4
1025	LBCS, LBLO		5(6)	4
1026	LBNE		5(6)	4
1027	LBEQ		5(6)	4
1028	LBVC		5(6)	4
1029	LBVS		5(6)	4
102A	LBPL		5(6)	4
102B	LBMI		5(6)	4
102C	LBGE		5(6)	4
102D	LBLT		5(6)	4
102E	LBGT		5(6)	4
102F	LBLE	Relative	5(6)	4
103F	SWI2	Inherent	20	2
1083	CMPD	Immed	5	4
108C	CMPY		5	4
108E	LDY	Immed	4	4
1093	CMPD	Direct	7	3
109C	CMPY		7	3
109E	LDY		6	3
109F	STY	Direct	6	3
10A3	CMPD	Indexed	7+	3+
10AC	CMPY		7+	3+
10AE	LDY		6+	3+
10AF	STY	Indexed	6+	3+
10B3	CMPD	Extended	8	4
10BC	CMPY		8	4
10BE	LDY		7	4
10BF	STY	Extended	7	4
10CE	LDS	Immed	4	4
10DE	LDS	Direct	6	3
10DF	STS	Direct	6	3
10EE	LDS	Indexed	6+	3+
10EF	STS	Indexed	6+	3+
10FE	LDS	Extended	7	4
10FF	STS	Extended	7	4
113F	SWI3	Inherent	20	2
1183	CMPU	Immed	5	4
118C	CMPS	Immed	5	4
1193	CMPU	Direct	7	3
119C	CMPS	Direct	7	3
11A3	CMPU	Indexed	7+	3+
11AC	CMPS	Indexed	7+	3+
11B3	CMPU	Extended	8	4
11BC	CMPS	Extended	8	4

Table A.1b. *Hexadecimal values of machine codes (continued)*

FIGURE 18 — PROGRAMMING AID

Instruction	Forms	Immediate Op	~	#	Direct Op	~	#	Indexed Op	~	#	Extended Op	~	#	Inherent Op	~	#	Description	5 H	3 N	2 Z	1 V	0 C
ABX														3A	3	1	B + X → X (Unsigned)	•	•	•	•	•
ADC	ADCA	89	2	2	99	4	2	A9	4+	2+	B9	5	3				A + M + C → A	↕	↕	↕	↕	↕
	ADCB	C9	2	2	D9	4	2	E9	4+	2+	F9	5	3				B + M + C → B	↕	↕	↕	↕	↕
ADD	ADDA	8B	2	2	9B	4	2	AB	4+	2+	BB	5	3				A + M → A	↕	↕	↕	↕	↕
	ADDB	CB	2	2	DB	4	2	EB	4+	2+	FB	5	3				B + M → B	↕	↕	↕	↕	↕
	ADDD	C3	4	3	D3	6	2	E3	6+	2+	F3	7	3				D + M:M + 1 → D	•	↕	↕	↕	↕
AND	ANDA	84	2	2	94	4	2	A4	4+	2+	B4	5	3				A Λ M → A	•	↕	↕	0	•
	ANDB	C4	2	2	D4	4	2	E4	4+	2+	F4	5	3				B Λ M → B	•	↕	↕	0	•
	ANDCC	1C	3	2													CC Λ IMM → CC					7
ASL	ASLA													48	2	1		8	↕	↕	↕	↕
	ASLB													58	2	1		8	↕	↕	↕	↕
	ASL				08	6	2	68	6+	2+	78	7	3					8	↕	↕	↕	↕
ASR	ASRA													47	2	1		8	↕	↕	•	↕
	ASRB													57	2	1		8	↕	↕	•	↕
	ASR				07	6	2	67	6+	2+	77	7	3					8	↕	↕	•	↕
BIT	BITA	85	2	2	95	4	2	A5	4+	2+	B5	5	3				Bit Test A (M Λ A)	•	↕	↕	0	•
	BITB	C5	2	2	D5	4	2	E5	4+	2+	F5	5	3				Bit Test B (M Λ B)	•	↕	↕	0	•
CLR	CLRA													4F	2	1	0 → A	•	0	1	0	0
	CLRB													5F	2	1	0 → B	•	0	1	0	0
	CLR				0F	6	2	6F	6+	2+	7F	7	3				0 → M	•	0	1	0	0
CMP	CMPA	81	2	2	91	4	2	A1	4+	2+	B1	5	3				Compare M from A	8	↕	↕	↕	↕
	CMPB	C1	2	2	D1	4	2	E1	4+	2+	F1	5	3				Compare M from B	8	↕	↕	↕	↕
	CMPD	10 83	5	4	10 93	7	3	10 A3	7+	3+	10 B3	8	4				Compare M:M + 1 from D	•	↕	↕	↕	↕
	CMPS	11 8C	5	4	11 9C	7	3	11 AC	7+	3+	11 BC	8	4				Compare M:M + 1 from S	•	↕	↕	↕	↕
	CMPU	11 83	5	4	11 93	7	3	11 A3	7+	3+	11 B3	8	4				Compare M:M + 1 from U	•	↕	↕	↕	↕
	CMPX	8C	4	3	9C	6	2	AC	6+	2+	BC	7	3				Compare M:M + 1 from X	•	↕	↕	↕	↕
	CMPY	10 8C	5	4	10 9C	7	3	10 AC	7+	3+	10 BC	8	4				Compare M:M + 1 from Y	•	↕	↕	↕	↕
COM	COMA													43	2	1	Ā → A	•	↕	↕	0	1
	COMB													53	2	1	B̄ → B	•	↕	↕	0	1
	COM				03	6	2	63	6+	2+	73	7	3				M̄ → M	•	↕	↕	0	1
CWAI		3C	≥20	2													CC Λ IMM → CC Wait for Interrupt					7
DAA														19	2	1	Decimal Adjust A	•	↕	↕	0	↕
DEC	DECA													4A	2	1	A − 1 → A	•	↕	↕	↕	•
	DECB													5A	2	1	B − 1 → B	•	↕	↕	↕	•
	DEC				0A	6	2	6A	6+	2+	7A	7	3				M − 1 → M	•	↕	↕	↕	•
EOR	EORA	88	2	2	98	4	2	A8	4+	2+	B8	5	3				A ⊻ M → A	•	↕	↕	0	•
	EORB	C8	2	2	D8	4	2	E8	4+	2+	F8	5	3				B ⊻ M → B	•	↕	↕	0	•
EXG	R1, R2	1E	8	2													R1 ↔ R2[2]	•	•	•	•	•
INC	INCA													4C	2	1	A + 1 → A	•	↕	↕	↕	•
	INCB													5C	2	1	B + 1 → B	•	↕	↕	↕	•
	INC				0C	6	2	6C	6+	2+	7C	7	3				M + 1 → M	•	↕	↕	↕	•
JMP					0E	3	2	6E	3+	2+	7E	4	3				EA[3] → PC	•	•	•	•	•
JSR					9D	7	2	AD	7+	2+	BD	8	3				Jump to Subroutine	•	•	•	•	•
LD	LDA	86	2	2	96	4	2	A6	4+	2+	B6	5	3				M → A	•	↕	↕	0	•
	LDB	C6	2	2	D6	4	2	E6	4+	2+	F6	5	3				M → B	•	↕	↕	0	•
	LDD	CC	3	3	DC	5	2	EC	5+	2+	FC	6	3				M:M + 1 → D	•	↕	↕	0	•
	LDS	10 CE	4	4	10 DE	6	3	10 EE	6+	3+	10 FE	7	4				M:M + 1 → S	•	↕	↕	0	•
	LDU	CE	3	3	DE	5	2	EE	5+	2+	FE	6	3				M:M + 1 → U	•	↕	↕	0	•
	LDX	8E	3	3	9E	5	2	AE	5+	2+	BE	6	3				M:M + 1 → X	•	↕	↕	0	•
	LDY	10 8E	4	4	10 9E	6	3	10 AE	6+	3+	10 BE	7	4				M:M + 1 → Y	•	↕	↕	0	•
LEA	LEAS							32	4+	2+							EA[3] → S	•	•	•	•	•
	LEAU							33	4+	2+							EA[3] → U	•	•	•	•	•
	LEAX							30	4+	2+							EA[3] → X	•	•	↕	•	•
	LEAY							31	4+	2+							EA[3] → Y	•	•	↕	•	•

LEGEND:

OP	Operation Code (Hexadecimal)	M̄ Complement of M	1 Test and set if true, cleared otherwise
~	Number of MPU Cycles	→ Transfer Into	• Not Affected
#	Number of Program Bytes	H Half-carry (from bit 3)	CC Condition Code Register
+	Arithmetic Plus	N Negative (sign bit)	: Concatenation
−	Arithmetic Minus	Z Zero result	V Logical or
•	Multiply	V Overflow, 2's complement	Λ Logical and
		C Carry from ALU	⊻ Logical Exclusive or

Ⓜ **MOTOROLA** Semiconductor Products Inc.

Table A.2a. *Programming aid*

FIGURE 18 — PROGRAMMING AID (CONTINUED)

Instruction	Forms	Immediate Op	~	#	Direct Op	~	#	Indexed[1] Op	~	#	Extended Op	~	#	Inherent Op	~	#	Description	5 H	3 N	2 Z	1 V	0 C
LSL	LSLA													48	2	1	A	•	↓	↓	↓	↓
	LSLB													58	2	1	B }	•	↓	↓	↓	↓
	LSL				08	6	2	68	6+	2+	78	7	3				M	•	↓	↓	↓	↓
LSR	LSRA													44	2	1	A	•	0	↓	•	↓
	LSRB													54	2	1	B }	•	0	↓	•	↓
	LSR				04	6	2	64	6+	2+	74	7	3				M	•	0	↓	•	↓
MUL														3D	11	1	A × B→D (Unsigned)	•	•	↓	•	9
NEG	NEGA													40	2	1	Ā + 1→A	8	↓	↓	↓	↓
	NEGB													50	2	1	B̄ + 1→B	8	↓	↓	↓	↓
	NEG				00	6	2	60	6+	2+	70	7	3				M̄ + 1→M	8	↓	↓	↓	↓
NOP														12	2	1	No Operation	•	•	•	•	•
OR	ORA	8A	2	2	9A	4	2	AA	4+	2+	BA	5	3				A V M→A	•	↓	↓	0	•
	ORB	CA	2	2	DA	4	2	EA	4+	2+	FA	5	3				B V M→B	•	↓	↓	0	•
	ORCC	1A	3	2													CC V IMM→CC				7	
PSH	PSHS	34	5+[4]	2													Push Registers on S Stack	•	•	•	•	•
	PSHU	36	5+[4]	2													Push Registers on U Stack	•	•	•	•	•
PUL	PULS	35	5+[4]	2													Pull Registers from S Stack	•	•	•	•	•
	PULU	37	5+[4]	2													Pull Registers from U Stack	•	•	•	•	•
ROL	ROLA													49	2	1	A	•	↓	↓	↓	↓
	ROLB													59	2	1	B }	•	↓	↓	↓	↓
	ROL				09	6	2	69	6+	2+	79	7	3				M	•	↓	↓	↓	↓
ROR	RORA													46	2	1	A	•	↓	↓	•	↓
	RORB													56	2	1	B }	•	↓	↓	•	↓
	ROR				06	6	2	66	6+	2+	76	7	3				M	•	↓	↓	•	↓
RTI														3B	6/15	1	Return From Interrupt					7
RTS														39	5	1	Return from Subroutine	•	•	•	•	•
SBC	SBCA	82	2	2	92	4	2	A2	4+	2+	B2	5	3				A – M – C→A	8	↓	↓	↓	↓
	SBCB	C2	2	2	D2	4	2	E2	4+	2+	F2	5	3				B – M – C→B	8	↓	↓	↓	↓
SEX														1D	2	1	Sign Extend B into A	•	↓	↓	0	•
ST	STA				97	4	2	A7	4+	2+	B7	5	3				A→M	•	↓	↓	0	•
	STB				D7	4	2	E7	4+	2+	F7	5	3				B→M	•	↓	↓	0	•
	STD				DD	5	2	ED	5+	2+	FD	6	3				D→M:M + 1	•	↓	↓	0	•
	STS				10 DF	6	3	10 EF	6+	3+	10 FF	7	4				S→M:M + 1	•	↓	↓	0	•
	STU				DF	5	2	EF	5+	2+	FF	6	3				U→M:M + 1	•	↓	↓	0	•
	STX				9F	5	2	AF	5+	2+	BF	6	3				X→M:M + 1	•	↓	↓	0	•
	STY				10 9F	6	3	10 AF	6+	3+	10 BF	7	4				Y→M:M + 1	•	↓	↓	0	•
SUB	SUBA	80	2	2	90	4	2	A0	4+	2+	B0	5	3				A – M→A	8	↓	↓	↓	↓
	SUBB	C0	2	2	D0	4	2	E0	4+	2+	F0	5	3				B – M→B	8	↓	↓	↓	↓
	SUBD	83	4	3	93	6	2	A3	6+	2+	B3	7	3				D – M:M + 1→D	•	↓	↓	↓	↓
SWI	SWI[6]													3F	19	1	Software Interrupt 1	•	•	•	•	•
	SWI2[6]													10 3F	20	2	Software Interrupt 2	•	•	•	•	•
	SWI3[6]													11 3F	20	1	Software Interrupt 3	•	•	•	•	•
SYNC														13	≥4	1	Synchronize to Interrupt	•	•	•	•	•
TFR	R1, R2	1F	6	2													R1→R2[2]	•	•	•	•	•
TST	TSTA													4D	2	1	Test A	•	↓	↓	0	•
	TSTB													5D	2	1	Test B	•	↓	↓	0	•
	TST				0D	6	2	6D	6+	2+	7D	7	3				Test M	•	↓	↓	0	•

NOTES:
1. This column gives a base cycle and byte count. To obtain total count, add the values obtained from the INDEXED ADDRESSING MODE table, Table 2.
2. R1 and R2 may be any pair of 8 bit or any pair of 16 bit registers.
   The 8 bit registers are: A, B, CC, DP
   The 16 bit registers are: X, Y, U, S, D, PC
3. EA is the effective address.
4. The PSH and PUL instructions require 5 cycles plus 1 cycle for each **byte** pushed or pulled.
5. 5(6) means: 5 cycles if branch not taken, 6 cycles if taken (Branch instructions).
6. SWI sets I and F bits. SWI2 and SWI3 do not affect I and F.
7. Conditions Codes set as a direct result of the instruction.
8. Value of half-carry flag is undefined.
9. Special Case — Carry set if b7 is SET.

 MOTOROLA Semiconductor Products Inc.

Table A.2b. *Programming aid (continued)*

FIGURE 18 — PROGRAMMING AID (CONTINUED)

Branch Instructions

Instruction	Forms	OP	~	#	Description	H	N	Z	V	C
BCC	BCC	24	3	2	Branch C=0	•	•	•	•	•
	LBCC	10	5(6)	4	Long Branch C=0	•	•	•	•	•
		24								
BCS	BCS	25	3	2	Branch C=1	•	•	•	•	•
	LBCS	10	5(6)	4	Long Branch C=1	•	•	•	•	•
		25								
BEQ	BEQ	27	3	2	Branch Z=1	•	•	•	•	•
	LBEQ	10	5(6)	4	Long Branch Z=1	•	•	•	•	•
		27								
BGE	BGE	2C	3	2	Branch ≥ Zero	•	•	•	•	•
	LBGE	10	5(6)	4	Long Branch ≥ Zero	•	•	•	•	•
		2C								
BGT	BGT	2E	3	2	Branch > Zero	•	•	•	•	•
	LBGT	10	5(6)	4	Long Branch > Zero	•	•	•	•	•
		2E								
BHI	BHI	22	3	2	Branch Higher	•	•	•	•	•
	LBHI	10	5(6)	4	Long Branch Higher	•	•	•	•	•
		22								
BHS	BHS	24	3	2	Branch Higher or Same	•	•	•	•	•
	LBHS	10	5(6)	4	Long Branch Higher or Same	•	•	•	•	•
		24								
BLE	BLE	2F	3	2	Branch ≤ Zero	•	•	•	•	•
	LBLE	10	5(6)	4	Long Branch ≤ Zero	•	•	•	•	•
		2F								
BLO	BLO	25	3	2	Branch lower	•	•	•	•	•
	LBLO	10	5(6)	4	Long Branch Lower	•	•	•	•	•
		25								

Instruction	Forms	OP	~	#	Description	H	N	Z	V	C
BLS	BLS	23	3	2	Branch Lower or Same	•	•	•	•	•
	LBLS	10	5(6)	4	Long Branch Lower or Same	•	•	•	•	•
		23								
BLT	BLT	2D	3	2	Branch < Zero	•	•	•	•	•
	LBLT	10	5(6)	4	Long Branch < Zero	•	•	•	•	•
		2D								
BMI	BMI	2B	3	2	Branch Minus	•	•	•	•	•
	LBMI	10	5(6)	4	Long Branch Minus	•	•	•	•	•
		2B								
BNE	BNE	26	3	2	Branch Z=0	•	•	•	•	•
	LBNE	10	5(6)	4	Long Branch Z=0	•	•	•	•	•
		26								
BPL	BPL	2A	3	2	Branch Plus	•	•	•	•	•
	LBPL	10	5(6)	4	Long Branch Plus	•	•	•	•	•
		2A								
BRA	BRA	20	3	2	Branch Always	•	•	•	•	•
	LBRA	16	5	3	Long Branch Always	•	•	•	•	•
BRN	BRN	21	3	2	Branch Never	•	•	•	•	•
	LBRN	10	5	4	Long Branch Never	•	•	•	•	•
		21								
BSR	BSR	8D	7	2	Branch to Subroutine	•	•	•	•	•
	LBSR	17	9	3	Long Branch to Subroutine	•	•	•	•	•
BVC	BVC	28	3	2	Branch V=0	•	•	•	•	•
	LBVC	10	5(6)	4	Long Branch V=0	•	•	•	•	•
		28								
BVS	BVS	29	3	2	Branch V=1	•	•	•	•	•
	LBVS	10	5(6)	4	Long Branch V=1	•	•	•	•	•
		29								

SIMPLE BRANCHES

	OP	~	#
BRA	20	3	2
LBRA	16	5	3
BRN	21	3	2
LBRN	1021	5	4
BSR	8D	7	2
LBSR	17	9	3

SIMPLE CONDITIONAL BRANCHES (Notes 1-4)

Test	True	OP	False	OP
N=1	BMI	2B	BPL	2A
Z=1	BEQ	27	BNE	26
V=1	BVS	29	BVC	28
C=1	BCS	25	BCC	24

SIGNED CONDITIONAL BRANCHES (Notes 1-4)

Test	True	OP	False	OP
r>m	BGT	2E	BLE	2F
r≥m	BGE	2C	BLT	2D
r=m	BEQ	27	BNE	26
r≤m	BLE	2F	BGT	2E
r<m	BLT	2D	BGE	2C

UNSIGNED CONDITIONAL BRANCHES (Notes 1-4)

Test	True	OP	False	OP
r>m	BHI	22	BLS	23
r≥m	BHS	24	BLO	25
r=m	BEQ	27	BNE	26
r≤m	BLS	23	BHI	22
r<m	BLO	25	BHS	24

NOTES:
1. All conditional branches have both short and long variations.
2. All short branches are 2 bytes and require 3 cycles.
3. All conditional long branches are formed by prefixing the short branch opcode with $10 and using a 16-bit destination offset.
4. All conditional long branches require 4 bytes and 6 cycles if the branch is taken or 5 cycles if the branch is not taken.
5. 5(6) means: 5 cycles if branch not taken, 6 cycles if taken.

 MOTOROLA *Semiconductor Products Inc.*

Table A.2c. *Programming aid (continued)*

Acronyms

This section includes all of the acronyms used in this volume. They range across chapters.

General

A

A   Address

AAPCS   Procedure Call Standard for the Arm® Architecture

AB   Available Bus (MC6809)

ABI   Application Binary Interface

ABM   Advanced Bit Manipulation (AMD technology)

ABT   ABorT

ACU   Address Computation Unit (synonyms: AGU, DAG)

AES   Advanced Encryption Standard

AES NI   AES New Instructions

AGU   Address Generation Unit (synonyms: ACU, DAG)

ALGOL   ALGOrithmic Language

AP	Application Processor
APCS	Arm® Procedure Call Standard
APIC	Advanced PIC (Intel)
ASCII	American Standard Code for Information Interchange
ASIP	Application-Specific Instruction set Processor
ASL	Arithmetic Shift Left
ASP	Application-Specific Processor
ATPCS	Arm® TPCS
AVX	Advanced Vector eXtensions (Intel technology)
AXP	Almost eXactly PRISM

B

b	bit (*cf.* BIT)
B	Byte
BCD	Binary-Coded Decimal
BE	Big Endian
BERT	Branch Effect Reduction Technique
BIOS	Basic Input/Output System
BIT	BInary digiT or Binary digIT
BMI	Bit Manipulation Instructions (Intel technology)
BP	Base Pointer (Intel)
BRAF	Block-Repeat-Active Flag
BRC	Block Repeat Counter

BS	Bus Status (MC6809)
BSP	BootStrap Processor
BSS	Block Started by Symbol (UNIX)
BTA	Branch Target Address
BTI	Branch Target Instruction

C

cc	condition code
CF	Carry Flag
CISC	Complex Instruction Set Computer
COBOL	COmmon Business Oriented Language
COP	Calculator-Oriented Processor (NS)
COPS	Controller-Oriented Processor System (NS), formerly COP
COSMAC	Complementary Symmetry Monolithic Array Computer
CPL	Current Privilege Level
CPSR	Current Program Status Register
CPU	Central Processing Unit
CR	Condition Register
CRC	Cyclic Redundancy Check
CS	Code Segment (Intel x86)
CTR	CounT Register
CU	Control Unit
CVT	ConVerT (AMD and Intel)

D

DAG	Data Address Generator (synonyms: ACU, AGU)
DFP	Decimal Floating-Point
DI	Destination Index (Intel x86)
DIF	Decimal-In-Frequency
DIL	Dual-In-Line
DIP	DIL Package
DISP	DISPlacement (i.e. offset)
DIT	Decimal-In-Time
DLL	Dynamic Link Library
DP	Direct Page
DRAM	Dynamic RAM
DXP	Decimal Fixed-Point
DYSEAC	Second SEAC

E

EA	Effective Address
EA	Empty Ascending
EBCDIC	Extended Binary-Coded Decimal Interchange Code (IBM)
ECC	Error Checking and Correcting/ Error-Correcting Code
ED	Empty Descending
EDC	Error-Detecting Circuit/Code
EDSAC	Electronic Delay Storage Automatic Calculator

EF	Entire Flag (MC6809)
EIC	External Interrupt Controller
EN	ENable
EOR	Exclusive OR (*cf.* EXOR and XOR)
EPC	Exception Program Counter (MIPS)
EQ	EQual
EXOR	EXclusive OR (*cf.* EOR and XOR)

F

FA	Full Ascending
FC	Function Code (MC68000)
FD	Full Descending
FFT	Fast Fourier Transform
FIFO	First In, First Out
FIQ	Fast Interrupt reQuest mode (ARM)
FIR	Finite Impulse Response
FIRQ	Fast IRQ
FMA	Fused Multiply-Accumulate
FORTRAN	FORmula TRANslation
FP	Floating Point
FPGA	Field-Programmable Gate Array
FPP	FP Processor

| FPU | FP Unit |
| FW | FirmWare |

G

GE	Greater than or Equal
GP FPP	General-Purpose FPP
GPP	General-Purpose Processor
GPR	General-Purpose Register
GT	Greater Than

H

HLL	High-Level (programming) Language
HW	HardWare
HWP	Heavy-Weight Process

I

IA	Intel Architecture
iAPX	Intel Advanced Performance Architecture
ICC	Interrupt Controller Communications
ID	Identification
IDT	Interrupt Descriptor Table (Intel)
IDTR	IDT Register (Intel)
IE	individual Interrupt Enable (PACE)
IF	Interrupt enable Flag

IIC	Internal Interrupt Controller
ILP	Instruction-Level Parallelism
INT	INTerrupt
INTA	INTerrupt Acknowledge
INTR	INTerrupt Request
I/O	Input/Output
IO	Input/Output (rarely used)
IOAPIC	I/O APIC
IOPL	I/O Privilege Level (flag)
IP	Instruction Pointer (Intel) (*cf.* PC)
IPL	Interrupt Priority Level (MC68000)
IR	Index Register
IRQ	Interrupt Request
IS	Instruction Set
ISA	IS Architecture
ISP	Instruction Set Processor
ISR	Interrupt Service Routine
ISSE	Intel SSE (AMD)
ISSE	Internet SSE (Intel)
IT	InTerruption (*cf.* INT)
IVT	Interrupt Vector Table

J

JTAG	Joint Test Action Group
JVM	Java Virtual Machine

K

KNI	Katmai New Instructions (Intel SSE1)

L

LA	end-of-Loop Address
LAPACK	Linear Algebra PACKage
LC	Loop Counter
LE	Less than or Equal/less or equal
LE	Little Endian
LE	Loop End
LED	Light-Emitting Diode
LEM	Lunar Excursion Module
LF	Loop Flag
LGC	LEM Guidance Computer
LGE	Less, Greater and Equal
LIFO	Last In, First Out
LINPACK	LINear Algebra PACKage
LINT	Local INT (APIC, Intel)
LIW	Long Instruction Word
LK	LinK (bit)

LR	Link Register (ARM)
LS	Loop Start
LSb	Least Significant bit
LSB	Least Significant Byte
LSL	Logical Shift Left
LSR	Logical Shift Right
LT	Less Than
LUT	LookUp Table
LWP	Light-Weight Process

M

MAC	Multiply-and-ACcumulate
MAX	Multimedia Acceleration eXtensions (PA-RISC 2.0)
MCS	Micro Computer Set (Intel)
MCU	MicroComputer Unit
MCU	MicroController Unit (preferable)
MDMX	MIPS Digital Media eXtensions
MIPS	Microprocessor without Interlocked Pipeline Stages from MIPS Technologies (then called MIPS Computer Systems)
MMR	Memory-Mapped Register
MMU	Memory Management Unit
MMX	MultiMedia eXtensions (Intel technology)
MOS	Metal-Oxide Semiconductor
MP	MultiProcesseur (MultiProcessor)

MPU	MicroProcessor Unit
MSb	Most Significant bit
MSB	Most Significant Byte
MSW	Machine Status Word
MUX	MUltipleXer
MVI	Motion Video Instructions (DEC Alpha)

N

N	Negative (flag)
NB	Natural Binary (*cf.* NBC)
NBC	Natural Binary Code (*cf.* NB)
NE	Not Equal
NI	New Instruction
NMI	Non-Maskable Interrupt
NNI	Nehalem New Instructions (Intel SSE4)
NOP	No Operation
NOS	Next-On-Stack

O

OF	Overflow Flag
OS	Operating System

P

PA	Physical Address
PA	Precision Architecture (HP)
PACE	Processing And Control Element (NS)
PA-RISC	Precision Architecture-RISC (HP)
PC	Personal Computer
PC	Program Counter (*cf.* IP)
PCR	Program Counter Register (MC6809)
PCS	Program Counter Stack
PDP	Programmable Data Processor (DEC)
PE	Protected Mode Enable
PIC	Peripheral Interface Controller (General Instrument)
PIC	Programmable Intelligent Computer (General Instrument)
PIC	Position-Independent Code
PIC	Programmable Interrupt Controller
PIE	Position-Independent Executable
PNI	Prescott New Instructions (Intel SSE3)
POWER	Performance Optimization With Enhanced RISC
PowerPC	POWER Performance Computing
PR	Predicate Register
PRISM	Parallel Reduced Instruction Set Machine (DEC Alpha AXP)
PSR	Processor Status Register

R

RAM	Random Access Memory
RC	Repeat Counter
RCA	Reverse-Carry Arithmetic
RCL	Rotate through Carry Left
RCR	Rotate through Carry Right
RE	Repeat End Address register
REA	Repeat End Address
REX	Register Extension (AMD, Intel)
RF	Register File
RGB	Red–Green–Blue
RIP	Instruction Pointer Register (Intel x86-64)
RISC	Reduced Instruction Set Computer
R/M	Register/Memory
R/M	modify Register or Memory
RMW	Read-Modify-Write
ROL	ROtate Left
ROLC	Rotate left through (the) carry (flag) (IEEE Std 694-1985)
ROM	Read-Only Memory
ROR	ROtate Right
RORC	Rotate right through (the) carry (flag) (IEEE Std 694-1985)
RS	Register Select
RS	Repeat Start Address register

RSA	Repeat Start Address
RSM	Resume from System Management Mode
RST	ReSeT

S

SAL	Shift Arithmetic Left
SAR	Shift Arithmetic Right
SEAC	Standards Electronic Automatic Computer
SEGT	SEGment Trap (request)
SHL	SHift arithmetic Left
SHLA	SHift Left Arithmetical (IEEE Std 694-1985)
SHLD	Shift Left Doublet
SHR	SHift logical Right
SHRA	SHift Right Arithmetical (IEEE Std 694-1985)
SHRD	Shift Right Double
SI	Source Index (Intel x86)
SIB	Scale-Index-Base
SIMD	Single Instruction stream/Multiple Data stream
SMI	System Management Interrupt
SMM	System Management Mode
SMP	Symmetric (shared memory) MultiProcessing
SP	Stack Pointer (x86 Intel)
SPARC	Scalable Processor ARChitecture

SR	Shift Register
SR	Status Register
SSE	Streaming SIMD Extensions (Intel)
SSSE3	Supplemental SSE3 (Intel)
SVC	SuperVisor Call
SW	SoftWare
SWI	SoftWare Interrupt
SYS	SYStem

T

TB	Test and Branch
TBM	Trailing Bit Manipulation (AMD technology)
TF	Trap Flag
TLB	Translation Lookaside Buffer
TNI	Tejas New Instructions (SSSE3)
TOS	Top-Of-Stack
TPCS	Thumb® Procedure Call Standard
TSS	Task State Segment

U

UCS	Universal Character Set
UND	UNDefined
UNICODE	UNIversal CODE
UNIVAC	Universal Automatic Computer

URL	Uniform Resource Locator
USB	Universal Serial Bus
USR	USeR
UTF	Unicode (or UCS) Transformation Format

V

VAX	Virtual Addressed eXtended (DEC)
VEX	Vector EXtensions
VHDL	VHSIC Hardware Description Language
VHSIC	Very High-Speed Integrated Circuit
VIC	Vectored Interrupt Controller (ARM)
VIS	Visual Instruction Set
VLIW	Very LIW
VM	Virtual Machine
VM	Virtual Memory
VMM	Virtual Machine Monitor
VMX	Vector Multimedia Extension

X

X	eXtend bit (MC68000)
XOP	eXtended OPerations
XOR	eXclusive OR (*cf.* EOR and EXOR)

Z

ZF   Zero Flag

Miscellaneous

μC   Microcontroller

μC   Microcomputer

μP   Microprocessor

2D or 2-D   Two-dimensional

3D or 3-D   Three-dimensional

Units of measurement or unit prefixes

CPI   (clock) Cycles Per Instruction

DMIPS   Dhrystone MIPS

FLOPS   Floating-Point Operations Per Second

iCOMP   Intel COmparative Microprocessor Performance

IPC   Instructions Per Cycle

IPS   Instructions Per Second

k   kilo (= 1000)

kWIPS   kiloWhetstone Instructions Per Second

M   mega (= 10^6)

MACS   Multiply-and-ACcumulates per Second

MFLOPS   megaFLOPS = Million FLoating-point Operations Per Second

MIPS   Million Instructions Per Second

MWIPS   Millions of or Mega-Whetstone Instructions Per Second

SPECflop	SPEC floating point
SPECfpxx	System Performance Evaluation Corporation floating point, xx = year
SPECintxx	System Performance Evaluation Corporation integer, xx = year

Electrical characteristics

| P_D | dissipated electrical power |

Temporal characteristics

| t_{exec} | execution time |
| T_{clock} | clock period |

Business or body

ACM	Association for Computing Machinery
AFISI	*Association Française d'Ingénierie des Systèmes d'Information* (French Association of Information Systems Engineering)
AIEE	American Institute of Electrical Engineers
AMD	Advanced Micro Devices, Inc.
ANSI	American National Standards Institute
ARM	Acorn RISC Machine (formerly Advanced RISC Machines)
AT&T	American Telephone and Telegraph Company
CSG	Commodore Semiconductor Group
DEC	Digital Equipment Corporation
HP	Hewlett-Packard
IBM	International Business Machines Corporation

IEC	International Electrotechnical Commission
IEEE	Institute of Electrical and Electronics Engineers
IRE	Institute of Radio Engineers
ISO	International Organization for Standardization
ISSCC	IEEE International Solid-State Circuits Conference
JEDEC	Joint Electron Device Engineering Council (Solid-State Technology Association)
MIT	Massachussets Institute of Technology
MPR	Microprocessor Report
NBS	National Bureau of Standards
NPL	National Physical Laboratory
NS	National Semiconductor
SGI	Silicon Graphics, Inc.
SPEC	Standard Performance Evaluation Corporation (formerly Cooperative)
TI	Texas Instruments
WDC	Western Digital Corporation, Western Digital Center
WTL	WeiTek Corporation

Trademark (™)

i486	Intel Corporation
Pentium	Intel Corporation
WeiTek	WeiTek Corporation

Registered trademark (®)

AMD	AMD
AT&T	AT&T
AVR	Microchip
Intel	Intel
Pentium	Intel
PIC	Microchip Technology
UNIX	AT&T
Xeon	Intel

References

For reasons of consistency in this domain, the references have been organized by chapter.

Preface and conclusion

Darche, P. (2000). *Architecture des ordinateurs – Représentation des nombres et codes – Cours avec exercices corrigés*. Éditions Gaëtan Morin.

Darche, P. (2002). *Architecture des ordinateurs – Fonctions booléennes, logiques combinatoire et séquentielle – Cours avec exercices et exemples en VHDL*. Éditions Vuibert.

Darche, P. (2003). *Architecture des ordinateurs - Interfaces et périphériques - Cours avec exercices corrigés*. Éditions Vuibert.

Darche, P. (2004). *Architecture des ordinateurs - Logique booléenne: implémentations et technologies*. Éditions Vuibert.

Darche, P. (2012). *Mémoires à semi-conducteurs: principe de fonctionnement et organisation interne des mémoires vives - Volume 1*. Éditions Vuibert. Un des quatre ouvrages sélectionnés pour le prix AFISI (Association Française d'Ingénierie des Systèmes d'Information) du meilleur livre informatique 2012.

IEEE (1996). The microprocessor is 25. *IEEE Micro*, 16(2).

Patt, Y.N. (1995). Scanning the issue, special issue on microprocessors. *Proceedings of the IEEE*, 83(12), 1599.

Chapters 1 to 3

Agarwal, V., Hrishikesh, M.S., Keckler, S.W., and Burger, D. (2000). Clock rate versus IPC: The end of the road for conventional microarchitectures. *27th Annual International Symposium on Computer Architecture (ISCA '00)*, 248–259. *ACM SIGARCH Computer Architecture News*, 28(2).

Aingaran, K., Jairath, S., Konstadinidis, G., Leung, S., Loewenstein, P., McAllister, C., Phillips, S., Radovic, Z., Sivaramakrishnan, R., Smentek, D., and Wicki, T. (2015). M7: Oracle's next-generation sparc processor. *IEEE Micro*, 35(2), 36–45.

AMD (2007). AMD64 Technology. 128-Bit SSE5 Instruction Set. Revision 3.1. Advanced Micro Devices, Inc.

AMD (2009). AMD64 Technology. AMD64 Architecture Programmer's Manual. Volume 6: 128-Bit and 256-Bit XOP and FMA4 Instructions. Publication n° 43479. Revision 3.04.

Anderson, W., Sparacio, F.J., and Tomasulo, R.M. (1967). The IBM System/360 Model 91: Machine philosophy and instruction-handling. *IBM Journal of Research and Development*, 11(1), 8–24. Also in CD-ROM by (Shriver and Smith 1998).

Anderson, E., Bai, Z., Dongarra, J., Greenbaum, A., McKenney, A., Du Croz, J., Hammarling, S., Demmel, J., Bischof, C., and Sorensen, D. (1990). LAPACK: A portable linear algebra library for high-performance computers. *1990 ACM/IEEE Conference on Supercomputing (Supercomputing '90)*, 2–11. November 12–16, 1990, New York, USA.

Arm (2000). Arm® Architecture Reference Manual. Arm® DDI 0100E. Arm® Limited 1996-2000.

Bannon, P. and Saito, Y. (1997). The Alpha 21164PC Microprocessor. *42nd IEEE International Computer Conference (COMPCON '97)*, 20–27, February 23–26, 1997, San Jose, California, USA.

Bayliss, J.A., Colley, S.R., Kravitz, R.H., McCormick, G.A., Richardson, W.S., Wilde, D.K., and Wittmer, L.L. (1981). The instruction decoding unit for the VLSI 432 General Data Processor. *IEEE Journal of Solid-State Circuits (JSSCC)*, SC-16(5), 531–537.

Beck, G.R., Yen, D.W.L., and Anderson, T.L. (1993). The Cydra 5 Minisupercomputer: Architecture and implementation. *The Journal of Supercomputing*, 7(1/2) Special Issue on Instruction-Level Parallelism, 143–180.

Benes, V.E. (1964). Optimal rearrangeable multistage connecting networks. *The Bell System Technical Journal*, 43(4), 1641–1656.

Blaauw, G.A. and Brooks, Jr. F.P. (1997). *Computer Architecture: Concepts and Evolution*. Addison-Wesley Professional.

Brooks, Jr. F.P. (1963). Advanced computer organization-addressing. *1962 International Federation For Information Processing Congress (IFIP 62)*, 564–565. August 27–September 1, 1962, Munich, Germany. North Holland Publishing Company.

Chow, F., Correll, S., Himelstein, M., Killian, E., and Weber, L. (1987). How many addressing modes are enough? *Second International Conference on Architectual Support for Programming Languages and Operating Systems (ASPLOS II)*, 117–121. *ACM SIGARCH Computer Architecture News*, 15(5), 117–121. *ACM SIGOPS Operating Systems Review*, 21(4), 117–121. *ACM SIGPLAN Notices*, 22(10), 117–121.

Clements, A. (2014). *Computer Organization and & Architecture: Themes and Variations*. CENGAGE Learning.

Cohen, D. (1981). On holy wars and a plea for peace. *IEEE Computer*, 14(10), 48–54. October First published in: Internet Engineering Note (IEN) 137. USC/ISI (University of Southern California/Information Sciences Institute), April 1, 1980.

Cooley, J.W. and Tukey, J.W. (1965). An algorithm for the machine calculation of complex Fourier series. *Mathematics of Computation*, 19(90), 297–301.

Cragon, H.G. (1992). *Branch Strategy Taxonomy and Performance Models*. IEEE Computer Society Press Monograph.

Creasy, R.J. (1981). The origin of the VM/370 time-sharing system. *IBM Journal of Research and Development*, 25(5), 483–490. September 1981.

Culler, D.E. and Singh, J.P. with Gupta, A. (1998). *Parallel Computer Architecture – A Hardware/Software Approach*. Mogan Kaufmann Publishers, Inc.

Curnow, H.J. and Wichman, B.A. (1976). A synthetic benchmark. *Computer Journal*, 19(1), 43–49. February 1976.

Cushman, R.H. (1975). 2-1/2-generation µP's-$10 parts that perform like low-end mini's. *EDN µP Design Series*. EDN, p. 36-41. September 20, 1975.

Darche, P. (2000). *Architecture des ordinateurs – Représentation des nombres et codes – Cours avec exercices corrigés*. Éditions Gaëtan Morin.

Darche, P. (2002). *Architecture des ordinateurs – Fonctions booléennes, logiques combinatoire et séquentielle – Cours avec exercices et exemples en VHDL*. Éditions Vuibert, 360 pages.

Darche, P. (2003). *Architecture des ordinateurs – Interfaces et périphériques – Cours avec exercices corrigés*. Éditions Vuibert.

Darche, P. (2004). *Architecture des ordinateurs – Logique booléenne: implémentations et technologies*. Éditions Vuibert.

Darche, P. (2012). *Mémoires à semi-conducteurs: principe de fonctionnement et organisation interne des mémoires vives – Volume 1*. Éditions Vuibert, 556 pages. Un des quatre ouvrages sélectionnés pour le prix AFISI (Association Française d'Ingénierie des Systèmes d'Information) du meilleur livre informatique 2012.

DEC (1983). PDP-11 Architecture Handbook. Order Code: EB-23657-18. Digital Equipment Corporation (DEC).

Diefendorff, K. (1999). Pentium III = Pentium II + SSE – Internet SSE Architecture Boosts Multimedia Performance. *Microprocessor Report (MPR)*, 13(3), 7 pages.

Diefendorff, K., Dubey, P.K., Hochsprung, R., and Scales, H. (2000). AltiVec extension to PowerPC accelerates media processing. *IEEE Micro*, 20(2), 85–95.

Dijkstra, E.W. (1975). Guarded commands, nondeterminacy and formal derivation of programs. *Communications of the ACM (CACM)*, 18(8), 453–457.

Dixit, K.M. (1991). The SPEC benchmarks. *Parallel Computing*, 17(10–11), 1195–1209.

Dongarra, J.J., Luszczek, P., and Petitet, A. (2003). The LINPACK benchmark: Past, present, and future. *Concurrency and Computation: Practice and Experience*, 15(9), 803–820.

Embleton, S., Sparks, S., and Zou, C. (2008). SMM rootkits: A new breed of OS independent malware. *4th International Conference on Security and Privacy in Communication Networks (SecureComm '08)*, 12 pages. September 22–25, 2008, Istanbul, Turkey.

Etiemble, D. (2016). Jeux d'instructions des processeurs. Article H1199. *Techniques de l'Ingénieur*.

Flynn, M.J. (1972). Some computer organizations and their effectiveness. *IEEE Transactions on Computers*, C-21(9), 948–960.

Giladi, R. (1996). Evaluating the Mflops measure. *IEEE Micro*, 16(4), 69–75.

Gosling, J., Joy, B., Steele, G., Bracha, G., Buckley, A., and Smith, D. (2018). *The Java® language specification. Java SE 10 edition*. Oracle America, Inc.

Gwennap, L. (1996). Digital, MIPS add multimedia extensions. *Microprocessor Report (MPR)*, 10(15), 5 pages.

Heidelberger, P. and Lavenberg, S.S. (1984). Computer performance evaluation methodology. *IEEE Transactions on Computers*, C-33(12), 1195–1220. In (Krishna 1996).

Hennessy, J.L. and Jouppi, N.P. (1991). Computer technology and architecture: An evolving interaction. *IEEE Computer*, 24(9), 18–29.

Hennessy, J.L. and Patterson, D.A. (2003a). *Computer Architecture. A Quantitative Approach*, 3rd edition. Morgan Kaufmann Publishers, Inc.

Hennessy, J.L. and Patterson, D.A. (2003b). *Architecture des ordinateurs - une approche quantitative*, 3rd edition. Vuibert Informatique.

Hennessy, J.L. and Patterson, D.A. (2011). *Computer Architecture. A Quantitative Approach*, 5th edition. The Morgan Kaufmann Series in Computer Architecture and Design.

Hilewitz, Y. and Lee, R.B. (2006). Fast bit compression and expansion with parallel extract and parallel deposit instructions. *IEEE International Conference on Application-Specific Systems, Architectures and Processors (ASAP '06)*, 65–72, September 11–13, 2006.

Hilewitz, Y. and Lee, R.B. (2008). Fast bit gather, bit scatter and bit permutation instructions for commodity microprocessors. *Journal of Signal Processing Systems*, 53(1–2), 145–169.

Horel, T. and Lauterbach, G. (1999). UltraSPARC-III: Designing third-generation 64-bit performance. *IEEE Micro*, 19(3), 73–85.

Hsu, P.Y.-T. (1986). Highly concurrent scalar processing. Doctoral Thesis, Coordinated Science Laboratory, University of Illinois at Urbana-Champaign.

Hsu, P.Y.T. and Davidson, E.S. (1986). Highly concurrent scalar processing. *13th Annual International Symposium on Computer Architecture (ISCA '86)*, 386–395. June 2–5, 1986, Tokyo, Japan. *ACM SIGARCH Computer Architecture News*, 14(2), 386–395.

Huffman, D.A. (1952). A method for the construction of minimum-redundancy codes. *Proceedings of IRE*, 40(9), 1098–1101.

Hunter, C. (1987). *Series 32000 Programmer's Reference Manual*. Prentice-Hall, Inc.

IEEE (1985). *IEEE Standard for Microprocessor Assembly Language*. IEEE Std 694-1985. The Institute of Electrical and Electronics Engineers (IEEE), New York, USA.

IEEE (2008). *IEEE Standard for Floating-Point Arithmetic*. IEEE Std 754™-2008. Revision of IEEE Std 754-1985.

Intel (1984). iAPX 286 Programmer's Reference Manual. Intel Corporation.

Intel (1986a). 80286 Operating Systems Writer's Guide. Intel Corporation.

Intel (1987a). 80286 Hardware Reference Manual. Intel Corporation.

Intel (1987b). 80286 Programmer's Reference Manual. Intel Corporation.

Intel (1989). 8086/8088 User's Manual, Programmer's and Hardware Reference. Intel Corporation.

Intel (1996). iCOMP® Index 2.0 Performance Brief – A Simplified Measure of Relative Microprocessor Performance. Order Number: 243127001. Intel Corporation.

Intel (1999). Intel® Pentium® II Processor Performance Brief. Order Number: 2433336-007. Intel Corporation.

Intel (2003). IA-32 Intel® Architecture Software Developer's Manual, Volume 3: System Programming Guide. Intel Corporation.

Intel (2007). Intel® SSE4 Programming Reference, Reference Number: D91561-003. Intel Corporation.

Intel (2012). Intel® Processor Identification and the CPUID Instruction. Application Note 485. Order Number: 241618-039. Intel Corporation.

Intel (2016). Intel® 64 and IA-32 Architectures Software Developer's Manual (Basic Architecture, Instruction Set Reference A-Z and System Programming Guide). Intel Corporation.

ISO/IEC (2014). Standard ISO/IEC 25000:2014. Systems and Software Engineering – Systems and Software Quality Requirements and Evaluation (SQuaRE) – Guide to SQuaRE.

ISO/IEC (2017). Information Technology – Universal Coded Character Set (UCS). Technologies de l'information – Jeu universel de caractères codés (JUC). International Standard ISO/IEC 10646:2017, 5th edition.

ISO/IEC/IEEE (2017). ISO/IEC/IEEE 24765-2017 – ISO/IEC/IEEE International Standard - Systems and Software Engineering – Vocabulary. Revision of ISO/IEC/IEEE 24765:2010.

John, L.K. and Eeckhout, L. (eds) (2006). *Performance Evaluation and Benchmarking*. Taylor & Francis Group, LLC.

Kaeli, D. and Yew, P.-C. (eds) (2005). *Speculative Execution in High Performance Computer Architectures*. Chapman & Hall/ CRC Computer and Information Science Series.

Kane, G. (1988). *MIPS RISC Architecture*. Prentice-Hall, Inc.

Kane, G. (1996). *PA-RISC 2.0 Architecture*. Prentice-Hall, Inc.

Kay, A.C. (1993). The early history of Smalltalk. *Second ACM SIGPLAN Conference on History of Programming Languages (HOPL-II)*, 69–95. April 20–23, 1993, Cambridge, Massachusetts, USA. Also in *ACM SIGPLAN Notices*, 28(3), 69–95.

Kessler, R.E. (1999). The Alpha 21264 microprocessor. *IEEE Micro*, 19(2), 24–36.

Kessler, R.E., McLellan, E.J., and Webb, D.A. (1998). The Alpha 21264 microprocessor architecture. *International Conference on Computer Design – VLSI in Computers and Processors*, 90–95, October 5–7, 1998, Austin, Texas, USA.

Kocher, P., Horn, J., Fogh, A., Genkin, D., Gruss, D., Haas, W., Hamburg, M., Lipp, M., Mangard, S., Prescher, T., Schwarz, M., and Yarom, Y. (2018). *Spectre Attacks: Exploiting Speculative Execution* [Online]. Available: https://spectreattack.com/spectre.pdf.

Kohn, L., Maturana, G., Tremblay, M., Prabhu, A., and Zyner, G. (1995). The visual instruction set (VIS) in UltraSPARC. *Compcon '95. Technologies for the Information Superhighway*, 462–469, March 5–9, 1995.

Konstadinidis, G.K., Li, H.P., Schumacher, F., Krishnaswamy, V., Cho, H., Dash, S., Masleid, R.P., Zheng, C., Yuanjung, D.L., Loewenstein, P., Park, H., Srinivasan, V., Huang, D., Hwang, C., Hsu, W., McAllister, C., Brooks, J., Pham, H., Turullols, S., Yanggong, Y., Golla, R., Smith, A.P., and Vahidsafa, A. (2016). SPARC M7: A 20nm 32-Core 64 MB L3 Cache Processor. *IEEE Journal of Solid-State Circuits (JSSCC)*, 51(1), 79–91.

Koopman, Jr., P.J. (1989). *Stack Computers: The New Wave*. Mountain View Press.

Krishna, C.M. (ed.) (1996). *Performance Modeling for Computer Architects*. IEEE Computer Society Press.

Kuhn, R.H. and Padua, D.A. (eds) (1981). *Tutorial on Parallel Processing*. IEEE Press.

Kumar, A. (1997). The HP PA-8000 RISC CPU. *IEEE Micro*, 2(17), 27–32.

Lee, R.B. (1996). Subword parallelism with MAX-2. *IEEE Micro*, 16(4), 51–59.

Lee, R.B. (1997). Multimedia extensions for general-purpose processors. *1997 IEEE Workshop on Signal Processing Systems (SiPS 97) – Design and Implementation (formerly VLSI Signal Processing)*, 9–23. November 3–5, 1997, Leicester, UK.

Lee, R.B. (1999). Efficiency of MicroSIMD architectures and index-mapped data for media processors. *Proceedings of the SPIE (The International Society for pOptical Engineering)*, 3655 (Media Processors '99), 34–46. *1999 IS&T/SPIE International Symposium on Electronic Imaging, Science and Technology*, January 28–29, 1999, San Jose, CA, USA.

Lee, R.B. and Huck, J. (1996). 64-bit and multimedia extensions in the PA-RISC 2.0 architecture. *Forty-First IEEE Computer Society International Conference Technologies for the Information Superhighway (Compcon '96)*, 152–160, February 25–28, 1996, Santa Clara, California, USA.

Lee, R.B., Fiskiran, A.M., and Bubshait, A. (2001). Multimedia instructions in IA-64. *2001 IEEE International Conference on Multimedia and Exposition (ICME '01)*, 281–284, August 22–25, 2001, Tokyo, Japan.

Leonard, J. and Kluth, E. (1989). Upward compatibility. *IEEE Potential*, 8(1), 35–36.

Levy, H.M. and Eckhouse, Jr., R.H. (1989). *Computer Programming and Architecture: The VAX*, 2nd edition. Digital Equipment Corporation (DEC) 1980, 1989.

Li, P., Shin, J.L., Konstadinidis, G., Schumacher, F., Krishnaswamy, V., Cho, H., Dash, S., Masleid, R., Zheng, C., Yuanjung, D.L., Loewenstein, P., Park, H., Srinivasan, V., Huang, D., Hwang, C., Hsu, W., and McAllister, C. (2015). 4.2 A 20nm 32-Core 64MB L3 Cache SPARC M7 Processor. *2015 IEEE International SolidState Circuits Conference (ISSCC)*, 72–73 etc. February 22–26, 2015, San Francisco, CA, USA.

Lindholm, T., Yellin, F., Bracha, G., and Buckley, A. (2018). *The Java® Virtual Machine Specification, Java SE 10 Edition*. Oracle America, Inc.

Lipp, M., Schwarz, M., Gruss, D., Prescher, T., Haas, W., Mangard, S., Kocher, P., Genkin, D., Yarom, Y., and Hamburg, M. (2018). Meltdown. arXiv.

Lua, K.T. (1989). Relative performance measurement of 80386, 80286 and 8088 Personal Computer Systems. *Microprocessing and Microprogramming*, 26(2), 85–95.

MacGregor, D. and Rubinstein, J. (1985). A performance analysis of MC68020-based systems. *IEEE Micro*, 5(6), 50–70.

McCalpin, J.D. (1995). Memory bandwidth and machine balance in current high performance computers. *IEEE Computer Society Technical Committee on Computer Architecture (TCCA) Newsletter*, 19–25.

McLellan, E. (1993). The Alpha AXP architecture and 21064 processor. *IEEE Micro*, 13(3), 36–47.

Motorola (1981, 1983). MC6809-MC6809E 8-Bit Microprocessor Programming Manual. M6809PM (AD). Motorola Semiconductor Products Inc. March 1, 1981. Republished in May 1983.

Motorola (1992). DSP56000 Digital Signal Processor Family Manual. Motorola Semiconductor Products Inc. Ref. DSP56KFAMUM/AD.

Peleg, A. and Weiser, U. (1996). MMX™ technology extension to the Intel architecture. *IEEE Micro*, 16(4), 42–50.

Peleg, A., Wilkie, S., and Weiser, U. (1997). Intel MMX for multimedia PCs. *Communications of the ACM (CACM)*, 40(1), 24–38.

Ponomarenko, A. and Rubanov, V. (2012). Backward compatibility of software interfaces: Steps towards automatic verification. *Programming and Computing Software*, 38(5), 257–267.

Randell, B. and Russell, L.J. (1964). *ALGOL 60 Implementation*. Academic Press.

Rao, D. (2001). Circular buffering on TMS320C6000. Application Report SPRA645A. Texas Instruments.

Rau, B.R., Yen, D.W.L., Yen, W., and Towle, R.A. (1989). The Cydra 5 departmental supercomputer. Design philosophies, decisions, and trade-offs. *IEEE Computer*, 22(1), 12–35.

Rubinfeld, P., Rose, B., and McCallig, M. (1996). Motion video instruction extensions for Alpha. White Paper. Digital Equipment Corporation.

Russel, R.M. (1978). The CRAY-1 computer system. *Communications of the ACM (CACM)*, 21(1), 63–72. Republished in (Kuhn and Padua 1981, 26–35).

Shah, M., Golla, R., Grohoski, G., Jordan, P., Barreh, J., Brooks, J., Greenberg, M., Levinsky, G., Luttrell, M., Olson, C., Samoail, Z., Smittle, M., and Ziaja, T. (2012). Sparc T4: A dynamically threaded server-on-a-chip. *IEEE Micro*, 32(2), 8–19.

Shanley, T. (1996). *Protected Mode Software Architecture*. MindShare, Inc. Addison-Wesley Developers Press.

Shanley, T. (2009). *x86 Instruction Set Architecture*. MindShare Technology Series. 1st edition. MindShare Press.

Shen, J.P. and Lipasti, M.H. (2005). *Modern Processor Design: Fundamentals of Superscalar Processors*. McGraw-Hill Series in Electrical and Computer Engineering. McGraw Hill Higher Education.

Shriver, B. and Smith, B. (1998). *The Anatomy of a High-Performance Microprocessor: A Systems Perspective*. IEEE Press.

Sima, D., Fountain, T., and Kacsuk, P. (1997). *Advanced Computer Architectures: A Design Space Approach*. Addison-Wesley Longman Limited.

Simpson, R.J. and Terrell, T.J. (1987). *Introduction to 6800/6802 Microprocessor Systems Hardware, Software and Experimentation*. First published by Newnes Technical Books Ltd 1982. Republished in 1985. First published by Heinemann Professional Publishing Ltd.

Sites, R.L. (ed.) (1992). Alpha Architecture Reference Manual. Digital Equipment Corporation. Digital Press.

Sites, R.L. (1993). Alpha AXP architecture. *Communications of the ACM (CACM)*, 36(2), 33–44.

Smith, J.E. and Nair, R. (2005). *Virtual Machines. Versatile Platforms for Systems and Processes*. Morgan Kaufmann Publishers. Elsevier Inc.

Song, P. (1997). Hal Packs Sparc64 onto single chip. *Microprocessor Report (MPR)*, 11(16), 4 pages.

SPEC (1989). SPEC, SPEC benchmark suite release 1.0. *SPEC (Standard Performance Evaluation Corporation) Newsletter*, 1(1), 5–9.

Thakkar, S.(T.) and Huff, T. (1999a). The Internet streaming SIMD extensions. *Intel Technology Journal*, 3(2), Q2.

Thakkar, S.(T.) and Huff, T. (1999b). Internet streaming SIMD extensions. *IEEE Computer*, 32(12), 26–34.

Toong, H.D. and Gupta, A. (1982). Evaluation kernels for microprocessor performance analyses. *Performance Evaluation*, 2(1), 1–8.

Tremblay, M., O'Connor, J.M., Narayanan, V., and He, L. (1996). VIS speeds new media processing. *IEEE Micro*, 16(4), 10-20.

Tsao, Y.-L., Chen, W.-H., Cheng, W.-S., Lin, M.-C., and Jou, S.-J. (2003). Hardware nested looping of parameterized and embedded DSP core. *2003 IEEE International SOC Conference*, 49–52, September 17–20, 2003, Portland, Oregon, USA.

Uht, A.K., Sindagi, V., and Somanathan, S. (1997). Branch effect reduction techniques. *IEEE Computer*, 30(5), 71–81.

Waterman, A.S. (2011). Improving energy efficiency and reducing code size with RISC-V compressed. Berkeley Technical Report N° UCB/EECS-2011-63. Department of Electrical Engineering and Computer Sciences, University of California at Berkeley.

Waterman, A.S. (2016). Design of the RISC-V instruction set architecture. PhD Dissertation, Technical Report N° UCB/EECS-2016-1, Electrical Engineering and Computer Sciences, University of California at Berkeley.

Weicker, R.P. (1984). Dhrystone: A synthetic systems programming benchmark. *Communications of the ACM (CACM)*, 27(10), 1013–1030.

Weicker, R.P. (1990). An overview of common benchmarks. *IEEE Computer*, 23(12), 65–75.

Williams, T., Patkar, N., and Shen, G. (1995). SPARC64: A 64-b 64-Active-Instruction out-of-order-execution MCM processor. *IEEE Journal of Solid-State Circuits (JSSC)*, 30(11), 1215–1226.

Wolfe, A. and Chanin, A. (1992). Executing compressed programs on an embedded RISC architecture. *25th Annual International Symposium on Microarchitecture*, 81–91.

William Wong (2016). What's the Difference Between Containers and Virtual Machines? *Electronic Design*. July 15, 2016.

William Wong (2017). VM, Containers, and Serverless Programming for Embedded Developers. *Electronic Design*. September 7, 2017.

Chapters 4 and 5

Blaauw, G.A. and Brooks, Jr., F.P. (1997). *Computer Architecture: Concepts and Evolution*. Addison-Wesley Professional.

Clark, W.A. (1957). The Lincoln TX-2 computer development. *Western Joint Computer Conference: Techniques for Reliability (IRE-AIEE-ACM '57)*, 143–145. February 26–28, 1957.

Clements, A. (1997). *Microprocessor Systems Design: 68000 Hardware, Software, and Interfacing*, 3rd edition. PWS Publishing Company.

Compaq (2002). *Alpha Architecture Reference Manual*, 4th edition. Compaq Computer Corporation.

Darche, P. (2000). *Architecture des ordinateurs – Représentation des nombres et codes – Cours avec exercices corrigés*. Éditions Gaëtan Morin.

Darche, P. (2003). *Architecture des ordinateurs - Interfaces et périphériques - Cours avec exercices corrigés*. Éditions Vuibert.

Darche, P. (2004). *Architecture des ordinateurs - Logique booléenne: implémentations et technologies*. Éditions Vuibert.

Darche, P. (2012). *Mémoires à semi-conducteurs: principe de fonctionnement et organisation interne des mémoires vives - Volume 1*. Éditions Vuibert. One of four books selected for the AFISI (Association Française d'Ingénierie des Systèmes d'Information) prize for the best computing book 2012.

Dumas II, J.D. (2006). *Computer Architecture - Fundamentals and Principles of Computer Design*. CRC Press.

Fox, W.A. and Reyling, Jr., G.F. (1975). A single chip 16-bit microprocessor for general application. *Microelectronics Reliability*, 14(4) Special Seminex '75 edition, 389–397.

Grohoski, G.F. (1990). Machine organization of the IBM RISC System/6000 processor. *IBM Journal of Research and Development*, 34(1), 37–58.

Hamacher, C., Vranesic, Z., Zaky, S., and Manjikian, N. (2012). *Computer Organization and Embedded Systems*, 6th edition. McGraw-Hill.

Harris, D.M. and Harris, S.L. (2007). *Digital Design and Computer Architecture*. Elsevier Inc.

Hennessy, J.L. and Patterson, D.A. (1990). *Computer Architecture. A Quantitative Approach.* Morgan Kaufmann Publishers, Inc.

Hennessy, J.L. and Patterson, D.A. (1994). *Architecture des ordinateurs - une approche quantitative.* EDISCIENCE International. Second edition published in International Thomson Publishing (ITP) France. English version: (Hennessy and Patterson 1990).

Hennessy, J.L. and Patterson, D.A. (2017). *Computer Architecture. A Quantitative Approach,* 6th edition. Morgan Kaufmann Publishers, Inc.

Hennessy, J., Jouppi, N., Baskett, F., Gross, T., and Gill, J. (1982). Hardware/software tradeoffs for increased performance. *First International Symposium on Architectural Support for Programming Languages and Operating Systems (ASPLOS I),* 2–11. *ACM SIGARCH Computer Architecture News,* 10(2), 2–11. *ACM SIGPLAN Notices,* 17(4), 2–11.

Hill, M.D., Jouppi, N.P., and Sohi, G.S. (eds) (2000). *Readings in Computer Architecture.* Morgan Kaufmann Publishers.

Hwu, W.-M.W. and Patt, Y.N. (1987a). Checkpoint repair for high-performance out-of-order execution machines. *IEEE Transactions on Computers,* C-36(12), 1496–1514.

Hwu, W.-M.W. and Patt, Y.N. (1987b). Checkpoint repair for out-of-order execution machines. *14th Annual International Symposium on Computer Architecture (ISCA '87),* 18–26, June 2–5, 1987, Pittsburgh, PA, USA.

IEEE (1985). *IEEE Standard for Binary Floating-Point Arithmetic.* ANSI/IEEE Std 754-1985. Republished in *SIGPLAN Notices,* 22(2), 9-25. February 1987.

IEEE (2008). *IEEE Standard for Floating-Point Arithmetic.* IEEE Std 754™-2008. Revision of IEEE Std 754-1985. 70 pages.

Intel (1980). Intel Fair Applications Handbook. Intel Corporation.

Intel (1986). 80386 Programmer's Reference Manual. Intel Corporation.

Intel (1988). 8259A Programamble Interrupt Controller (8259A/8259A-2). Intel Corporation.

Intel (1989). 8086/8088 User's Manual, Programmer's and Hardware Reference. Intel Corporation.

Intel (2003a). System Programming Guide. Order Number 245472-012. Intel Corporation.

Intel (2003b). IA-32 Intel® Architecture Software Developer's Manual, Volume 3: System Programming Guide. Intel Corporation.

Intel (2005). IA-32 Intel® Architecture Software Developer's Manual, Volume 3: System Programming Guide. Intel Corporation.

JEDEC (2002). Terms, Definitions, and Letter Symbols for Microcomputers, Microprocessors, and Memory Integrated Circuits. JEDEC Standard JESD100B.01 (Minor Revision of JESD100-B, December 1999).

JEDEC (2013). Dictionary of Terms for Solid-State Technology. JEDEC Standard n° 88-E. (JESD88E), 6th edition. JEDEC Solid State Technology Association.

Kane, G. (1988). *MIPS RISC Architecture*. Prentice-Hall, Inc.

Kane, G. and Heinrich, J. (1992). *MIPS RISC Architecture*, 2nd edition. Prentice-Hall.

Keller, R.M. (1975). Look-ahead processors. *ACM Computing Surveys*, 7(4), 177–195.

Kuck, D.J. (1978). *The Structure of Computers and Computations*. Vol. 1. John Wiley & Sons, Inc.

Leiner, A.L. (1954). System specifications for the DYSEAC. *Journal of the ACM*, 1(2), 57–81.

Macauley, M.W.S. (1998). Interrupt latency in systems based on Intel 80x86 Processors. *Microprocessors and Microsystems*, 22(2), 121–126. June 1998.

Meinadier, J.-P. (1971, 1988). *Structure et Fonctionnement des Ordinateurs*. Série Informatique. Librairie Larousse, Paris.

Melliar-Smith, P.M. and Randell, B. (1977). Software reliability: The role of programmed exception handling. *Proceedings of an ACM Conference on Language Design for Reliable Software*, 95–100, March 28–30, 1977. Raleigh, North Carolina, USA. *ACM SIGOPS Operating Systems Review*, 11(2) *Proceedings of an ACM Conference on Language Design for Reliable Software*, 95–100. April 1977. *ACM SIGPLAN Notices*, 12(3) *Proceedings of an ACM Conference on Language Design for Reliable Software*, 95–100. March 1977. *ACM SIGSOFT Software Engineering Notes*, 2(2) *Proceedings of an ACM Conference on Language Design for Reliable Software*, 95–100.

Mersel, J. (1956). Program interrupt on the Univac scientific computer. *Joint ACM-AIEE-IRE Western Computer Conference (AIEE-IRE '56)*, 52–53, February 7–9, 1956, San Francisco, California, USA.

Motorola (1981, 1983). MC6809-MC6809E 8-Bit Microprocessor Programming Manual. M6809PM (AD). Motorola Semiconductor Products Inc. March 1, 1981. Republished in May 1983.

Motorola (1984). MC6809E datasheet. DS9846-R2. Motorola Inc.

Motorola (1996). PowerPC™ Microprocessor Family: The Programming Environments. Rev 0.1. Motorola Inc.

Moudgill, M. and Vassiliadis, S. (1996). Precise interrupts. *IEEE Micro*, 16(1), 58–67. In CD-ROM by (Shriver and Smith 1998).

O'Connor, J.M. and Tremblay, M. (1997). picoJava-I: The Java virtual machine in hardware. *IEEE Micro*, 17(2), 45–53.

Pajari, G.E. (1989). Interrupts aren't always best. *Byte Magazine*, 13(5), 261–264.

Rau, B.R. and Fisher, J.A. (1992). Instruction-level parallel processing: History, overview, and perspective. Report HPL92-132. Computer Systems Laboratory, Hewlett Packard.

Rau, B.R. and Fisher, J.A. (1993). Instruction-level parallel processing: History, overview, and perspective. *The Journal of Supercomputing*, 7(1–2) Special Issue on Instruction-Level-Parallelism, 9–50. Republished in (Hill *et al.* 2000, p. 288–308).

Rojas, R. and Hashagen, U. (eds) (2000). *The First Computers: History and Architectures*. MIT Press.

Rudd, K.W. (1997). Efficient exception handling techniques for high-performance processor architectures. Technical Report CSLTR-97-732.

Samadzadeh, M.H. and Garanabi, L.E. (2001). Hardware/software cost analysis of interrupt processing strategies. *IEEE Micro*, 21(3), 69–76.

Schlansker, M.S. and Rau, B.R. (2000). EPIC: Explicitly parallel instruction computing. *IEEE Computer*, 33(2), 37–45.

Scott, M.L. (2016). *Programming Language Pragmatics*, 4th edition. Morgan Kaufmann.

Shriver, B. and Smith, B. (1998). *The Anatomy of a High-Performance Microprocessor: A Systems Perspective*. IEEE Press.

Smith, M.D. (1992). Support for speculative execution in high-performance processors. Technical Report CSL-TR-93-556. Computer Systems Laboratory, Stanford University, Stanford, California, USA.

Smith, J.E. and Pleszkun, A.R. (1988). Implementing precise interrupts in pipelined processors. *IEEE Transactions on Computers*, 37(5), 562–573.

Smith, M.D., Horowitz, M., and Lam, M.S. (1992). Efficient superscalar performance through boosting. *Fifth International Conference on Architectural Support for Programming Languages and Operating Systems (ASPLOS V)*, 248–259, October 12–15, 1992, Boston, Massachusetts, USA. *ACM SIGPLAN Notices*, 27(9), 248–259.

Smotherman, M. (1989a). A sequencing-based taxonomy of I/O systems and a review of historical machines. *ACM SIGARCH Computer Architecture News*, 17(5), 5–15.

Smotherman, M. (1989b). A sequencing-based taxonomy of I/O systems and review of historical machines. Paper 1 of Chapter 7 in (Hill *et al.* 2000). Originally published in (Smotherman 1989a).

Walker, W.A. (1992). A taxonomy of interrupt processing strategies in pipelined microprocessors. Master's Thesis, Department of Computer Science, University of Texas at Austin, USA.

Walker, W. and Cragon, H.G. (1995). Interrupt processing in concurrent processors. *IEEE Computer*, 28(6), 36–46.

Wilkes, M.V., Wheeler, D.J., and Gill, S. (1951). *The Preparation of Programs for an Electronic Digital Computer, with Special Reference to the EDSAC and the Use of a Library of Subroutines*. Addison-Wesley Press, Inc.

Yang, J., Minturn, D.B., and Frank Hady, F. (2012). When Poll is Better than Interrupt. *10th USENIX Conference on File and Storage Technologies (Fast '12)*, February 14–17, 2012, San Jose, California, USA.

Index

This index covers all 5 volumes in this series of books.

T

technology
  electronic, *cf. electronic technology*
  integration, *cf. integration technology*
test, § V5-2.3
  BIST, § V5-2.2.5
  bus, § V2-3.5
  instruction, *cf. instruction/atomic,*
    instruction/branching
  interface, *cf. debugging hardware*
    interface
  register, *cf. register/test*
  self-test, § V3-5.3
  test program, *cf. performance/ program*
    and firmware/POST
time, § V1-1.4
  access, § V1-1.2, V1-1.4, V1-2.1, V2-
    1.2, V2-1.5, V3-2.4.2, V3-3.1.11.1
    and V3-3.2
  bus settling, § V2-1.2, V2-1.3, V2-1.5
    and V2-3.1
  execution, *cf. execution/time*
  cycle, § V1-1.4, V1-2.1, V1-2.3, V1-2.4,
    V3-1.2, V3-2.4.1 *and* V3-3.4.3.2
  hold, § V2-1.5 *and* V2-3.1
  reaction, § V4-5.3
  starvation, § V4-5.3
  switching, § V4-3.4.5
  transfer, § V2-1.1 *and* V2-1.3
time (linked to software development)
  assembly, § V5-1.1.2
  compilation, § V5-1.1.2
  loading, § V2-2.1.1
TLP (Thread-Level Parallelism), § V1-
  3.4.3.2 *and* V3-4.7
transistor, § V1-1.2, V1-1.4 to V1-1.6,
  V1-3.1.4, V2-2.2.1 *and* V2-3.3.4
  bipolar junction (BJT), § V1-1.2
  density, § V1-1.2
  field effect (FET), § V1-1.2
  gate, *cf.* § V1-1.5 *and* V4-3.4.5
TTL, *cf. electronic technology*

U

UEFI, *cf. firmware*
ULSI, *cf. integration technology*
UMA, *cf. memory (concepts)/unified*
UMB, *cf. memory (concepts)*
unit
  central, *cf.* § V1-1.2 *and* V3-1.1
  logical
    AGU, § V3-3.4.4 *and*
      V4-1.2.4.5.2
    control unit, § V1-3.2.2.1,
      V1-3.3.1.2, V1-3.3.1.2.2 *and*
      V3-3.4
    hardwired, § V1-3.2.3
    microprogrammed, § V3-3.4,
      V3-3.4.3.2 *and* V4-1.1
      (footnote)
    DPU, § V5-3.3.1
    FMAC, § V3-5.2
    functional, § V3-1.2
    Integer Processing (IPU), §
      V1-1.2, V1-3.3.1.2,
      V1-3.3.1.2.1, V3-3.3, V3-5.1
      and V3-5.2
    MAC, § V4-2.8.4.2 *and*
      V3-5.2
    vector-based, § V1-1.2, V4-2.3.2
      and V4-2.7.1
  of measurement, § V1-1.2, V1-2.1 *and*
    V4-3.4
  processing, *cf. element/processing unit*
UNIVAC, *cf. computer model*

V

verification
  cycle, § V3-5.3
  exchange, § V2-1.3
  machine, § V2-2.5.7
  memory, § V5-2.2.4.3 *and* V5-2.2.5
  result, § V2-2.4.1

Other titles from

in

Computer Engineering

2020

DUVAUT Patrick, DALLOZ Xavier, MENGA David, KOEHL François, CHRIQUI Vidal, BRILL Joerg
Internet of Augmented Me, I.AM: Empowering Innovation for a New Sustainable Future

LAFFLY Dominique
TORUS 1 – Toward an Open Resource Using Services: Cloud Computing for Environmental Data
TORUS 2 – Toward an Open Resource Using Services: Cloud Computing for Environmental Data
TORUS 3 – Toward an Open Resource Using Services: Cloud Computing for Environmental Data

LAURENT Anne, LAURENT Dominique, MADERA Cédrine
Data Lakes
(Databases and Big Data Set – Volume 2)

OULHADJ Hamouche, DAACHI Boubaker, MENASRI Riad
Metaheuristics for Robotics
(Optimization Heuristics Set – Volume 2)

SADIQUI Ali
Computer Network Security

VENTRE Daniel
Artificial Intelligence, Cybersecurity and Cyber Defense

2019

BESBES Walid, DHOUIB Diala, WASSAN Niaz, MARREKCHI Emna
Solving Transport Problems: Towards Green Logistics

CLERC Maurice
Iterative Optimizers: Difficulty Measures and Benchmarks

GHLALA Riadh
Analytic SQL in SQL Server 2014/2016

TOUNSI Wiem
Cyber-Vigilance and Digital Trust: Cyber Security in the Era of Cloud Computing and IoT

2018

ANDRO Mathieu
Digital Libraries and Crowdsourcing
(Digital Tools and Uses Set – Volume 5)

ARNALDI Bruno, GUITTON Pascal, MOREAU Guillaume
Virtual Reality and Augmented Reality: Myths and Realities

BERTHIER Thierry, TEBOUL Bruno
From Digital Traces to Algorithmic Projections

CARDON Alain
Beyond Artificial Intelligence: From Human Consciousness to Artificial Consciousness

HOMAYOUNI S. Mahdi, FONTES Dalila B.M.M.
Metaheuristics for Maritime Operations
(Optimization Heuristics Set – Volume 1)

Jeansoulin Robert
JavaScript and Open Data

Pivert Olivier
NoSQL Data Models: Trends and Challenges
(Databases and Big Data Set – Volume 1)

Sedkaoui Soraya
Data Analytics and Big Data

Saleh Imad, Ammi Mehdi, Szoniecky Samuel
Challenges of the Internet of Things: Technology, Use, Ethics
(Digital Tools and Uses Set – Volume 7)

Szoniecky Samuel
Ecosystems Knowledge: Modeling and Analysis Method for Information and Communication
(Digital Tools and Uses Set – Volume 6)

2017

Benmammar Badr
Concurrent, Real-Time and Distributed Programming in Java

Héliodore Frédéric, Nakib Amir, Ismail Boussaad, Ouchraa Salma, Schmitt Laurent
Metaheuristics for Intelligent Electrical Networks
(Metaheuristics Set – Volume 10)

Ma Haiping, Simon Dan
Evolutionary Computation with Biogeography-based Optimization
(Metaheuristics Set – Volume 8)

Pétrowski Alain, Ben-Hamida Sana
Evolutionary Algorithms
(Metaheuristics Set – Volume 9)

Pai G A Vijayalakshmi
Metaheuristics for Portfolio Optimization
(Metaheuristics Set – Volume 11)

2016

BLUM Christian, FESTA Paola
Metaheuristics for String Problems in Bio-informatics
(Metaheuristics Set – Volume 6)

DEROUSSI Laurent
Metaheuristics for Logistics
(Metaheuristics Set – Volume 4)

DHAENENS Clarisse and JOURDAN Laetitia
Metaheuristics for Big Data
(Metaheuristics Set – Volume 5)

LABADIE Nacima, PRINS Christian, PRODHON Caroline
Metaheuristics for Vehicle Routing Problems
(Metaheuristics Set – Volume 3)

LEROY Laure
Eyestrain Reduction in Stereoscopy

LUTTON Evelyne, PERROT Nathalie, TONDA Albert
Evolutionary Algorithms for Food Science and Technology
(Metaheuristics Set – Volume 7)

MAGOULÈS Frédéric, ZHAO Hai-Xiang
Data Mining and Machine Learning in Building Energy Analysis

RIGO Michel
Advanced Graph Theory and Combinatorics

2015

BARBIER Franck, RECOUSSINE Jean-Luc
COBOL Software Modernization: From Principles to Implementation with the BLU AGE® Method

CHEN Ken
Performance Evaluation by Simulation and Analysis with Applications to Computer Networks

CLERC Maurice
Guided Randomness in Optimization
(Metaheuristics Set – Volume 1)

DURAND Nicolas, GIANAZZA David, GOTTELAND Jean-Baptiste,
ALLIOT Jean-Marc
Metaheuristics for Air Traffic Management
(Metaheuristics Set – Volume 2)

MAGOULÈS Frédéric, ROUX François-Xavier, HOUZEAUX Guillaume
Parallel Scientific Computing

MUNEESAWANG Paisarn, YAMMEN Suchart
Visual Inspection Technology in the Hard Disk Drive Industry

2014

BOULANGER Jean-Louis
Formal Methods Applied to Industrial Complex Systems

BOULANGER Jean-Louis
Formal Methods Applied to Complex Systems:Implementation of the B Method

GARDI Frédéric, BENOIST Thierry, DARLAY Julien, ESTELLON Bertrand,
MEGEL Romain
Mathematical Programming Solver based on Local Search

KRICHEN Saoussen, CHAOUACHI Jouhaina
Graph-related Optimization and Decision Support Systems

LARRIEU Nicolas, VARET Antoine
Rapid Prototyping of Software for Avionics Systems: Model-oriented Approaches for Complex Systems Certification

OUSSALAH Mourad Chabane
Software Architecture 1
Software Architecture 2

2013

BOULANGER Jean-Louis
Static Analysis of Software: The Abstract Interpretation

CAFERRA Ricardo
Logic for Computer Science and Artificial Intelligence

HOMES Bernard
Fundamentals of Software Testing

KORDON Fabrice, HADDAD Serge, PAUTET Laurent, PETRUCCI Laure
Distributed Systems: Design and Algorithms

KORDON Fabrice, HADDAD Serge, PAUTET Laurent, PETRUCCI Laure
Models and Analysis in Distributed Systems

LORCA Xavier
Tree-based Graph Partitioning Constraint

TRUCHET Charlotte, ASSAYAG Gerard
Constraint Programming in Music

VICAT-BLANC PRIMET Pascale *et al.*
Computing Networks: From Cluster to Cloud Computing

2010

AUDIBERT Pierre
Mathematics for Informatics and Computer Science

BABAU Jean-Philippe *et al.*
Model Driven Engineering for Distributed Real-Time Embedded Systems

BOULANGER Jean-Louis
Safety of Computer Architectures

MONMARCHE Nicolas *et al.*
Artificial Ants

PANETTO Hervé, BOUDJLIDA Nacer
Interoperability for Enterprise Software and Applications 2010

SIGAUD Olivier *et al.*
Markov Decision Processes in Artificial Intelligence

SOLNON Christine
Ant Colony Optimization and Constraint Programming

AUBRUN Christophe, SIMON Daniel, SONG Ye-Qiong *et al.*
Co-design Approaches for Dependable Networked Control Systems

2009

FOURNIER Jean-Claude
Graph Theory and Applications

GUEDON Jeanpierre
The Mojette Transform / Theory and Applications

JARD Claude, ROUX Olivier
Communicating Embedded Systems / Software and Design

LECOUTRE Christophe
Constraint Networks / Targeting Simplicity for Techniques and Algorithms

2008

BANÂTRE Michel, MARRÓN Pedro José, OLLERO Hannibal, WOLITZ Adam
Cooperating Embedded Systems and Wireless Sensor Networks

MERZ Stephan, NAVET Nicolas
Modeling and Verification of Real-time Systems

PASCHOS Vangelis Th
Combinatorial Optimization and Theoretical Computer Science: Interfaces and Perspectives

WALDNER Jean-Baptiste
Nanocomputers and Swarm Intelligence

2007

BENHAMOU Frédéric, JUSSIEN Narendra, O'SULLIVAN Barry
Trends in Constraint Programming

JUSSIEN Narendra
A TO Z OF SUDOKU

2006

BABAU Jean-Philippe *et al.*
From MDD Concepts to Experiments and Illustrations – DRES 2006

HABRIAS Henri, FRAPPIER Marc
Software Specification Methods

MURAT Cecile, PASCHOS Vangelis Th
Probabilistic Combinatorial Optimization on Graphs

PANETTO Hervé, BOUDJLIDA Nacer
Interoperability for Enterprise Software and Applications 2006 / IFAC-IFIP I-ESA'2006

2005

GÉRARD Sébastien *et al.*
Model Driven Engineering for Distributed Real Time Embedded Systems

PANETTO Hervé
Interoperability of Enterprise Software and Applications 2005